James Payn

**Union Hymnal**

Songs and prayers fpr yewish worship

James Payn

**Union Hymnal**
*Songs and prayers fpr yewish worship*

ISBN/EAN: 9783744781367

Printed in Europe, USA, Canada, Australia, Japan

Cover: Foto ©Thomas Meinert / pixelio.de

More available books at **www.hansebooks.com**

# UNION HYMNAL

## SONGS AND PRAYERS

### FOR

## JEWISH WORSHIP

THIRD EDITION
REVISED AND ENLARGED

COMPILED AND PUBLISHED
BY
THE CENTRAL CONFERENCE OF AMERICAN RABBIS
1936

# CONTENTS

|  |  | PAGE |
|---|---|---|
| PREFACE | | V |
| HYMNS | | I |
| MUSICAL SERVICES | | 315 |

SERVICES FOR THE RELIGIOUS SCHOOL

| Assembly Services | 432 |
|---|---|
| Assembly Service for Younger Children | 454 |

Service for:

| Sabbath | 461 |
|---|---|
| Passover | 475 |
| Pentecost | 488 |
| Tabernacles | 499 |
| New Year | 510 |
| Atonement | 526 |
| Purim and Chanukkoh | 541 |
| Youth and High School | 546 |

| INDEXES | 569 |
|---|---|

# PREFACE

**T**HE present edition of the Union Hymnal is the second revision of a work published originally by the Central Conference of American Rabbis in 1892. At that time the need of a Hymn Book that would answer the religious requirements of Reform congregations was apparent. In the discussion of the subject, the founder and first president of the Conference, Isaac M. Wise, said: "It is not the prayer coming from the spirit of Judaism which is fundamental, so much as it is the indestructible element in the psalmody of the people." (Year Book, vol. III, p. 23.) The late Maurice H. Harris added this significant word to the discussion: "The choir has driven the congregation out as far as worship is concerned. It is time the congregation be given a hearing before God."

Several attempts to create a Jewish Hymn Book had been previously made. The first attempt in the United States was the so-called Charleston collection, which appeared about the fourth decade of the nineteenth century, and of which Miss Penina Moise was the author of all the hymns except a few that had been written at her request by some of her friends. In the year 1868, Temple Emanu-El of New York published a collection of forty hymns, thirty-six of which were translations from the German by James K. Gutheim and Felix Adler. Coincident with the Temple Emanu-El collection, were similar collections by Isaac M. Wise and Marcus Jastrow. In the year 1877, the Union of American Hebrew Congregations offered a prize for a Jewish Hymn Book, but the offer failed to induce competition, and the prize was never awarded. Encouraged by the offer of the Union, and as the only contestant for the announced reward, Simon Hecht of Evansville, Ind., published a small hymnal for Jewish Sunday Schools. In 1882, Gustav Gottheil compiled a hymnal from Jewish and non-Jewish sources. Other collections of hymns had been published by F. de Sola Mendes, Joseph Krauskopf, Max Landsberg, Adolph Guttman, Louis Stern, Louis Grossmann, J. Leonard Levy, Jacob Voorsanger, and Isaac S. Moses.

The first edition of the Union Hymnal was compiled by the Conference and Society of American Cantors in 1897. With various changes, it contained hymns from the Gottheil and Temple Emanu-El hymnals, as well as from the Moise and Hecht collections.

In 1914, the first revision of the Union Hymnal was published by the Central Conference of American Rabbis. It contained two hundred and twenty-six hymns as compared with one hundred and twenty-nine in the original edition. Three years later, there was a very widespread demand for another revision. Studies

were made by several committees from that time until 1924, when the present Committee on Revision was appointed. The work was brought to completion with the presentation of the manuscript to the Conference in Providence, R. I., in 1930.

The Committee sought to meet the requirements of our congregations and religious schools by providing a revision which "should ring true to the Jewish spirit." As against two hundred and twenty-six hymns in the second edition, the present compilation has two hundred and sixty-six hymns, many of which are entirely new. Considerable use was made of the second edition, many favorite hymns were retained, but many were eliminated, because they did not answer the special needs of our congregations and religious schools; others were re-harmonized or separated, or the language of the poetry revised so as to give more appropriate expression to the demands of Jewish theology. Jewish composers contributed melodies and settings that were inspired by traditional Jewish music. Many Jewish poems were introduced into our hymnology for the first time. The Committee on Revision was actuated by a desire to produce a hymn book which would stimulate congregational singing, inspire Jewish devotion, revive the value of Jewish melody, make use of neglected Jewish poetry, lean heavily where possible upon Jewish motifs, awaken in the children of our religious schools a love for Jewish poetry and song, and encourage in the religious schools an earnest study of Jewish music, and finally contribute to the field of hymnology a publication which would be essentially Jewish in color, spirit and purpose.

One of the main purposes kept constantly in view was to make it as Jewish as possible, and thus meet one of the needs of our modern synagogal life, namely the adaptation of Jewish traditional music to the usage and taste of our own days. This involves a two-fold question: what elements of synagogal melody best express our religious life in music employed by our congregations; and how shall we clothe them in harmony that shall reveal their own peculiar modal character and melodic contours? We would not assert that we have solved these two problems. Not only in this Hymnal, but in our religious-musical life in general, they are still far from a solution. But we have made an earnest effort to proceed in this direction. We have called upon Jewish composers for aid. As noted elsewhere in this Preface, a considerable number of them contributed compositions to this collection. Composers were urged to utilize some of the wealth of synagogal melody. This plea found a ready response. Even a superficial glance through the contents of this volume indicates how many of the hymns are based upon traditional melodies.

The Committee moreover adopted a liberal attitude toward experiments in harmonization. Some of the hymns are not intended to be sung by four voices. Some are experiments, and attempt to make use of modern harmonic discoveries and apply them to the original or synagogal melodies employed. Some original compositions are frankly in the style of traditional Jewish music, and with varying success adopt its characteristic mood.

But we recognize that the needs and tastes of our congregations are not one, but many. A number of old and new hymns have been included which are in the

general tone, but which are not specifically Jewish. In the case of these, too, the Committee has exercised the utmost care. Although we must rely upon our own judgment and recognize our fallibility, we have tried to exclude all trivial and unworthy music. Every hymn was scrutinized with genuine care and accepted only after repeated tests had been made. In some cases hymns had to be set to music three or four times before the Committee was satisfied.

Above all we fully recognize that the hymns should be singable, within the gamut of the average voice, and garbed with easy, intelligible harmony. In contrast with previous editions of the Hymnal, many songs for young children are included. Musical responses for almost every service in the year have been added.

It has been our aim to combine Jewish and general musical values. Such a Hymnal as this is not an end, but an advance on the road toward the achievement of a difficult goal. It is our ardent hope that it will help educate our congregations in the beauties of our musical heritage, and lead them God-ward "on the wings of song."

The aim of the Services in the Hymn Book are spiritual and intellectual; namely to develop in the children a spirit of prayerful devotion and to acquaint them with the regular Jewish Liturgy. These aims were attained with considerable success in the old Hymn Book. The Committee felt, however, that the Services could be made more prayerful and educational.

To have scope for experimentation, the number of Services was increased (nineteen instead of eight). This permitted the grouping of an adequate number of Services according to the ages of the children. There are Services for very young children, Services for the intermediate grades and Services for the High School Department. In addition, simple phrasing of the Services, departing from the language of the Union Prayer Book, is attempted. However, in those Services in which the adult language has been modified, the traditional framework of the Liturgy has been retained. Because of the number, some Services are experimental and others similar to the Union Prayer Book, thus permitting every school principal to have a wide choice of service.

### The Transliteration of the Hebrew Text

The transliteration of Hebrew into other languages has been attempted a number of times since Origen made the first one into Greek at the beginning of the third century.

In the present transliteration there is no principle of science or scholarship involved. It does not follow the French, Italian, or any other continental system of pronunciation. It is not intended for professional singers, for choirs, or for those familiar with Hebrew itself. It is arranged for American congregations, adults and children, whose vernacular is English as it is spoken in the United States of America. It is based upon the American and not the continental pronunciation, particularly of vowel sounds. It seeks to reproduce the Hebrew consonants and vowels into English, along lines that are easily understood and consist-

vii

ent in their application. The pronunciation of the Hebrew adopted was according to the Ashkenazic method, not because it was supposed to be philologically superior, but simply because it is the pronunciation used by the majority of those who will make use of the hymnal.

The music of the following hymn numbers is entirely new, and is exclusively the property of the Central Conference of American Rabbis, and the Conference reserves all rights in the use of these hymns: 5, 6, 7, 10, 11, 12, 13, 15, 16, 17, 19, 21, 24, 27, 28, 30, 31, 32, 33, 34, 35, 36, 38, 39, 41, 42, 46, 48, 49, 52, 55, 56, 57, 62, 63, 64, 65, 66, 67, 68, 69, 70, 72, 73, 74, 75, 78, 79, 80, 81, 82, 83, 85, 86, 90, 91, 92, 93, 94, 95, 97, 98, 99, 100, 101, 105, 106, 107, 108, 109, 111, 112, 113, 114, 116, 117, 118, 119, 121, 122, 123, 126, 127, 128, 131, 132, 134, 135, 137, 139, 142, 143, 144, 145, 148, 152, 153, 154, 155, 156, 157, 158, 159, 161, 162, 163, 164, 166, 167, 168, 169, 171, 172, 174, 176, 177, 178, 179, 180, 181, 182, 183, 184, 185, 186, 187, 188, 189, 190, 191, 192, 193, 194, 195, 197, 198, 199, 200, 201, 203, 204, 205, 206, 210, 211, 213, 215, 216, 217, 218, 219, 220, 221, 223, 225, 231, 232, 233, 234, 235, 236, 237, 238, 240, 241, 242, 243, 244, 245, 246, 247, 248, 249, 250, 251.

## ACKNOWLEDGMENTS

The Central Conference of American Rabbis and its Committee on Synagog Music wish to make acknowledgment to the following: Abraham W. Binder of New York, who served the Committee as its Musical Editor, and who in that capacity directed all of the work of the musical section of this hymn book, and who himself contributed many new musical settings; to N. Lindsay Norden of Philadelphia, for a painstaking reading of the proofs; to Mrs. Alice Lucas, Solomon Solis-Cohen, Joseph Leiser, Louis Newman, John Haynes Holmes, the late David Levy (whose poems are a memorial to his service on the Committee on Revision), Barbara Joan Singer (whose poem on "The Harvest" is a memorial to the daughter of one of the Committee on Revision, who passed away while her father was journeying to a meeting of the Committee), Harry H. Mayer, Isabella R. Hess, Nathan Stern, Mrs. Claude G. Montefiore, Max D. Klein, Mrs. Elma Ehrlich Levinger, for their contribution of poems; to Jacob Singer, James G. Heller, Henry Gideon, J. Goldfarb, and Lewis M. Isaacs for generous contributions of original musical settings; to Mrs. Isaac S. Moses for permission to use "Blessed Be Ye Who Come," "The Sabbath Bride," and "Flower Offering" from the Sabbath School Hymnal of Isaac S. Moses; to the Bloch Publishing Co. for permission to use "The Lulab," "Evening Prayer," and "Sabbath Blessing" from Miss Jessie R. Sampter's "Around the Year in Rhymes for the Jewish Child"; to A. S. Barnes & Co., Inc., for permission to use "We Build Our School on Thee" by Sebastian W. Meyer, from *Hymns of the Christian Life* by Milton S. Littlefield; to the Boston Music Co. for permission to use "Adonai Mo Odom" from the *Z'miroth Ut'filoth Yisroel* by Rev. M. Halpern; to G. Schirmer, Inc., for permission to use "V'al Kulom"; to Eton & Mains for permission to use "God of the Nations Near and Far" and to Morris S. Lazaron for the High School services taken from his *Religious Services for Jewish Youth*.

COMMITTEE ON SYNAGOG MUSIC

# UNION HYMNAL

## Part I

## HYMNS

# Call to Worship

## How Goodly is Thy House

Henry S. Jacobs

W. A. Mozart

*mf Andante Moderato*

*mf*

1. How good - ly is Thy house, O Lord! With -
2. Hith - er we come to praise Thy name, And
3. Ac - cord us, then, Thy ten - der love; Un -

in its courts we turn to Thee, Who
hum - bly seek Thy gra - cious face; Thy
to our prayer - ful words give ear; Grant

art by Is - rael's sons a - dor'd As
truth and great - ness to pro - claim In
them ac - cept - ance from a - bove, And

God, to all e - ter - ni - ty.
this, Thy ho - ly dwell - ing place.
to our plaint be ev - er near.

# Call to Worship

## How Lovely are Thy Dwellings

PSALM 82

John Milton  St. 1 and st. 2, l. 3, alt.

Arr. fr. Schumann

1. How love - ly are Thy dwell - ings, Lord, From
2. Lord God of Hosts, that reign'st on high, They
3. For God, the Lord, both sun and shield, Gives

noise ... and troub - le free; How beau - ti - ful the
are .... the tru - ly blest Who on Thee on - ly
grace .... and glo - ry bright; No good from him shall

sweet ac - cord Of those ... who pray to Thee.
will re - ly, In Thee ... a - lone will rest.
be with-held, Whose ways ... are just and right.

# Call to Worship

## How Lovely are Thy Dwellings

### PSALM 84

Stanza 1 John Milton    Stanza 2, 3, 4. composite

Felix Mendelssohn

*mf* *Andante con moto*

1. How love - ly are Thy dwel - lings fair, O
2. My soul doth long, yea, ev - en faint Thy
3. Be - hold, the spar - row find - eth out A
4. Blest all who dwell with - in Thy house; They

*mf*

Lord of Hosts, how dear . . , The pleas - ant tab - er -
courts, O Lord, to see; . . . My heart and flesh are
house where-in to rest; . . . The swal - low al - so
ev - er give Thee praise; . . . And blest the man whose

nac - les are, Where Thou dost dwell so near.
cry - ing out, O liv - ing God, for Thee.
for her - self Hath found a peace - ful nest.
strength Thou art, Who, faith - ful, loves Thy ways.

# Call to Worship

## God is in His Holy Temple

Anonymous

H. W. Hawkes

f *Allegretto*

1. God is in His ho - ly tem - ple,
2. He is with us, now and ev - er,
3. God is in His ho - ly tem - ple,
4. Ban - ish then each base e - mo - tion,

Earth - ly thoughts, be si - lent now, While with rev' - rence
When we call up - on His name, Aid - ing ev' - ry
In the pure and ho - ly mind; In the rev' - rent
Lift us up, O Lord, to Thee, Let our souls, in

we as - sem - ble, And be - fore His pres - ence bow.
good en - deav - or, Guid - ing ev' - ry up - ward aim.
heart and sim - ple; In the soul from sense re - fined.
pure de - vo - tion, Tem - ples for Thy wor - ship be.

# Call to Worship
## Here Let Thy People

Robert Loveman

A. W. Binder

5

*mf   Andante espressivo*

1. Here let Thy peo - ple come, dear Lord, To
2. Here let Thy child - ren come, dear Lord, Bring -
3. E - ter - nal, Fa - ther, and our Guide, A -
4. We yield our hearts, our souls, our love, With -

*mf*

love, to trust, to pray, To learn the wis - dom
ing their hearts to Thee, The depths of be - ing
down the dawn - ing years, Through these, Thy sa - cred
in this ho - ly place, Smile on Thy peo - ple

of Thy word From peace - ful day to day.
sweet - ly stirr'd To faith and char - i - ty.
por - tals wide, We bring our joys, our fears.
from a - bove, Bless them with Thy vast grace.

# Morning

## Almighty Father

Heinrich Schalit

mf Religioso

1. Al - might - y Fa - ther, God of love, Look
3. As child - ren guid - ed by Thine arm, We

down in mer - cy from a - bove, And be Thy gra - cious
feel our - selves se - cure from harm, And go re - joic - ing

hands out - spread In bless - ing o'er Thy child - ren's head.
on our way, Thy pres - ence all our joy and stay.

# Almighty Father
## Continued

2. We thank Thee    for    the    care which    kept   Our homes   in
4. Then, when the    even - ing    comes once    more,    We   shall

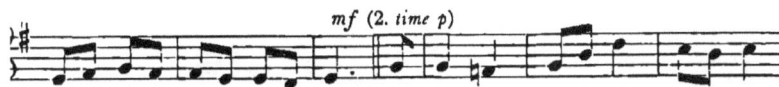

safe - ty    while   we   slept; And now we    pray, that    thro' the
a-gain Thy    grace im - plore, And lay   us    down in    peace and

day   Thy   lov - ing    eye   would    guide   our    way.
sleep, For Thou   wilt    watch   a - round   us    keep.

# Morning

## Once More, O Lord

Lily Weitzman

Jacob Weinberg

*p Adagio religioso*

1. Once more, O Lord, do I a - wak - en, Mine eyes be -
2. With ho - ly joy my heart is bound - ing, I chant a -
3. Thy boun - ty, Lord, a - gain per - mits me An - oth - er
4. Help me, my God, to trust and serve Thee, Nor from the

*mf*

hold the glo - rious light, Once more her flight has dark - ness
loud sweet hymns of praise, Thanks be to Thee, my God, my
sun - rise to be - hold, Let me not pass the day un -
path of right to stray, And when at last Thou call'st me

*espress.* *p* *rall.*

ta - ken, A - gain I bid fare - well to night.
Fa - ther, Who hast in love pro - longed my days.
heed - ful, Let me not waste its hours of gold.
hence... A - wake my soul to end - less day.

*espress.*

*p* *rall.*

8

# Morning

## Pray When the Morn Unveileth

Penina Moise

F. Brandeis

*mf Moderato*

1. Pray when the morn un - veil - - eth, Her glor - ies to thine eye;...... Pray when the sun - light fail - eth, And stars u - surp the sky.
2. Far from thy bos - om fling - - ing Each world - ly thought im - pure,..... The praise of God be sing - ing, Mor - tal for - ev - er - more.
3. Pray for the friend whose kind - - ness Ne'er fail'd in word or deed;..... Pray for the foe whose blind - ness Hath caus'd thy heart to bleed.
4. A bles - sing for thy neigh - - bor Ask thou of God a - bove;..... And on thy hal - lowed la - bor Shall fall His smile of love.

# Morning

## Splendor of the Morning Sunlight

Felix Adler

M. Tintner

*f Moderato*

1. Splen - dor of the morn - ing sun - light,
2. Let me use the gold - en hours . . . .
3. *Let me prompt be in my dut - ies,
4. And when even - ing comes and 'twink - ling

Shine in - to my heart to - day; Flood each cran - ny
As they glide so swift - ly by; Freight them with a
Ear - nest to im - prove my mind; Grate - ful to my
Stars my con - duct seem to ask, May I look a -

of my be - ing With new strength and spir - it gay.
pre - cious freight of Truth and love and knowl - edge high.
guides and teach - ers And to all my com - rades kind.
loft and tell them I have fin - ished well my task.

*Stanza 3 for children only

10

# Morning

## May He Who Kept Us

Alice Lucas                                    J. H. Rogers

*p Andante*

1. May He who kept us through the hours of night
2. How could we else our heav - y bur - den bear,
3. For un - to all, how - ev - er bright - ly rise The
4. May He who know - eth ev - er - y hu - man need,

Cause us to greet in peace the morn - ing light, While we im -
Search-ings of heart, and doubt and fear and care, If un - to
sun, there comes the hour of al - tered skies, When to the
And ev' - ry heart's de - sire, hear and heed, And through life's

plore His mer - cy in - fin - ite To guard us through the day.
Him we raised not hands of prayer For guid - ance day by day?
hills they lift their long - ing eyes, And mark the wan - ing day.
change - ful hours His child - ren lead Un - to the per - fect day.

II

# Evening

## Again, as Evening's Shadow Falls

S. Longfellow

A. W. Binder

*mf Andante religioso*

*mf*

1. A - gain, as eve - ning's sha - dow falls,
2. May strug - gling hearts that seek re - lease
3. O God, our Light, to Thee we bow!
4. Life's tu - mult we must meet a - gain,

We gath - er in these hal - lowed walls,
Here find the rest of God's own peace,
With - in all sha - dows stand - est Thou.
We can - not at the shrine re - main;

And eve - ning hymn and eve - ning prayer
And strength - ened here by hymn and prayer,
Give deep - er calm than night can bring,
But in the spir - it's se - cret cell

Rise, ming gling on the ho - ly air.
Lay down the bur - den and the care.
Give sweet - er songs than lips can sing.
May hymn and prayer for ev - er dwell!

# Evening

## The Day is Done

Lily Weitzman

Boris Levenson

*p* *Molto moderato*

1. The day is done, the night draws nigh, A
2. What though be - set with doubt and fear, What
3. To Thee a - lone my soul I bare, And
4. Give me the light of faith, I pray, To

myr - i - ad stars be - deck the sky; My droop - ing soul is
though my days seem dark and drear; Though cold the world nor
Thou a-lone can'st soothe my care; The cal - lous world may
guide me on life's wear - y way; Grant me the light that

*poco rit.*

*pp*

sore op - pressed, For I am tired and fain would rest.
heeds my pain, I shall not cry to Thee in vain.
pass me by, But Thou, O Lord, art ev - er nigh.
will not wane E'en in the dark - est night of pain.

*poco rit.*

*pp*

# Evening

## Unto the Hills

Alice Lucas        PSALM 121        Jacob Beimel

*Andante*

1. Un - to the hills I lift mine eyes, Whence
3. He is thy rock, thy shield and stay, On

comes my help that lies in God, Who is en-throned a-
thy right hand a shade al-way, The sun ne'er smit-eth

bove the skies, Who made the heav-ens and earth to be.
thee by day, The moon at night ne'er troub-les thee.

14

2. He guides thy foot o'er moun - tain steeps, He
4. The Lord will guard thy soul from sin, Thy

slum - bers not, thy soul He keeps, Be - hold He slum - bers
life from harm with - out, with - in, Thy go - ing out and

not, nor sleeps, Of Is - ra - el the guard - ian He.
com - ing in, From this time forth e - ter - nal - ly.

# Evening

## Into Thy Hands

Lily Weitzman

Cecile Hartog

*mf Andante*

1. In - to Thy hands my spir - it I com - mend,
2. And when at last life's bat - tles I have fought,

As when I wake, so when I sleep - ing lie,
Down death's dark vale my path in peace I wend,

In love di - vine my sleep Thou wilt de - fend,
My mor - tal ash - es in mine eyes are naught,

I fear not night, O God, . . . since Thou art nigh.
My soul in - to Thy hands . . . do I com - mend.

1. night . . . . . . . O God,
2. to . . . . . . . . Thy hands

16

# Evening

## Evening Prayer

15

Author unknown—Tr. Alice Lucas

David Nowakowsky—adapted by A. W. Binder

*mf* *Adagio*

1. Bless - ed art Thou, O Lord of all, Who
2. God of my fa - thers, may it be Thy
3. From thoughts of ill my slum - ber keep, And,
4. Bless - ed art Thou, O Lord most high, Who

mak - est the bands of sleep to fall Up - on mine eyes, and
will, this night to suf - fer me To lay me down in
lest the sleep of death I sleep, O light-en Thou mine
in Thy glo - rious ma - jes - ty, And in Thy gra-cious

slum - ber press Mine eye - lids down with heav-i - ness.
peace and rise In peace, when morning gilds the skies;
eyes, for Thou, Lord, dost with light the eye en - dow.
love hast giv - en Light up-on earth and light in heav'n.

17

# Evening
## When There is Peace

T. A. Davis

A. W. Binder

*p Tranquillo*

*p*

1. When there is peace, where praise hath been, And
2. When all the birds are fast a - sleep In
3. And, Lord, may those who wake - ful lie, Or
4. When shep - herds in the sun - set lands Their
5. O Fa - ther, Shep - herd, King of Love! Men

flow'rs are gent - ly clos - ing, Fa - ther on
nests of count - less num - ber, Thy watch a -
trem - ble, weak and lone - ly, Look up and
wear - ied flocks are fold - ing, Then may Thy
fail, -- Thou fail - est nev - er, -- One God, a -

Thee our hearts would lean, Re - pos - ing.
bove Thy chil - dren keep, Who slum - ber.
feel Thee stand - ing by, Thee on - ly!
Hand, O Lord, our hands Be hold - ing!
round, with - in, a - bove, For ev - er!

# Evening
## Around the Weary World

17

David Levy

N. Lindsay Norden

*Andante religioso*
*p legato*

1. A - round the wear - y world are gent - ly drawn
2. To Thee, O Lord, the fold - ed hours we leave,
3. And when, at last, our wear - y eye - lids close,

The som - ber cur - tains of ap - proach - ing night,
And to Thy care our slum - b'ring souls con - fide,
Our lat - est prayer as now in trust shall be;

To tran - quil rest the si - lent hours per - suade,
Bright vis - ions from on high our dreams at - tend,
"In peace and safe - ty I will lay me down,

'Til wak - 'ning hours to life and work in - vite.
An - gel - ic vi - gils guard on ev - 'ry side.
As - sured that Thy strong arm still keep - eth me."

19

# Aspiration

**18**

## Early Will I Seek Thee

Gustav Gottheil—Tr. fr. the Heb. of Solomon ibn Gabirol

S. Sabel

*mf Andante Religioso*

1. Ear - ly will I seek Thee, God, my ref - uge strong; Late pre-pare to
2. What this frail heart dream-eth And my tongue's poor speech, Can they ev - en

meet Thee With my even-ing song. Though un - to Thy great - ness
dis - tant To Thy great-ness reach? Be - ing great in mer - cy,

I with trembling soar, - - Yet my in-most think-ing Lies Thine eyes before.
Thou wilt not de - spise Prais-es which till death's hour From my soul shall rise.

# Aspiration

**19**

## O Lord, Be Near Me

Harry Rowe Shelley

*p* *Moderato*

1. O   Lord, be near me  when  I pray,  And guide  my thoughts a-right;
2. I   am not wise, or  brave, or strong, But grant  this pray'r to  me,
3. Teach me to come with  ear - nest mind To  wor - ship  at  Thy throne,
4. And  e - ven  if  the  songs I sing  Be naught but sim - ple lays,

*p*

*cresc.*     *dim.*

I   call  up - on Thee ev' - ry  day,   I   praise Thee ev' - ry  night.
If   I   am tempt - ed  to  do  wrong,   That I   may think of  Thee.
With words and ho - ly thoughts com-bined, And  not with words a - lone.
Still they are off - 'rings that  I  bring   In thanks  to Thee  and praise.

*cresc.*     *dim.*

**20**

## To the God of all Creation

W. W. Hull              PSALM 95          Arr. from Ludwig van Beethoven

*mf* *Andante*

1. To  the God  of  all  cre - a - tion  Let  us sing  with cheer-ful voice;
2. In  his pres - ence let  us gath - er  With glad hearts and thank-ful lays,
3. He  is King  a - mong  all  na-tions,  God  a - bove all gods is  He;
4. He  cre - a - ted land  and o-ceans,  He with beaut - y clothes the sod;

*mf*

In  the Rock  of  our  sal - va - tion  Let  us  heart-i - ly  re - joice.
And  to God, our heaven - ly  Fa - ther  Show our  joy  with psalms of praise.
In  His hand are earth's foun - da-tions,  The strong  hills and roll - ing sea.
Let  us bow  in  deep  de - vo - tion,  Bless our  Mak-er  and  our God.

21

# Aspiration

## O Lord, Where Shall I Find Thee?

Judah ben Samuel Halevi—tr. by Solomon Solis-Cohen          Jacob Weinberg

1. O Lord, where shall I find Thee? Hid is Thy lof-ty place; And where shall I not find Thee. Whose glo-ry fills all space? Who formed the world, a-bid-eth With-in man's soul al-way; ...
2. O, how shall mor-tals praise Thee. When an-gels strive in vain-- Or build for Thee a dwell-ing. Whom worlds can-not con-tain? I find Thee in the mar-vels Of Thy cre-at-ive, might, ..
3. Who saith he hath not seen Thee. Thy heavens re-fute his word; Their hosts de-clare Thy glo-ry, Though nev-er voice be heard. That Thou, tran-scend-ent, ho-ly, Joy-est in Thy creat-ures' praise,

22

Ref - uge to them that seek Him, Ran - som for them that stray.
In vis-ions in Thy Tem - ple, In dreams that bless the night.
And com - est where men are gath - ered, To glor - i - fy Thy ways.

**22**

## Lord, Do Thou Guide Me

Words by Alice Lucas—2nd st., alt.

James G. Heller

*mf* *Lento*

1. Lord, do Thou guide me on my pil-grim way, Then shall I be at
2. Pierce Thou my gloom with mer-cy's gol-den ray, Let not the mists of
3. O'er rug-ged paths be Thou my staff and stay, Be-neath Thy wings from

*mf*

peace, what - e'er be - tide me; The morn is dark and
sin from Thee di - vide me; Teach Thou my lips 'mid
storm and tem - pest hide me: Through life to death, through

clouds hang low and gray, Lord, do Thou guide me; Lord, do Thou guide.
doubts and fear to say. Lord, do Thou guide me; Lord, do Thou guide.
death to heav'n-ly day, Lord, do Thou guide me; Lord, do Thou guide.

23

# Aspiration

**23**

## Hymn of Glory

Alice Lucas,—Tr. fr. the Heb., Author unknown, 13th Cent.     Traditional "Omnom Kayn"

*f Maestoso*

1. Sweet hymns and songs will I re - cite To sing of Thee, by day and night, Of Thee, who art my soul's de - light, Of Thee, who art my soul's de - light.
2. How doth my soul with - in me yearn Be - neath Thy shad - ow to re - turn, Thy se - cret mys - ter - ies to learn, Thy se - cret mys - ter - ies to learn.
3. And e'en while yet Thy glo - ry fires My words, and hymns of praise in - spires, Thy love it is my heart de - sires, Thy love it is my heart de - sires.
4. O Thou whose word is truth al - way, Thy peo - ple see Thy face this day, O be Thou near them when they pray, O be Thou near them when they pray.
5. O may my words of bless - ings rise To Thee, who throned a - bove the skies, Art just and might - y, great and wise! Art just and might - y, great and wise!
6. My med - i - ta - tion day and night, May it be pleas - ant in Thy sight, For Thou art all my soul's de - light, For Thou art all my soul's de - light.

24

# Aspiration

## Gird Us, O God

Wm. H. Foulkes

Jacob Singer

*ff* *Moderato*

1. Gird us, O God, with hum-ble might, To serve the souls who tire;
2. Guard us, O God, with conqu'ring light, To hedge a - bout our way;

Give us stout hearts a - blaze with right To kin - dle far its fire.
Give us sure faith in dark-est night To see the dawn-ing day.

Guide us, O God, with swift-winged feet, To find the souls a - stray;
Grant us, O God, Thy death-less love, To set our spir - its free;

Give us Thy pa- tience, we en - treat, To fol - low all the way.
Give us Thy Spir - it from a - bove To bind our souls to Thee.

# Aspiration

## Happy He Who Walketh Ever

### PSALM 1

Jacob Voorsanger

H. Fabisch

*Allegro moderato*

1. Hap-py he who walk-eth ev-er In the ways of God, our Lord;
2. He shall flour-ish like a flow-er, Plant-ed by the wa-ter-side;

Hap-py he who sin-neth nev-er 'Gainst the teach-ings of His word;
God will give him grace and pow-er, In his vir-tue to a-bide.

Whose de-light is Him to serve, Day by day and year by year;
By the help of God, most tender, Shall he pros-per in his ways;

From His pre-cepts ne'er to swerve; Un-to peace shall he be near.
Vir-tue shall be his de-fend-er, Bless-ed shall be all his days.

# Aspiration
## Happy He Who Walketh Ever
### PSALM 1

Jacob Voorsanger

A. W. Binder

f   *Marcato*

1. Hap-py he who walk-eth ev-er   In the ways of God, our Lord;
2. He shall flour-ish like a flow-er,   Plant-ed by the wa-ter side;

Hap-py he who sin-neth nev-er   'Gainst the teach-ings of His word;
God will give him grace and pow-er,   In his vir-tue to a-bide.

Whose de-light is Him to serve,   Day by day and year by year;
By the help of God, most ten-der,   Shall he pros-per in his ways;

From His pre-cepts ne'er to swerve;   Un-to peace shall he be near.
Vir-tue shall be his de-fen-der,   Bless-ed shall be all his days.

# Aspiration

## How Blest the Man

### PSALM 1

B. H. Kennedy

J. Kinross

*Lento non troppo*

1. How blest the man, who fears to stray Where God-less peo-ple meet,
2. As some fair tree, which has its root The flow-ing wa-ters nigh,

Nor tar-ries in the sin-ner's way, Nor fills the scorn-er's seat:
Brings forth its sea-son-a-ble fruit And leaves that nev-er die,

But tak-ing for his sole de-light The Lord's all-per-fect law,
Thus all he do-eth pros-pers well: Not so the wick-ed fare:

He mus-es on it day and night With love and ho-ly awe.
Like chaff be-fore the driv-ing gale, They wa-ver here and there.

# Aspiration

### Prayer for Wisdom

James Montgomery

C. Hugo Grimm

*mf Maestoso*

1. Al - might - y God, in hum - ble prayer To Thee our souls we lift;
3. We ask not hon - ors, which the hours May bring and take a - way;

*mf*

Do Thou
We ask

Do Thou our wait - ing minds pre-pare For Thy most need-ful gift.
We ask not pleas - ure, pomp or power Lest we should go a - stray.

our wait - ing
not pleas - ure

2. We ask, that if Thou grant - est wealth Our alms may rich - ly
4. We ask for wis - dom; Lord, im - part The knowl - edge how to

flow; And that we may, in years of health, Good works in plen - ty sow.
live; A wise and un - der - stand-ing heart To all be - fore Thee give.

# Aspiration

**29**

## O Lord, My God

J. K. Gutheim—Tr. fr. The Hamburg Temple Hymnal

Arr. from S. Sulzer

*f Andante moderato*

1. O Lord, my God, to Thee I pray For know-ledge and for light,
2. O shed Thy light in - to my soul That I may un - der - stand

That from Thy path I may not stray When dark - ness veils my sight.
To reach my be - ing's hap - py goal, Di - rect - ed by Thy hand.

For Thee I yearn, I deep - ly long; Be Thou my guide ere I choose wrong,
Each du - ty be my soul's de-light, My cour-age true to do the right

So that my will be firm and just, My heart up - held with con-stant trust.
In weal and woe, in joy and pain, May faith and hope my heart sus - tain.

# Aspiration

## PSALM XLII

"New" Version

Reuben R. Rinder

p Andante

1. As pants the hart for cool-ing streams When heat-ed in the chase,
2. For Thee, my God, the liv-ing God, My thirst-ing soul doth pine,
3. Why rest-less, why cast down, my soul, Trust God who will em - ploy
4. Why rest-less, why cast down, my soul, Hope still and thou shalt sing

So longs my soul for Thee, O God, And Thy re-fresh-ing grace.
Oh, when shall I be - hold Thy face, Thy ma - jes - ty di - vine!
His aid for thee, and change these sighs To thank - ful hymns of joy.
The praise of Him who is thy Lord, Thy health's e - ter - nal spring.

## The Cry of Israel

Solomon Ibn Gabirol—Tr. by Solomon Solis-Cohen

James G. Heller

mf Andante

1. Thou know'st my tongue, O God, Fain would it bring
2. Thou guid'st my steps from old; If boon too high
3. My thought hast Thou made pure, As whit - est fleece;
4. Oh, be my ref - uge now, Ev'n as of yore.

A pre - cious gift - - the songs Thou mak'st me sing.
I ask - - Thou gav'st me speech, Spurn not my cry!
Thou wilt not that my heart Shall ne'er have peace.
My God, my Sav - ior, Thou - - Tar - ry no more!

31

# Aspiration

## O God, the Rock of Ages,

Edward H. Bickersteth      PSALM 90      Joseph Achron

*mf*   Andante   (♩ = 50-52)

1. O God, the Rock of A - ges, Who e - ver-more hast been,
2. Our years are like the sha -dows On sun - ny hills that lie,
3. O Thou, who canst not slumb- er, Whose light grows ne - ver pale,

*mf*

What time the temp - est ra - ges, Our dwell - ing place se - rene;
Or grass - es in the mea - dows, That bloss - om but to die --
Teach us a - right to num - ber Our years be - fore they fail;

## O God, the Rock of Ages

### Continued

Be-fore Thy first cre - a - tion, O Lord, the same as now,
A sleep, a dream, a sto - ry By strang-ers quick - ly told,
On us Thy mer - cy light - en, On us Thy good - ness rest,

To end - less ge - ne - ra - tions The e - ver - last - ing Thou.
An un - re-main - ing glo - ry Of things that soon are old.
And let Thy spi - rit bright - en The hearts Thy - self hast blessed.

# Aspiration

**33**

## I Lift Mine Eyes

C. M. C.     PSALM 121     Joseph Achron

1. I lift mine eyes un-to the hills, And to the bound-less sky;

2. The burn-ing rays of noon-tide sun, Shall smite me not by day; -

Through all life's sad and var-ied ills, Our help is from on high.

And while the e-vil path I shun, God will pro-tect my way.

# I Lift My Eyes

## Continued

The heav'n - ly King, who aye shall be,    In might  e - ter - nal reigns;

On  ev - 'ry side He  is  my  shade, And still pre-serves my soul;

When sor - row's darts en - com-pass  me,  He  ev - 'ry  hope sus-tains.

His  great-ness  e - ver  is  dis - played Through years that on-ward roll.

# Aspiration
## The Cry of Israel

Solomon Solis-Cohen—Trans. fr. the Hebrew of Solomon Ibn Gabirol

Heinrich Schalit

**34**

*ff Andante maestoso*

1. Thou know-est my tongue, O God, Fain would it bring A
3. My thought.. hast Thou made pure As whit-est fleece; Thou

pre - cious gift ... the songs Thou mak'st me sing! 2. Thou
wilt not that mine heart Shall ne'er have peace. 4. O,

guid-est my steps from eld; If boon too high I
be... my re - fuge now, E'en as of yore. My

ask.. Thou gav'st me speech. Spurn not my cry!
God, my Sa - vior, Thou -- Tar - ry no more!

# Aspiration
## Bow Down Thine Ear, Lord

**35**

Harry H. Mayer

PSALM 86

Jacob Beimel

*mp Sostenuto*

1. Bow down Thine ear, Lord, hear Thou my cry,
2. Dai - ly my pray'r soars a - loft to the sky,
3. Kind and for - giv - ing, ev - er art Thou,

Need - y, af - flict - ed, on Thee I re - ly;
Dai - ly I hope for Thy grace from on high;
Plen - teous in grace when Thy name we a - vow;

Guard Thou my life, let my faith plead for me;
Mer - ci - ful show Thy - self, Lord, un - to me,
Heark - en, O Lord, to my sor - row - ful plea,

Save Thou Thy ser - vant that trust - eth in Thee.
Glad - den Thy ser - vant that trust - eth in Thee.
Fa - ther! Re - deem - er! My trust is in Thee.

# Aspiration
## Thy Word is to My Feet a Lamp

36

"New" Version     PSALM 119     Pinchas Jassinowsky

*mf* *Andante religioso*

1. Thy word is to my feet a lamp,    The way of truth to show;
2. When I with griefs am so op-prest    That I can bear no more,
3. O let my sac-ri-fice of praise    With Thee ac-cept-ance find;
4. Thy tes-ti-mo-nies I have made    My her-i-tage and choice;

*mf*

A cheer-ing light to mark the path Where-in I ought to go,
Ac-cord-ing to Thy word, do Thou My faint-ing soul re-store,
And in Thy right-eous judg-ments, Lord, In-struct my will-ing mind,
For they, when oth-er com-forts fail, My droop-ing heart re-joice,

A cheer-ing light to mark the path Where-in I ought to go.
Ac-cord-ing to Thy word, do Thou My faint-ing soul re-store.
And in Thy right-eous judg-ments, Lord, In-struct my will-ing mind.
For they, when oth-er com-forts fail, My droop-ing heart re-joice.

38

# Aspiration

## Prayer

**37**

Alice Lucas

Theme from D'Andrieux (XVII Century)

*p  Andantino*

1. Lord God, whose breath the un - i - verse con - trols Guide
2. Fit us for what thou giv - est, Lord of all, And
3. For - give us all our sins, O King of Kings, Teach

thou the ves - sel of my life t'wards Thee, Thou tran - quil ha - ven
what thou deem - est fit on us be - stow, On us, thy chil - dren,
us to do thy will—thou knowest best— And grant us, 'neath the

*rit.*

of all storm-tossed souls, Who long at rest to be.
when to Thee we call, A - midst life's ebb and flow.
shad-ow of Thy wings In per - fect peace to rest.

*rit.*

# Aspiration

## O Lord, Thy All Discerning Eyes

John Quincy Adams      PSALM 139      Harry Rowe Shelley

*mf Maestoso*

1. O Lord, Thy all dis - cern - ing eyes My in-most pur-pose see;
2. Be - fore, be-hind, I meet Thine eye And feel Thy might - y hand;
3. If I as-cend to heav'n on high, Or make my bed be - low,

*mf*

My deeds, my words, my thoughts a - rise, A - like dis-closed to Thee.
Such know-ledge is for me too high To reach or un - der-stand;
Or take the morn - ing wings and fly O'er o - cean's ebb and flow,

# O Lord, Thy All Discerning Eyes
## Continued

My sit - ting down, my ris - ing up, Broad noon and deep - est night;
What of Thy won - ders can I know? What of Thy pur - pose see?
Or seek from Thee a hid - ing - place A - mid the gloom of night—

My path, my pil - low, and my cup Are o - pen to Thy sight.
Where from Thy spir - it shall I go? Where from Thy pres - ence flee?
A - like to Thee are time and space The dark - ness and the light.

# Aspiration

**39**

## Lord, Be Thou With Us Still

Isabella R. Hess

James G. Heller

*ff Moderato*

1. Lord, writ-ten in rocks and in wood-land, In mount-ain, and plain, and in sea,
2. And now, with a wid - er vi - sion, Made heirs of the van -ish-ed years,
3. New path-ways are o - pen be-fore us, New won-ders our eyes ev-er see,

Is the sto - ry of earth's long ex-is - tence, The sto - ry of man-kind and Thee!
Men search out the age - old se - crets, Un-known to the an-cient seers!
But the new on the old is ev-er build - ed! And man must re-ly - e'er on Thee!

For Thine is the fin-ger that wrote it, — Thy sym - bol each val-ley and hill,
And with a new rev - er-ence throb-bing, With a sense of Thy glo - ry a - thrill,
Keep Thou our spir-its un-daunt - ed Keep glow-ing our faith in Thy will

## Lord, Be Thou With Us Still
### Continued

And we are a part of the sto - ry! O Lord, may'st Thou be with us still.
They know the pow'r of Thy guid-ance O Lord, may'st Thou be with us still.
That the right is the law of Thy King-dom, O Lord, may'st Thou be with us still.

**40** As Pants the Hart
PSALM 42
Alois Kaiser

"New" version
*p   Andante con moto*

1. As pants the hart for cool-ing streams When heat-ed in the chase,
2. For Thee, my God, the liv-ing God, My thirst-ing soul doth pine,
3. Why rest-less, why cast down, my soul, Trust God who will em-ploy
4. Why rest-less, why cast down, my soul, Hope still and thou shalt sing

So longs my soul for Thee, O God, And Thy re - fresh-ing grace.
Oh, when shall I be - hold Thy face, Thy maj-es - ty... di-vine!
His aid for thee and change these sighs To thank-ful hymns of joy.
The praise of Him who is... thy Lord, Thy health's e - ter - nal spring.

# Aspiration

## Thou Ever Present Perfect Friend

Louis I. Newman

Reuben R. Rinder

*f* *Con spirito*

1. Thou ev - er - pre-sent Per - fect Friend, To Whom we ut - ter pray'r;
2. Our wrongs toward self and oth - ers are Dis - loy - al - ty to Thee,
3. O Com-rade of our in - ner life, In - spired by Thee we dream

*f*

Our souls with Thee in un - ion blend, Thy spir - it God, we share.
And friend-ship's o - pen gates they bar, Till Thou hast set us free.
Of peace that o - ver - com - eth strife, Of fel - low-ship su-preme.

# Thou Ever Present Perfect Friend
## Continued

Di - vine Com-pan -ion, near to us, I - deal of all we are,

When we with con-trite hearts re-pent, And cleanse our-selves from sin,

Thou art be - gin - ing, Thou art end, The so - lace of our years,

Thine aid is ev - er gen - er - ous, Thy coun - sel nev - er far.

We know that Thou art made con-tent, And love has en - ter'd in.

Thou ev - er - pres - ent Per - fect Friend, Who dry - est all our tears.

# Aspiration

## Father Hear

L. M. Willis

Jacob Singer
Adapted from folk-melody of "Eliyahu Hanavi"

1. Fa - ther, hear the pray'r we of - fer! Not for ease that pray'r shall be,
2. Not for - ev - er by still wa - ters Would we i - dly qui - et stay,
3. Be our strength in hours of weak-ness, In our wand'r-ings be our guide;

But for strength that we may ev - er Live our lives cour - age-ous-ly.
But would smite the liv-ing foun - tains From the rocks a - long our way.
Through en-deav-or, fail - ure, dan - ger, Fa - ther, be Thou at our side.

# Aspiration

## Haste not! Haste not! Do not Rest!

**43**

C. C. Cox—Tr. fr. v. Goethe

Arr. fr. Jacques Blumenthal

*f* *Allegro moderato*

1. Haste not! haste not! do not rest! Bind the mot - to to thy breast;
2. Haste not! let no thought-less deed Mar for aye the spir- it's speed;
3. Rest not! life is sweep-ing by, Go and dare be - fore you die;
4. Haste not! rest not! calm - ly wait; Meek-ly bear the storms of fate!

Bear it with thee as a spell; Storm or sun - shine, guard it well!
Pon - der well and know the right, On - ward then with all thy might,
Some-thing might-y and sub-lime Leave be-hind to con-quer time!
Du - ty be the po - lar guide, Do the right what-e'er be-tide!

Heed not flow'rs that 'round thee bloom, Bear it on - ward to the tomb.
Haste not, years can ne'er a - tone For one reck - less ac - tion done.
Grand it is to live for aye When these forms have passed a - way.
Haste not! rest not! con - flicts past, God shall crown thy work at last.

Heed not flow'rs that 'round thee bloom, Bear it on - ward to the tomb.
Haste not, years can ne'er a - tone For one reck - less ac - tion done.
Grand it is to live for aye When these forms have passed a - way.
Haste not! rest not! con-flicts past, God shall crown thy work at last.

47

# Aspiration

## Remember Him, the Only One

Emma Lazarus

M. Henle

*mf Larghetto*

1. Re - mem - ber Him,  the  On - ly  One,  Now,
2. Now,  ere  for  thee  the  sun  has  lost  His
3. Now,  while  thou  lov - est  all  on  earth,  And
4. Re - mem - ber Him,  the  On - ly  One,  Be -

*mf*

ere  the  years  flow  by;  Now,  while  the  smile  is
glo - ry  and  his  light;  Or  earth  re - joice  thee
deem - est  all  will  last,  Be - fore  thy  hope  has
fore  the  days  draw  nigh,  When  thou  shalt  have  no

on  thy  lip,  The  light  with - in  thine  eye:
not  with  flowers,  Nor  with  its  stars  the  night
van - ished  quite,  And  ev' - ry  joy  has  past.
joy  in  them,  And  pray - ing  yearn  to  die.

# Aspiration

## O God, All Gracious!

**45**

Penina Moise st. 1, l. 1, 3. l. 3-4, alt.

Ferdinand Dunkley

*mf*  *Andante*

*mf*

1. O God, all gra - cious! In Thy gift
2. I ask but for the prec - ious ore
3. Let wis - dom of the heart, O Lord!

Though count - less bless - ings lie,
Con - tained in vir - tue's mine;
Be now and ev - er mine;

My voice for one a - lone I lift,
And for her wreath that will en - dure
Naught else is life's sub - lime re - ward,

In pray'r to Thee on high.
When di - a - dems de - cline.
We love Thy law di - vine.

# Aspiration
## "Oh Soul Supreme!"

46
Louis I. Newman

A. W. Binder

*mf Andante espressivo*

1. O Soul su-preme a-bove us, O Life be-yond our life,
2. We hun-ger for the mean-ing With-in our world of pain;
3. For har-mo-ny and or-der, For per-fect law we seek;
4. O Lord of bound-less spa-ces, Though days be dim and drear,

*mf*

*p poco rit.*

O Heart that yearns to love us, O Guard-ian in our strife.
We tread our path-way glean-ing Thy spir-it's rich do-main.
Yet hail-ing Thee as Ward-er, To whom the low-ly speak.
Thy light is on our fa-ces, Thy heal-ing pres-ence near.

*p poco rit.*

47
Isaac Watts

O God, Our Help

PSALM 90

William Croft

*f Largo*

1. O God, our help in a-ges past, Our hope for years to come,
2. Be-fore the hills in or-der stood, Or earth re-ceived her frame,
3. Be-neath the shad-ow of Thy throne Thy chil-dren dwell se-cure;
4. O God, our help in a-ges past, Our hope for years to come,

*f*

Our shel-ter from the storm-y blast, And our e-ter-nal home.
From ev-er-last-ing Thou art God, To end-less years the same.
Suf-fi-cient is Thine arm a-lone, And our de-fence is sure.
Be Thou our guide while trou-bles last, And our e-ter-nal home.

# Aspiration
## Grant Me Strength

Lily Weitzman

Jacob Weinberg

*p  Andantino*

1. Grant me strength when skies are a - zure   And the world is   fair,
2. Grant me hope when storm-clouds gath-er,   And the skies are   gray;
3. Grant me peace when death's grim shad-ow   Looms with-in my   sight;

That the glit-ter  of earth's tin-sel,  May not me en - snare,   That the glit-ter
Grant me hope's di-vin-est prom-ise  Of  e - ter - nal   day.   Grant me hope's di-
Grant me peace till Thou dost wake me To e - ter - nal   light.   Grant me peace till

*poco rit.*   |1  2   |3

of earth's tin-sel  May not me en - snare.
vin-est prom-ise   Of  e - ter-nal   day.
Thou dost wake me To e - ter-nal   light.   light. ——

*poco rit.*   *rit.*

# Aspiration

## Jacob's Ladder

Stanzas 1 and 2, Fred. de Sola Mendes
Stanza 3, Nathan Stern

Max Grauman

1. To Beth-el came the pa-tri-arch, A dream to him re-veals
2. The gates of prayer were opened there, And an-gels bore the word
3. The praise which Ja-cob of-fered then, Be-came a faith and flame

The path by which man's soul di-rects To Heav-en its ap-peals.
The wand'rer breathed forth from his heart, By deep e-mo-tion stirred.
Which we, his heirs, still keep a-live To glo-ri-fy God's name.

# Aspiration

## O God All Gracious

**50**

Penina Moise St. 1, l. 1, 3, l. 3, 4 alt.

Composer Unknown

*f Con moto*

1. O God, all gra - cious! In Thy gift Though countless bless - ings lie,
2. I ask but for the pre - cious ore Con - tained in Vir - tue's mine;
3. Let wis - dom of the heart, O Lord! Be now and ev - er mine;

My voice for one a - lone I lift, In pray'r to Thee on high.
And for her wreath that will en - dure When di - a - dems de - cline.
Naught else is life's sub - lime re - ward , We love Thy Law di - vine.

**51**

## The Sanctity of Sorrow

W. H. Burleigh

L. Spohr

*f Moderato*          *f*

1. Oh, deem not that earth's crown - ing bliss Is found in joy a - lone,
2. As blos - soms smit - ten by the rain Their sweet - est o - dors yield;
3. So to the hopes by sor - row crushed A nob - ler faith suc - ceeds;
4. How rich and sweet and full of strength Our hu - man spir - its are,

*mf*

For sor - row, bit - ter though it be, Hath bless - ings all its own.
As where the plough - share deep - est strikes, Rich har - vests crown the field,—
And life, by tri - als fur - rowed, bears The fruit of lov - ing deeds.
In - struct - ed in the sanc - ti - ties Of suff' - ring and of prayer!

*mf*

53

# Aspiration

## God of Israel

May also be used for Confirmation or Bar Mitzwoh

Harry H. Mayer
A. W. Binder

*f Con spirito*

1. God of Is-rael, keep us faith-ful to Thy ho - ly laws; We would join with
3. Let no world-ly pomp or pleas-ure lead our hearts a - stray, Kind -er make us,

earn - est broth-ers In Thy cause. 2. We would strive to be a bless-ing
Lord, more faith-ful, Day by day. 4. Sold - iers of the light, up-hold-ing

to the hu-man race, .... Thee, be-fore all men professing, God of grace.
Is - ra- el's sacred cause, We would battle, God and Father, For Thy laws.

# Praise

## Almighty God

Alice Lucas, 2 l. each st. alt.

53

L. Lewandowski

*f  Allegro moderato*

1. Al-might - y God, who hear-est pray'r, Thou to whom we hum - bly bring
2. O Lord, our God, be with us still As  we tread life's darken-ing road;
3. Grant us Thy peace, O Lord most High, Teach us, Thou whose name we bless,

The  bur - den of our dai - ly care, The joy of prais-e's of - fer-ing,
Through com-ing days of toil and ill  Give Thou us  strength to bear our load.
With right - eous-ness to sanc - ti - fy  Our task, our joys with thank - ful-ness.

Hear, we be-seech Thee once a - gain, When we our sup-pliant voic - es raise,
Yea, and en-light - en Thou our eyes, That we, the clear - er vis - ion won,
Hear us  in mer - cy when we pray, And guide us, that each day may be

Do Thou with faith our souls sus-tain, And gra - cious-ly ac-cept  our praise.
May know Thy love, as great as wise, It  is  that laid the bur - den  on.
An - o-ther step up - on the way, Lead-ing us near-er un - to  Thee.

# Praise

## Praise to the Living God

Newton Mann, fr. Heb. att. to Daniel B. Judah (13th cent.)    Traditional Leoni "Yigdal"

*mf Maestoso*

1. Praise to the liv-ing God! All prais-ed be His name, Who
2. Form-less, all love-ly forms De-clare His lov-li-ness; Ho-
3. His spir-it flow-eth free, High surg-ing where it will, In
4. He know-eth ev-'ry thought, Our se-crets o-pen lie, End
5. E-ter-nal life hath He Im-plant-ed in the soul; His

was, and is and is to be, For aye the same! The One E-ter-nal God, Ere
ly, no ho-li-ness of earth Can His ex-press. Lo, He is Lord of all! Cre-
pro-phet's word He spake of old— He speaketh still. Es-tablish'd is His law, And
as be-gin-ning clear to His All-see-ing eye. With perfect poise He binds, Ac-
love shall be our strength and stay, While a-ges roll. Praise to the liv-ing God! All

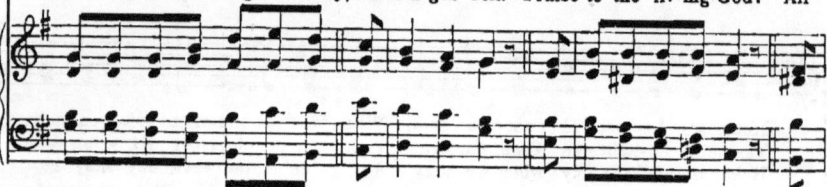

aught that now ap-pears: The First, the Last, beyond all thought His time-less years!
a-tion speaks His praise, And ev-'ry-where, a-bove, be-low, His will o-beys.
changeless it shall stand, Deep writ up-on the hu-man heart, On sea, on land.
cord-ant to the deed, To wrong the doom, to right the joy, In measured meed.
prais-ed be His name, Who was, and is, and is to be, For aye the same!

# Praise

## Nishmas

Penina Moise

Samuel Alman

*p*  *Andante con spirito*

1. All liv-ing souls shall bless Thy name, O just and grac-ious God!
3. Young men and maidens lift the voice, Thy wis-dom to ex - tol,
5. Though songs, like sounding bil-lows, too, Should from our lips pro - ceed,

*mf*

All flesh Thy pro-vid - ence pro-claim, Thy hol - y works ap - plaud.
And chil-dren in Thy praise re-joice, Fa - ther and Friend of all!
How large a debt would yet be due To Thee, from Jac-ob's seed!

*f*

2. From age to age will we re-late The wond-ers Thou hast wrought,
4. But though our hands should be out-spread, As are the ea - gle's wings,
6. Thrice ho - ly, Lord of hosts, art Thou, In - ef - fa - ble and pure!

*dim. e rall.*

De - light - ing to ex - pa - ti - ate On all which Thou hast taught.
To thank Thee for the dai - ly bread, That from Thy boun - ty springs.
Be - fore Thy Ma - jes - ty we bow, Great King, whom we a - dore.

*dim. e rall.*

# Praise

## How Wond'rous

Alice Lucas

(AKDOMUS)

Jacob Singer

Based on cantillation mode of "Akdamus"

*mf* *Andante*

1. How wond'rous is Thy world, O Lord, How great its love - li - ness!
2. How might - i - ly in flower and star Thy mar - vels are displayed,
3. Cre - a - tion's glo - ries si - lent - ly Thy sov - ereign might ac - claim
4. And in Thy grac - ious Fa - therhood Thou dost on him be - stow,
5. Lord in all men Thy spir - it lives, Thy chil - dren, Lord, are we
6. Let us in sol - emn glad - ness then The In - fi - nite a - dore,

The heavens with their star - ry horde, Earth's beau - ties num - ber - less.
Yet man is still most wond'rous far Of all that Thou hast made.
Man, man a - lone, can wor - ship Thee, And praise Thy ho - ly name.
The power to will, the will for good, (Gift great - er than we know).
And end - less peace Thy mer - cy gives To all that trust in Thee.
And reverence in our fel - low - men Thine im - age ev - er - more.

*dim.*

# Praise

## 57    The Heavens, O God, Thy Glory Tell

B. H. Kennedy                    PSALM 19                    Lewis M. Isaacs

*f Andante maestoso*

1. The heav'ns, O God, Thy glo-ry tell, Thy skill the star-ry firm-a-ment;
2. To all the earth their les-sons run, To ut-most shores their her-ald-cry: A
3. Pure is Thy soul-con-vert-ing word, Thy law which makes the sim-ple wise;

Day un-to day re-peats the spell, And night to day is el-o-quent;
tent a-midst them for the sun The hand di-vine hath set on high.
Heart-sooth-ing are Thy stat-utes, Lord; Thy truth is light un-to the eyes;

They breathe no sound, they shape no word, The list'-ning ear no voice hath heard.
As bride-groom from his cham-ber, he Comes forth in dazz-ling bril-lian-cy.
Thy fear a-bides for ev-er clean, Thy judg-ments true and right are seen.

59

# Praise

**58**
John Milton

PSALM 136

Ashkenazi Tune from Braham and Nathan's "Hebrew Melodies"

*f Lento*

1. Let us with a glad-some mind    Praise the Lord, for He is kind;
2. Let us blaze His name a - broad,    For of gods He is the God,
3. He the gold - en tress - èd sun,    Caused all day his course to run,
4. He His cho - sen race did bless,    In the waste-ful wil - der - ness,
5. All things liv - ing He doth feed;    His full hand sup-plies their need;

For His mer-cies aye en - dure,    Ev - er faith - ful, ev - er sure.
Who by all com-mand - ing might,    Filled the world with new-made light.
Th' horn-ed moon to shine by night,    'Mid her spangl-ed sis - ters bright.
He hath with a pit - eous eye,    Looked up - on our mis - er - y.
For His mer-cies aye en - dure,    Ev - er faith - ful, ev - er sure.

**59**

## Magnify the Eternal's Name

J. Montgomery St. 1, l. 1 alt.    PSALM 107

Arr. fr. G. F. Händel

*f Moderato*

1. Mag - ni - fy th' E - ter-nal's name,    For His mer-cies ev - er sure,
2. Let His ran - somed flock re - joice,    Gath-ered out of E-gypt's land,
3. In the wil - der - ness a - stray,    In the lone - ly waste they roam,
4. To the Lord, their God, they cry,    He in-clines a grac-ious ear;
5. Them to pleas - ant lands He brings,    Where the wine and ol - ive grow;
6. Come then, Is - rael, praise the Lord,    In His ho - ly dwell-ing - place,

From e - ter - ni - ty the same,    To e - ter - ni - ty en - dure.
As the peo-ple of His choice,    Plucked from the de - stroy - er's hand.
Hun - gry, faint-ing by the way,    Far from ref - uge, shel - ter, home.
Sends de-liv'r-ance from on high,    Res-cues them from all their fear.
Where from verd-ant hills the springs    Through lux-ur - iant val - leys flow.
For the wond-er of His word    And the rich - es of His grace.

# Praise

## O Worship the King
### PSALM 104

Robert Grant

Franz J. Haydn

*f Allegro*

1. O wor-ship the King, all - glo-rious a - bove! O grate-ful - ly
2. O tell of His might, O sing of His grace, Whose robe is the
3. The earth, with its stores of won-ders un - told, Al - migh - ty, Thy
4. Thy boun - ti - ful care what tongue can re - cite? It breathes in the
5. Frail chil-dren of dust, and fee - ble as frail, In Thee do we

sing His pow'r and His love! Our Shield and De - fend - er, the
light, Whose can - o - py space! His char - iots of wrath the deep
power hath found-ed of old; Hath 'stab-lished it fast by a
air, it shines in the light, It streams from the hills, it de -
trust, nor find Thee to fail; Thy mer - cies how ten - der, how

An - cient of Days, Pa - vil-ioned In splen-dor and gird - ed with praise.
thun - der-clouds form, And dark is His path on the wings of the storm.
change-less de - cree, And 'round it hath cast, like a man-tle, the sea.
scends to the plain, And sweet-ly dis - tils in the dew and the rain.
firm to the end, Our Mak-er, De - fend - er, Re - deem-er and Friend!

# Praise

## There Lives a God!

James K. Gutheim
Tr. fr. the Hamburg Temple Hymnal

Otto Lob

*f  Allegretto*

1. There lives a God! Each fi - nite crea-ture  Pro-claims His rule on  sea and
2. There lives  a God! Though storms are sweeping A-cross our  pil-grim paths of
3. There is   a God! When life is wan-ing,  His love   is near from dread to

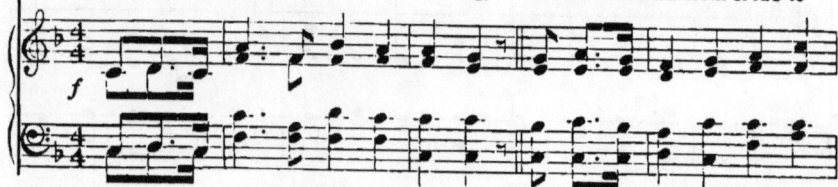

land; Throughout all changing forms of  na-ture  Is clear - ly shown His mighty
life,  More bright the morn that ends the weep-ing Through nights of el - e-men - tal
save;  My years are all  of His  or - dain-ing He on - ly tak-eth what He

hand.  In  ev' - ry place  is heard the  call: "The Lord of Hosts has made us all."
strife.  Wher-ev-er God does choose my way,  I  fol - low Him without dis-may.
gave.  The grave shall not end all  for  me,  Thou liv-est, God, I live in Thee.

# Praise

## O Bless the Lord, My Soul

Isaac Watts      PSALM 103      Traditional "Az Yasheer" melody
Arr. by A. W. Binder

*f Con moto*

1. O bless the Lord, my soul!    His grace to thee pro-claim,
2. O bless the Lord, my soul!    His mer-cies bear in mind;
3. He will not al-ways chide;    He will with patience wait;
4. He par-dons all thy sins;    Pro-longs thy fee-ble breath;
5. He clothes thee with His love,    Up-holds thee with His truth,
6. Then bless His ho-ly name,    Whose grace has made thee whole,

*f*

And all that is with-in me join    To bless His ho-ly name.
For-get not all His ben-e-fits:    The Lord to thee is kind.
His wrath is ev-er slow to rise,    And read-y to a-bate.
He heals all thine in-firm-i-ties    And ran-soms thee from death.
And like the ea-gle He re-news    The vig-or of thy youth.
Whose lov-ing kind-ness crowns thy days:    O bless the Lord, my soul!

# Praise

## All the World

Israel Zangwill
Tr. tr. the Hebrew "Vaye-esayu"

A. W. Binder

*f   Andante Maestoso*

1. All the world shall come to serve Thee, And bless Thy glo-rious name,
2. They shall build for Thee their al - tars, Their i - dols o - ver-thrown,
3. With the com - ing of Thy king- dom The hills will shout with song,

And Thy right - eous-ness tri - um - phant The is - lands shall ac - claim.
And their grav - en gods shall shame them As they turn to Thee a - lone.
And the is - lands laugh ex - ul - tant, That they to God be - long.

Yea the peo - ples shall go seek - ing, Who knew Thee not be - fore,
They shall wor - ship Thee at sun - rise And feel Thy kingdom's might
And through all Thy con-gre - ga - tions, So loud Thy praise shall ring,

And the ends  of earth shall praise Thee,    And    tell    Thy greatness o'er.
And im-part Thy  un- der-stand - ing,       To     those   a-stray  in  night.
That the  ut - most peoples, hear - ing,     Shall   hail    Thee crown-ed King.

**64**          Earth, With All Thy Thousand Voices

Edward Churton, abridged          PSALM 66          Adapted from
                                   Lewandowski's "S'u Sh'oreem" by A. W. B.

*f  Animato*

1. Earth, with  all  thy  thousand voic-es    Praise  in songs th' e - ter - nal King;
2. Lord, from each far - peo-pled dwelling   Earth shall raise the   glad ac-claim;
3. Bless  the Lord, who ev - er  liv - eth;  Sound His praise through ev'ry land.

Praise His name, whose praise re - joic - es    Ears that hear, and tongues that sing.
All    shall come, Thy great-ness tell - ing,   Sing Thy praise, and bless Thy name.
Who    our dy - ing  souls re - viv - eth,      By  whose arm  up- held we stand.

# Praise

## Praise Ye the Lord!

Penina Moise

Lewis M. Isaacs

*f Allegro*

1. Praise ye the Lord! for it is good   His might-y acts to mag - ni - fy,
2. Break forth, O Is - rael, in - to song,   Let hymns as-cend to heav-en's vault;
3. Let hal - le - lu - jah loud-ly rise!   Let hal - le - lu - jah soft - ly fall!

And make those mer - cies un - der - stood,   His hand de-lights to mul - ti -
No sweet - er task has mor - tal tongue   Than its Cre - a - tor to ex -
Un - til on an - gel lips it dies,   As they un - to each oth - er

ply.   Praise ye the Lord!   Praise ye the Lord!
alt.   Praise ye the Lord!   Praise ye the Lord!
call,   Praise ye the Lord!   Praise ye the Lord!

# Praise

## God is the Giver of All

Christopher Wordsworth

Max Grauman

*mf Moderato*

1. O Lord of heaven, and earth, and sea, To
2. For peace - ful homes, and health - ful days, For
3. We lose what on our - selves we spend, We
4. To Thee, from whom we all de - rive Our

Thee all praise and glo - ry be; How shall we show our
all the bless-ings earth dis - plays, We owe Thee thank-ful -
have as treas - ure with - out end What ev - er, Lord, to
life, our gifts, our pow'r to give; O may we ev - er

love to Thee, Who giv - - est all?
ness and praise, Who giv - - est all.
Thee we lend, Who giv - - est all.
with Thee live, Who giv - - est all.

# Praise

## Sing to the Sovereign of the Skies

Hamburg Temple Hymnal, Translated by Felix Adler

Boris Levenson

*Tempo di marcia*

1. Sing to the Sov'reign of the skies, To His great name a - lone,
2. Praise be to Thee, who didst com-mand, Thy first-born Is - ra - el,

Let wing - ed words of praise a - rise    To the Al-might-y's throne.
In ev-'ry clime, in ev - 'ry land,    Thy liv-ing truths to tell.

For He has given His law of light    A rad - i - ant star to be;
O may these ev-er be our guide, And bear us safe - ly o'er

## Sing to the Sovereign of the Skies
### Continued

*f*   *dim. e rit.*

To guide thine err-ing  steps a - right,  Make it  a  law  for  thee.
Life's dark and swift-ly flow-ing tide,  Un - til it flows  no  more.

*f*   *dim. e rit.*

**68**                                   **God**

James Cowden Wallace  1793 (?) –1841                    Eugen Haile

*mf* *Andante*

1. There is   an Eye   that nev - er sleeps   Be - neath the wing  of night; of night;
2. There is   an Arm  that nev - er tires    When hu-man strength gives way; gives way;
3. That Eye  un-seen o'er-watch-eth all;    That Arm up-holds the sky; the sky,

*mf*

There is    an  Ear   that nev - er shuts  When sink the beams of  light.
There is     a  love  that nev - er fails   When earth - ly  loves  de - cay.
That   Ear doth hear the spar-rows call;  That  love is   ev   er   nigh.

# Praise

## Who is Like Thee, O Universal Lord

James K. Gutheim

A. W. Binder

*f* Con spirito

1. Who is like Thee, O U - ni-ver-sal Lord, Who dare Thy praise and glory share,
2. Thy ten-der love em-brac-es all man-kind, Thy chil-dren all by Thee are blest;

Who is in heav'n, Most High, like Thee adored, Who can on earth with Thee compare?
Re - pen-tant sin -ners with Thee mercy find; Thy hand up-hold-eth the oppressed;

Thou art the One true God a - lone, And firm - ly found-ed is Thy throne.
All worlds at - test Thy pow'r sub - lime; Thy glo - ry shines in ev - 'ry clime.

70

# Praise

## With the Voice of Sweet Song

Harry H. Mayer

Frederic H. Cowen

*f* *Andante con moto*

1. With the voice of sweet song, In a hymn, clear and strong,
2. Where the sun's rays are shed, Or the moon-beams are spread,
3. Then, to God be our song, In a hymn, clear and strong,

To God let us ren - der our prais - - - es!
His gen - er - ous boun - ty pro - vid - - - eth;
Un - ceas - ing the bless - ings he sends us;

From His store of de-lights All our days, all our nights,
Through the win-ter's wild wrath, Through the sum - mer's still path,
In His care we a - bide, In His love we con - fide,

How rich - ly with pleas - ures He gra - - - ces.
Our foot - steps se - cure - ly He guid - - - eth.
His mer - cy for - ev - er at - tends us.

71

# Praise

## The Lord—the Lord of Glory Reigns

Mrs. Follen      PSALM 93      S. Rappaport

1. The Lord—the Lord of glo - ry reigns In maj - es - ty ar - rayed;
2. Thou art from ev - er - last - ing, Lord; For - ev - er fixed Thy throne;
3. The might - y waves are roll - ing high, The floods lift up their voice;
4. But Thou, O Lord, art might - ier far, The tem-pests bow to Thee;
5. He who can calm the storm - y deep Will give His ser-vants peace;

His pow'r the un - i - verse sus-tains; By Him it first was made.
All sprang from Thy cre - a - tive word; Thou art the Ho - ly One.
They seem to meet the bend - ing sky; The roar - ing storms re - joice.
Thy voice can still their rag - ing war, And smooth the troub-led sea.
His prom - is - es He'll ev - er keep; His mer - cies nev - er cease.

## O Lord, Our King

B. H. Kennedy      PSALM 8      Samuel Alman

f Maestoso (M. M. ♩ = 108)

1. O Lord our King how bright Thy fame In all the earth, how
2. Lord what is man, that in Thy mind, His works and ways re -
3. To man's do - min - ion all must yield, The sheep and ox - en

# O Lord, Our King
## Continued

great Thy name, Thou who hast made the hea-ven-ly height
mem-brance find? Or what the child of man, to share,
of the field, The wild beast in the for - est lair,

The dwell-ing of Thy glo-ri-ous light! Full oft I muse, with
Thy ten-der love, Thy guard-ian care? He stands, Thy chos-en
The wild bird scud - ding through the air, The fish-es that in

rev-e-rent eyes, Read-ing the beau-ty of the skies, The moon and
de - pu-ty To rule the creat-ures formed by Thee: Thy power be-
o - cean glide, And myr-iad na--tions of the tide,— O Lord, our

stars, that ord - ered stand O-be-di-ent to Thy fram-ing hand.
neath his feet has laid, What e'er on earth that power has made.
King, how bright Thy fame, In all the earth, how great Thy name!

# Praise

## In God, the Holy

Penina Moise

Harry Rowe Shelley

*f Larghissimo*

1. In God the ho - ly, wise and just, From child-hood's ten-der years,
2. From ev - 'ry page that time has turned, Since that bright sea-son fled,
3. Oh, should my term of life ex-ceed Frail man's al - lot - ted days,

Have I re - posed with per - fect trust, My chang-ing hopes and fears.

Some use - ful les-sons have I learned, Some whole-some mor-al read.

Un - til the last my pray'r would plead For strength my God to praise.

# Praise

## Arise to Praise the Lord

James K. Gutheim, Tr. fr. Hamburg Temple Hymnal

A. W. Binder

*f Spirited*

1. A - rise to praise the Lord, A - wake my slum-b'ring soul,
2. He is thy rock, thy shield And will not fail to be;

Strike deep the stir - ring chord, Thy Mak - er to ex - tol.
What off - 'ring canst thou yield For so much love to thee?

For He pre-served thy life When dark - ness closed a - round,
If but sin - cere thy gift, It will His fa - vor find,

'Midst dan - gers ev - er rife, He was thy re - fuge found.
Thy heart to Him up - lift, And be to Him re - signed.

75

# Praise

## God of Grace

Edward Churton · PSALM 67 · Eugen Haile

*f Andante*

1. God of grace, O let Thy light Bless our dim and blind - ed sight;
2. Praise to Thee, the faith-ful Lord; Let all tongues in glad ac-cord
3. Praise to Thee, all-faith - ful Lord! Let all tongues in glad ac-cord

Like the day-spring on the night Bid Thy grace ... to shine......
Learn the good thanks-giv - ing word, Ev - er prais - - ing Thee:.....
Speak the good thanks-giv - ing word, Praise Thee ev - - er - more:.....

To the na - tions led a -stray Thine e - ter - nal love dis - play;
Let them, moved to glad - ness, sing, Own - ing Thee their Judge and King;
So the fruit - ful earth's in-crease God shall give, the God of peace,

*p · cresc. · ff*

Let Thy truth di - rect their way, Till the world be Thine.
Right-eous truth shall bloom and spring Where Thy rule shall be.
Whom the world shall nev - - er cease Hum-bly to a - - dore.

# Praise

## The Lord of All

F. De Sola Mendes. Tr. fr. the "Adon Olam," page 328.  S. Sulzer

*f  Andante con moto*

1. The Lord of all, who reigned su - preme  Ere first cre -
2. When this, our world, shall be no more,  In maj - es -
3. A - lone is He be - yond com - pare,  With - out div -
4. He is my God, my Sav - ior He,  To whom I
5. Then in His hand my - self I lay,  And trust - ing

a - - tion's form was framed;  When all was fin - ished
ty......  He still shall reign,  Who was, Who is, Who
i - - sion or al - ly,  With - out in - i - tial
turn in sor - row's hour—  My ban - ner proud, my
sleep, and wake with cheer;  My soul and bod - y

by His will His name  Al - might - y was pro-claimed.
will for aye In end - less glor - y still re - main.
date or end, Om - nip - o - tent He rules on high.
ref - uge sure, Who hears and an - swers with His pow'r.
are His care; The Lord doth guard, I have no fear.

# Praise

## The Heavens, O God,

B. H. Kennedy

PSALM 19

Ludwig van Beethoven
Arr. by A. W. B.

1. The heav'ns O God, Thy glo - ry tell, Thy skill the star - ry
2. Pure is Thy soul-con-vert - ing word, Thy law which makes the

fir - ma-ment; Day un - to day re-peats the spell, And night to
sim - ple wise; Heart-soothing are Thy stat - utes, Lord; Thy truth is

day is el - o-quent; They breathe no sound, they shape no
light un - to the eyes; Thy fear a-bides for-ev - er

78

The Heavens, O God,
Continued

word,
The list - - ening ear no voice hath heard.
clean,
Thy judg - ments true and right are seen.

They beathe no sound, they shape no word, The list-ening ear no
Thy fear a - bides for - ev - er clean, Thy judgments true and

voice hath heard, The list - ening ear no voice hath heard.
right are seen, Thy judg-ments true and right are seen.

# Praise

## Loud Let the Swelling Anthems Rise

Felix Adler, Tr. fr. Hamburg Temple Hymnal

N. Lindsay Norden

1. Loud let the swell - ing an - thems rise, Let all the na - tions sing
2. Praise ye the Lord, pro - claim His might, Who made our fath - ers free;
3. Then let your hymns of thanks as - cend To the Al - might - y's throne,

To Him who rules a - bove the skies, Un - to the Lord, our King.
Who gave to us a heaven - ly light, The sun of lib - er - ty.
To whom in grat - i - tude we bend, Who reigns su - preme a - lone.

The sun, at His com - mand, Re - newed the bar - ren ground,
A pros-p'rous peo - ple hails Its bright and gen - ial ray,
Of His great mer - cies tell, Whom earth and heaven a - dore,

Rich har - vest decks the land, And plen - ty smiles a - round.
And gold - en peace pre - vails Wide o'er the land to - day.
Let hal - le - lu - jahs swell His praise for ev - er - more.

**79**   Israel's Song
A HYMN OF PRAISE

Robert Loveman                                           Boris Levenson

*f Allegro moderato*

1. There is a joy the heart can feel, That earth does not pos - sess,
2. Sing, nat - ions of the globe, re-joice, For Is - rael's God is King:
3. And in our heart of right-eous birth, Thy last - ing love hold sway,

*rit.*

It com - eth from a true ap-peal, To God for hap - pi - ness.
Let man-kind rise with joy - ous voice, And earth his tem-ple, ring.
Un - til this night of life on earth, Is changed to hea-ven's day.

*rit.*

# Praise
## The Lord of All

F. De Sola Mendes, Tr. fr. the "Adon Olam"     Sephardic Melody.   A. W. Binder

**80**

*f  A dante maestoso*

1. The Lord of all, who reigned su - preme Ere
2. When this, our world, shall be no more, In
3. A - lone is He, be - yond com - pare, With -
4. He is my God, my Sav - ior He, To
5. Then in His hand my - self I lay, And

first cre - a - tion's form was framed; When all was fin - ish'd
maj - es - ty--- He still shall reign, Who was, Who is, Who
out di - vi-- sion or al - ly, With - out in - i - tial
Whom I turn-- in sor-row's hour— My ban - ner proud, my
trust - ing sleep,- - and wake with cheer; My soul and bod - y

*Ped.*

by His will His name Al - might - y was pro-claimed.
will for aye In end - less glo - ry still re - main.
date or end, Om - ni - po - tent He rules on high.
ref - uge sure-- Who hears and an - swers with His pow'r.
are His care; The Lord doth guard, I have no fear.

# Praise

## Now Bless the God of All

Israel Abrahams

Frederic H. Cowen

*f* Moderato

1. Now bless the God of all, Who peace to us has giv - en;
2. From our first days of life, When peace-ful - ly we rest - ed
3. O grant, Lord, that our hearts In joy may ev - er treas - ure

Whose light up - on us shines, And grace from high - est heav - en.
With - in our mo - ther's arms, Un - troub - led, un - mo - lest - ed,
That peace which Thou dost grant To men in boun-teous meas - ure.

The God of Is - rael, He Up - on all men be - stows
Thy love did bear us up, Thy mer - cy nev - er failed;
And, Lord, our hands con - firm To work for all men's peace,

The won - ders of that Hand, From which all bless - ing flows.
When we were weak Thy strength To make us strong a - vail'd.
Our God, whose love is sure, Whose mer - cies nev - er cease.

# Providence

## Lo, Our Father's Tender Care

James K. Gutheim

James H. Rogers

1. Lo, our Fath-er's ten-der care Slum-bers not, nor sleep-eth;
2. Lo, our Fath-er's gra-cious love Slum-bers not, nor sleep-eth;

Gra-cious gifts His lav-ish hand Dai-ly on us heap-eth.
Trust with all thy heart in Him, Who thy por-tion keep-eth;

Though fierce storms, though per-ils low-er
Who till now pro-tec-tion grant-ed

# Lo, Our Father's Tender Care
## Continued

Is    not  God   our   shelt'-ring   tow'r?   Trem - ble   not!
And   thy   for - tune  wise - ly   plant-ed. Fear   thou   not!

At  His word the storm  is  still,   Per - ils van - ish  at   His  will;
God, who life  and be - ing grants,   Kind - ly,  too, sup-plies  our wants;

And  His love   or-dains  our  lot,   Lo,   our Guard-ian slum - bers not.
Let   but du - ty guide  our  lot   Lo,   our Guard-ian slum - bers not.

# Providence

## God Moves in a Mysterious Way

William Cowper

A. W. Binder

*mf* *Lento*

1. God moves in a mys - ter - ious way. His won - ders
2. Deep in un - fath - om - a - ble mines Of nev - er -
3. Ye fear - ful saints, fresh cour - age take, The clouds ye
4. Judge not the Lord by fee - ble sense, But trust Him
5. His pur - pos - es will rip - en fast, Un - fold - ing
6. Blind un - be - lief is sure to err, And scan His

to per - form; -- He plants His foot - steps
fail - ing skill -- He treas - ures up His
so much dread -- Are big with mer - cy,
for His grace; -- Be - hind a frown - ing
ev - 'ry hour; -- The bud may have a
work in vain; -- God is His own in -

in the sea, And rides u - pon the storm.
bright de - signs, And works His sov - ereign will.
and shall break In bless - ings on your head.
Prov - i - dence He hides a smil - ing face.
bit - ter taste But sweet will be the flower.
ter - pre - ter And He will make it plain.

# Providence

## Our Shepherd is the Lord

Felix Adler  
Tr. fr. the Hamburg Temple Hymnal

PSALM 23

P. C. Lutkin

f Moderato

1. Our Shep - herd is the Lord, And us His flock He lead - eth;
2. Through night of death and fear We pass with - out dis - may; --
3. Thus hap - py is our lot With - in this earth - ly sphere, --

His earth, with beau - ty stored, Yields all that man-kind need - eth.
His light re - ful - gent shines To guard us on our way, --
While heav - en's bless - ings smile In rich - ness, far and near. --

Is there a thirst - ing heart? His staff to wa - ters leads it;
His arm grants vic - to - ry, Dis - pen - ses joy and bliss, --
God decks our life with gifts Of His a - bun - dant grace, --

To soothe its ach - ing smart, With joy and light He feeds it.
And trust - ing in His help We can - not step a - miss. --
Un - til e - ter - nal rest Com - pletes our pil - grim race. --

# Faith, Trust and Courage

### Father, to Thy Dear Name

J. Leonard Levy

A. W. Binder

*p Andante*

1. Fa - ther, to Thy dear name I lift my voice in praise, For Thou hast
2. As I may jour - ney on Life's high-way, smooth or rough, If Thou wilt

been my guide Through all my days. What-e'er on earth is mine Came from Thy
be my help, It were e - nough. Though time may take from me Much that I

lov - ing hand, Right - ly to use and share At Thy com-mand.
now hold dear, Let it not take the hope That Thou art near.

# Faith, Trust and Courage

## The Lord, My Shepherd Still Has Been

Alice Lucas        PSALM 23        A. W. Binder

1. The Lord, my Shep-herd still has been, There-fore no want I know;
2. He makes my soul at peace to be From pain and sore dis-tress,
3. Yea, though death's dark-some vale I trod, Yet would I fear no ill,
4. Thou dost for me a ta-ble spread In pres-ence of my foes,
5. Good-ness and mer-cy stead-fast-ly Shall fol-low me al-ways,

He lead-eth me in pas-tures green And where calm wa-ters flow.
And for His name's sake guid-eth me In paths of right-eous-ness.
For e-ven there Thy staff and rod Would be my com-fort still.
With oil an-noint-est Thou my head, My cup it o-ver-flows.
And in the house of God shall I Dwell to the end of days.

89

# Faith, Trust and Courage
## Our Guiding Star

**87**

Norman Macleod

PSALM 37, 3

F. Mendelssohn

*f* Maestoso

1. Cour-age, broth-er, do not stum-ble, Though the path be dark as night;
2. Let the road be rough and drear-y, And its end far out of sight,
3. Per - ish pol - i - cy and cun-ning! Per - ish all that fears the light!
4. Sim - ple rule and saf - est guid-ing, In - ward peace and in - ward might,

There's a star to guide the hum-ble, "Trust in God and do the right."
Press on brave-ly! strong, or wea - ry, "Trust in God and do the right."
Wheth - er los - ing, wheth-er winning, "Trust in God and do the right."
Star up - on our path a - bid-ing, "Trust in God and do the right."

**88**
## All as God Wills

John Greenleaf Whittier

Joseph Barnby

*mf* Moderato

1. All as God wills, who wise - ly heeds To give or to with - hold,
2. E - nough, that bless-ings un - de-served Have mark'd my err - ing track;
3. That more and more a prov - i-dence Of love is un - der - stood,
4. No long - er for-ward or be-hind I look, in hope or fear,

And know-eth more of all my needs Than all my pray'rs have told.
That, where-so - e'er my feet have swerved, Thy chast'ning turned me back;
Mak - ing the springs of time and sense Sweet with e - ter - nal good;
But grate - ful take the good I find, God's bless-ing, now and here.

# Faith, Trust and Courage
## Ah, Well It Is That God Should Read

Grace Aguilar
Stanza 1, lines 5 and 6, and st. 2, alt.

Georg Neumark, har. J. S. Bach

*p Grave*

1. Ah, well it is that God should read, And none but
2. Lift but to God the tear - dimmed eye And bend in
3. Come, then, and seek the Fount of love, Whose liv - ing

God, our in-most soul, That He a-lone can see it bleed
prayer the sink-ing knee, He will re-ceive each swell-ing sigh
wa - ters all may share; The Friend who sits en-shrined a - bove

'Neath its dark veil of self-con-trol. Grieve not that man can
And heed our wants what-e'er they be. In hearts that trust Him
Will all our sor - rows soothe and bear. Come but to Him and

nev - er know Our spir - it's deep - est joy or woe.
He or - dains A love no earth - ly doubt e'er stains.
He will give Us fitt - ing grace for Him to live.

# Faith, Trust and Courage
## As God Wills

Harry H. Mayer

Boris Levenson

*mf Moderato*

1. In sun - shine and in storm, O God, I lean con - tent up - on Thine arm, Thy lov - ing kind - ness com - forts me, And guards my soul from ev - 'ry harm.

2. I can - not fa - thom Thy de - signs, But wheth - er life seem good or ill, I calm - ly rest up - on Thy love, And humb - ly strive to do Thy will.

3. Could I but clear - ly see as Thou, And un - der - stand, come joy or woe, The hid - den pur - pose of Thy plan, Then should I choose Thy way to go.

4. In sor - row and in joy, a - like, Thy will is on - ly for my good, My bless - ings and my bur - dens all Are gifts by Wis - dom un - der - stood.

*rit.*

92

# Faith, Trust and Courage

## Rest in the Lord, My Soul

Maltbie D. Babcock      PSALM 37, 7, 8      A. W. Binder

*mf Andante*

1. Rest in the Lord, my soul; — Com - mit to Him thy way; — What to thy sight seems dark as night, To Him is bright as day. —

2. Rest in the Lord, my soul; — He planned for thee thy life; — Brings fruit from rain, brings good from pain, And peace and joy from strife. —

3. Rest in the Lord, my soul; — This fret - ting weak - ens thee; — Why not be still? Ac - cept His will, Thou shalt His glo - ry see. —

*mf*

93

# Faith, Trust and Courage

## Resignation

Abraham Ibn Ezra.— Tr. by Alice Lucas

James G. Heller

*p Andante*

1. I hope for the sal - va - tion of the Lord, In
2. Hence doubt - ing heart! I will the Lord ex - tol With
3. All that is hid - den, shall mine eyes be - hold, And
4. Sweet is ev'n sor - row com - ing in His name, Now

Him I trust, when fears my be - ing thrill, Come life, come
glad - ness, for in Him is my de - sire, Who, as with
the great Lord of all be known to me, Him will I
will I seek its pur - pose to ex - plore, His praise will

death, ac - cord - ing to His word, He is my por - tion still.
fat - ness, sat - is - fies my soul, That doth to heav'n as - pire.
serve, His am I as of old; I ask not to be free.
I con - tin - ual - ly pro - claim, And bless Him ev - er - more.

94

# Faith, Trust and Courage

## God Supreme!

**93**

Penina Moise, St. 1 and 2;
Edward N. Calisch, St. 3 and 4;
Last line of each stanza alt.

Joseph Achron

*p Andante (♩ = 58-60)*

1. God su-preme! to Thee we pray: Let our lips be taught to say,
2. What Thy wis-dom may dic-tate, Let Thy ser-vant vin-di-cate,
3. Thou a-lone dost best de-cide What-so-e'er shall us be-tide;
4. When our sky is o-ver-cast, When our life-work's o'er at last,

*p*

Whe-ther good or ill may flow,
Though it may our hopes o'er-throw,
Be our stat-ion high or low,
When Thou call'st for us to go, Hea-ven-ly Fa-ther

be it so, Hea-ven-ly Fa-ther be it so.

95

# Faith, Trust and Courage

## 94
### O Sometimes Gleams

John G. Whittier

A. W. Binder

mf Lento

1. O sometimes gleams up-on my sight, Through present wrong, th' eternal Right!
2. That all of good the past hath had Re-mains to make our own time glad,
3. Through the harsh nois-es of our day A low, sweet pre-lude finds its way;
4. Henceforth my heart shall sigh no more For old-en time and ho-lier shore;

And, step by step, since time be-gan, I see the stead-y gain of man.
Our com-mon dai-ly life di-vine, And ev-'ry land a Pal-es-tine.
Thru clouds of doubt and creeds of fear A light is break-ing, calm and clear.
God's love and bless-ing, then and there, Are now and here and ev-'ry-where.

## 95
### God Is My Strong Salvation

James Montgomery

PSALM 27

A. W. Binder

f Moderate tempo, but spirited

1. God is my strong sal-va-tion; Of whom shall I fear?
2. Place on the Lord re-li-ance, My soul, with cour-age wait,

# God Is My Strong Salvation
## Continued

In dark-ness and temp - ta - tion, My light, my help is near.
His truth be thine af - fi - ance, When faint and des - o - late.

Though hosts en - camp a - round me, Firm to the fight I stand;
His might thine heart shall strengthen, His love thy joy in-crease,

What ter - ror can con - found me With God at my right hand?
Mer - cy thy days shall leugth - en, The Lord will give thee peace.

# Faith, Trust and Courage

## Father, to Thee We Look in All Our Sorrow

**96**

F. L. Hosmer

F. Mendelssohn

*mf Adagio non troppo*

1. Fa - ther, to Thee we look in all our sor - row; Thou art the
2. Naught shall af - fright us on Thy good-ness lean - ing; Low in the
3. Pa - tient, O heart, though heav-y be thy sor - rows! Be not cast

foun - tain whence our heal - ing flows; Dark though the night, joy
heart faith sing - eth still her song; Chas - tened by pain, we
down, dis - qui - et - ed in vain; Yet shalt thou praise Him,

com-eth with the mor - row; Safe - ly they rest who in Thy love re - pose.
learn life's deeper mean-ing, And in our weak-ness Thou dost make us strong.
when these darkened furrows, Where now He plougheth, wave with golden grain.

98

# Faith, Trust and Courage

**97**

## O God, Whose Law from Age to Age

John Haynes Holmes

Jacob Singer

*Maestoso*

1. O God, whose law from age to age, No chance or change can know,
2. The winds, Thy faith-ful mes-sen-gers, Are guid-ed by Thy hand,
3. Thy ho-ly pur-pose moves be-fore The na-tions on their way,
4. Dear Fa-ther, we would learn to trust The do-ing of Thy will,

Whose love for-e-ver more a-bides, While ae-ons come and go;
Thy min-i-sters, the flames of fire, O-bey Thy stern com-mand;
And leads the stumbling hosts of men From dark-ness in-to day.
And in Thy per-fect law of love Our doubts and fears would still.

From all the strife of earth-ly life, To Thine em-brace we flee;
The seas resound with-in the bound Where Thy do-min-ion reigns,
No cap-tain's sword, no prophet's word, But Thy great mer-cy prove;
Help us to know, in joy or woe, Thy ways are al-ways best.

And 'mid our crowd-ing doubts and fears Would put our trust in Thee.
And wheel-ing plan-ets seek the paths Thy might-y will or-dains.
No clime or kin-dred but at-test Thy prov-i-dence of love.
And we, Thy chil-dren ev-er-more, By Thy great good-ness blest.

# Faith, Trust and Courage

## The Worth of Suffering

William Henry Burleigh

J. H. Rogers

*mf Con moto*

1. O deem not that earth's crown - ing bliss Is
2. As blos - soms smit - ten by the rain, Their
3. So the hopes by sor - row crushed, A

found in joy a - lone; — For sor - row, bit - ter
sweet - est o - dors yield, — As where the plough has
no - bler faith suc - ceeds, — And life by tri - als

though it be, Hath bless - ings all its own.
deep - est struck, Rich har - vests crown the field.
fur - rowed, bears The fruit of lov - ing deeds.

# Truth and Light
## Let There be Light

Mrs. I. L. Rypins                                    Jacob Singer

*f Maestoso*

1. While yet the earth mid'st cha - os whirled, And all was
2. Forth flashed the sun's ma - jes - tic rays, The orb of
3. List for God's voice; 'twill pierce the night; The light of

clothed in - night God's might - y voice the dark - ness
day was - born, And —— night, of name - less
Truth will - shine, So shall thy soul, its dark - ness

pierc - ed, He said, "Let there be light."
ter - rors, by — A star - ry host, was shorn.
fled, —— Be cloth'd with light di - vine.

# Truth and Light

## Happy He That Never Wanders

Felix Adler, tr. fr. the Hamburg Temple Hymnal

A. W. Binder

*f* *Andante marcatissimo*

1. Hap - py    he    that    nev - er wan - ders    From    the    path of
2. In    the    des - ert    of    our wand'r-ings,    O'er    life's wide and
3. O    E - ter - nal    Fa - ther, teach us    Well    Thy sa - cred

truth    a - stray,    Whom    the    light    of    knowl - edge guid - eth
track - less    sand,    But    a    sin - gle    path    can lead us
word    to    know;    Light    up - on    the    soul,    and    qui - et

## Happy He That Never Wanders
### Continued

On  life's dark  and  storm - y  way.  Joy - ful - ly  and
Safe - ly  to  the  prom - ised  land.  But  be strong, O
On  the anx - ious  heart  be - stow.  May  our  life  be

well  he  la - bors,  Till  his  toil  and  cares  are  past,
man,  and doubt not;  Look  a - loft!  the  ra - diant  light
pure  be - fore Thee,  Till  its  race  on  earth  is  o'er;

And  the wea - ry  pil - grim rest - eth  In  e - ter - nal bliss  at last.
Of  the star of  truth will guide thee  In  thy troub-led course a - right.
May Thy bless - ings  rest  up-on  us,  And Thy peace for - ev - er more.

# Truth and Light

## Come, Ye Faithful Servants

J. Leonard Levy

Boris Levenson
Free adaptation of a Synagogue Chant

f Moderato

1. Come, ye faith - ful ser - vants Of God's ho - ly cause,
2. Sin and mis - deed tri - umph, Er - ror leads a - stray;
3. Earth's down-trod-den chil - dren Look for help - ing hands;
4. Ye, who are of Is - rael, Zi - on's cho - sen sons,

Truth and Light your wea - pons, Ye need nev - er pause.
False - hood oft is hon - ored, Truth is kept at bay;
Up, then, aid your breth - ren, Scatter-ed through all lands;
Bear - ing words of com - fort To earth's mourn-ing ones,

On the side of vir - tue Be ye ev - er found,
Yet, lose not your cour - age, Men and wom-en true,
Let your plea be Jus - tice, Love be your de - light,
Rise and speed your mes - sage To the hu - man race,

poco rit.  p

Bring - ing all things e - vil / Down - ward to the ground.
God's cause still shall tri - umph, / If your part ye do.
Right - eous-ness, your watch-word, / Eq - ui - ty, your might.
So that earth may soon be / Joy's a - bid - ing place.

poco rit.

## Close of Service
### Father, Let Thy Blessing

102

Althea A. Ogden

Russell King Miller

mf Lento

1. Fa - ther, let Thy bless - ing Touch us and re - main,
2. Fa - ther, keep us lov - ing, Brave and true and free,
3. Un - to all Thy child - ren, Here and ev - 'ry - where,

mf

rall.

Guid - ing all our ac - tions Till we meet a - gain.
Kind to ev - 'ry crea - ture — All be - long to Thee.
Fa - ther give the com - fort Of Thy lov - ing care.

rall.

# Close of Service

## When This Song of Praise Shall Cease

William Cullen Bryant

E. J. Stark

*mf Con moto*

1. When this song of praise shall cease, Let Thy
2. Oh, wher - e'er our path may lie, Fa - ther,

chil - dren, Lord, de - part With the bless - ing
let us not for - get That we walk be -

of Thy peace, And Thy love in ev - 'ry
neath Thine eye, That Thy care up - holds us

heart, And Thy love in ev - 'ry heart.
yet, That Thy care up - holds us yet.

# Close of Service

## Grateful Praises

104

Alois Kaiser

**Allegretto**

1. O ho - ly joy that rais - es A - gain each pray-ing heart!
2. O what a heaven-ly bless - ing Moves o - ver us this hour!
3. Like shad - ows, days are fly - ing Thou, Lord, wilt e'er en-dure;

Give to the Lord new prais - es, Ere from this house we part;
Oh joy, we are pos - ses - sing A new and ho - lier power.
A foun - tain nev - er dry - ing Is Thy word, clear and pure.

Good seeds have been im - plant - ed In bo-soms young and pure,
O Fa - ther, make us will - ing To glo - ri - fy Thy name
To Thee, the bount - eous don - or Of truths that nev - er end,

Let growth to them be grant - ed, O Lord, make them ma - ture.
Through deeds of truth ful - fill - ing The law Thou didst pro - claim.
Shall songs of praise and hon - or, From pi - ous lips as - cend.

# Sabbath Eve

## Sabbath Eve

Harry H. Mayer

Pinchos Jassinowsky
Based on cantillation mode of "Sheer Hasheerecm"

*mf Andante cantabile*

1. Come, O ho - ly Sab - bath eve - ning,
2. Weave your mys - tic spell a - round me,
3. Come, O ho - ly Sab - bath spir - it,

Crown my toil with well earn - ed rest, Bring me hal - lowed
Lift my soul o'er care's dark tide, Shad - ow forth the
Ra - diant shine from ev - 'ry eye, Give to all man -

hours of glad - ness, Day of days be - loved and blest.
joy man pic - tures Where the an - gel hosts a - bide.
kind a fore - taste Of our spir - it's home on high.

# Sabbath Eve

## Sabbath Blessing

Jessie E. Sampter

A. W. Binder

*mf Andante*

1. The Sab - bath light is burn - ing bright; Our pret - tiest cloth is
2. At set of sun our work is done; The ha - py Sab - bath
3. O Sab - bath guest, dear Sab - bath guest, Come, share the bless - ing

clean and white, With wine and bread for Fri - day night.
has be - gun; Now bless us, Fa - ther, ev - 'ry one.
with the rest, For all our house to - night is blest.

# Sabbath Eve

### Descend, O Sabbath Princess

Aaron Cohen

David Nowakowsky
Adapted by A. W. B.

1. De - scend, de - scend, O Sab - bath Prin - - cess, She -
ki - nah's rays with - in thine eyes, De - scend and bring Thy
peace - ful tid - ings, From yon - der o - ver - arch - ing skies.

2. De - scend, de - scend, O Sab - bath Prin - - cess, For
we are wear - y here and blind, De - scend and light - en
all the bur - dens Of anx - ious soul and trou - bled mind;

Be - hold, in dark - ness and in sad - ness, We
The path of life is rough and thorn - y, Our

wan - der here, we stray, we grope; De - scend and give us faith and
feet are bruised and wounded sore, De - scend and bring us Hea - ven's

glad - ness, De - scend and give Thy light and hope.
prom - ise Of Sab - bath peace for ev - er - more.

# Sabbath Eve

**108**

## Sabbath Hymn

Alice Lucas, Tr. fr. Solomon Alkabetz

David Nowakowsky
Adapted by A. W. B.

*f  Marcato con moto*

Come forth, my friend, the bride to meet, Come, O my friend, the
Sab - bath greet! 

1. "Ob - serve ye" and "re - mem - ber" still The
2. Greet we the Sab - bath at our door, Well-
3. A - rouse thy - self, a - wake and shine, For
4. Crown of thy hus - band, come in peace, Come,

Sab - bath-thus His ho - ly will God in one ut-t'rance did pro-
spring of bless-ing ev - er-more, With ev - er - last - ing glad-ness
lo, it comes, the light di-vine. Give forth a song, for ov - er
bid - ding toil and trou - ble cease! With joy and cheer-ful-ness a-

# Sabbath Hymn
## Continued

claim. The Lord is One, and One His name To

fraught. Of old or-dained, di-vine-ly taught, Last

thee The glo-ry of the Lord shall be Re-

bide A-mong Thy peo-ple true and tried, Thy

His re-nown and praise and fame. Come forth, my friend, the

in cre-a-tion, first in thought. Come forth, my friend, the

vealed in beau-ty speed-i-ly. Come forth, my friend, the

faith-ful peo-ple-come, O bride! Come forth, my friend, the

*dal segno*

bride to meet, Come, O my friend, the Sab-bath greet!

bride to meet, Come, O my friend, the Sab-bath greet!

bride to meet, Come, O my friend, the Sab-bath greet!

bride to meet, Come, O my friend, the Sab-bath greet!

113

# Sabbath Eve

## How Good it is to Thank the Lord

### PSALM 92

Florence Weisberg

Henry Gideon

*mf Moderato*

1. How good it is to thank the Lord, To praise Thy name, O Thou Most High; To tell Thy kind-ness through the day, Thy faith-ful-ness when night draws nigh.

2. With joy-ous psalms and with the harp, Will I Thy mar-vels glad-ly sing; Thy works have made my heart re-joice; I tri-umph in Thy work, my King!

3. Like state-ly palm the right-eous thrive, As ce-dar fair they flour-ish free In God's own house; His courts a-lone Their dwell-ing-place and home shall be.

4. Still, in old age, ripe fruit they bear, Ver-dant and fresh they still re-main To prove that God, my Rock of Help, His right-eous-ness doth e'er main-tain.

# Sabbath Eve

## How Good it is to Thank the Lord

Florence Weisberg      PSALM 92      From Lewandowski's "L'cho Dodee"

*f Largamente*

1. How good it is to thank the Lord, To praise Thy
2. With joy-ous psalms and with the harp, Will I Thy
3. Like state-ly palm the right-eous thrive, As ce - dar
4. Still, in old age, ripe fruit they bear, Ver - dant and

name, O Thou Most High; To tell Thy kind - ness
mar - vels glad - ly sing; Thy works have made my
fair they flour - ish free In God's own house; His
fresh they still re - main To prove that God, my

through the day, Thy faith - ful - ness when night draws nigh.
heart re - joice; I tri - umph in Thy work, my King!
courts a - lone Their dwell - ing - place and home shall be.
Rock of Help, His right-eous - ness doth e'er main - tain.

# Grace

## Grace After Meals

Author Unknown—Tr. by Alice Lucas

Traditional "Grace" Melody
Adapted by Max Grauman

1. His flock our Shep - herd feeds, With
2. There - fore with one ac - cord We
3. Our Rock, with lov - ing care, Ac -

gra - cious - ness di - vine, He sa - tis - fies our
will His name a - dore, Pro - claim - ing ev - er -
cord - ing to His word, Bids all His boun - ty

needs With gifts of bread and wine.
more None ho - ly as the Lord.
share, Then let us bless the Lord.

# The Sabbath

## Lord, In This Sacred Hour

Stephen Greenleaf Bulfinch

Harry Rowe Shelley

*mf Andante con moto*

1. Lord, in this sa - cred hour, With - in Thy courts we bend, And
2. Thy tem - ple is the arch Of yon un-meas-ured sky; Thy
3. Lord, may that ho - lier day Dawn on thy ser-vant's sight; And

bless Thy love, and own Thy pow'r, Our Fa - ther and our Friend!
Sab - bath, the stu - pen-dous march Of grand e - ter - ni - ty.
pur - er wor-ship may we pay In heav'n's un - cloud - ed light!

# Sabbath

## Sabbath Hymn

David Levy

Max Grauman

*f Andante*

1. As birds un-to the gen-ial home-land fly, The win-ter's
2. Here at Thy shrine we leave all vex-ing care, For-get the dis-ap-
3. Bless all who spend this night in pain and woe, The bur-dened
4. Come, Sabbath joy, each trust-ing heart now fill, And bliss-ful

cold and low'r-ing skies to flee, So seeks my soul Thy
point-ment, grief—— and tear, And on the wings of hope-ful
heart, the faint-ing, and dis-tressed, Thy com-fort send to
peace with-in our homes a-bide, May thank-ful praise each

gracious presence here And finds, —— O God, its rest and peace in Thee.
song and prayer We rise, and ris-ing feel Thy Spir-it here.
darkened homes bereaved, Thy sav—ing help to those by want oppressed.
grateful heart now thrill, And to God's lov-ing care their lives — con-fide.

# The Sabbath
## When the Sabbath

114

Marcus Jastrow, alt.

Jacob Beimel
Based on a Traditional Sabbath Mode

*Moderato*

1. When the Sab-bath, peace-in-vit-ing, Fills our hearts with sa - cred mirth,
2. Here, where wor-ship-pers as-sem-ble, Where God's spir-it 'mongst us dwells,

Then from hea-ven, soul-de-light-ing, Man-na rain-eth down on earth;
Where all lips, re-joic-ing, tremble, And with thanks each bo-som swells,

Then to song all sor-row yield-eth, Loud to God rings up the strain,
Here the dust-born man per-ceiv-eth How to con-quer fear and woe,

Heav-en-born de-vo-tion wield-eth O'er each soul her sway a-gain.
Cho-sen when this earth he leav-eth, End-less Sab-bath bliss to know.

# Sabbath

I Bless Thee, Father, for the Grace

Grace Aguilar

A. Epstein

*mf* Andante

1. I bless Thee, Fa - ther, for the grace Thou me this day hast giv - en,
2. Oh! 'tis as some re - viv - ing dew Were o'er each sor-row steal - ing,

Strength'ning my soul to seek Thy face And list the theme of heav - en.
Fold- ing in heav - en's az-ure hue Each dark and wear - y feel - ing.

I bless Thee that each work-day care Thy love has lulled to rest, ...
Come, then, if God, 'tis Thy de - cree, My work-day thoughts feel care, ...

And ev - 'ry thought whose wing is pray'r Thine answering word hath blessed.
Thy day of rest is still for me Thy pres-ence then to share.

# Sabbath

## Sweet Sabbath!

**116**

Bertha Helena Maurice

Russell King Miller

*mf Moderato*

1. Sweet Sab - bath! day of sa - cred joy and rest,
2. The mean - est hearth is new - ly swept for thee,
3. We wor - ship at Thy throne, O might - y King,

We haste to meet thee, ev - er - wel - come guest.
Fair chil - dren, clust - 'ring at their mo - ther's knee.
Thou source from whom all life and be - ing spring;

At thine ap - proach, dull care is cast a - side,
In sweet com - bine, with thoughts in - tent, re - hearse,
En - shrine this ho - ly day, that it may be

And, decked in smiles, we greet thee, heav'n - ly bride.
The Bi - ble text and joy - ous hym - nal verse.
The crown - ing gift to all pos - ter - i - ty.

# The Sabbath

## The Sabbath Bride

Isaac S. Moses

Jacob Beimel
Based on a traditional Sabbath mode

*p Tranquillo*

1. O ho - ly Sab - bath-day, draw near, Thou art the source of bliss and cheer;
2. Re - joice ye now with all your might: The Sab-bath, free-dom brings and light;
3. Now come thou bles-sed Sabbath-Bride, Our joy, our com-fort and our pride;

The first in God's cre - a - tive thought, The fi - nal aim of all He wrought,
Let songs of praise to God as - cend, And voic - es sweet in cho-rus blend.
All cares and sor - rows bid thou cease, And fill our waiting hearts with peace.

Wel - come, wel - come, day of rest, Day of joy the Lord hath bless'd.
Wel - come, wel - come, day of rest, Day of joy the Lord hath bless'd.
Wel - come, wel - come, day of rest, Day of joy the Lord hath bless'd.

# Sabbath

## Come, O Sabbath Day

Gustav Gottheil

A. W. Binder

*mf Larghetto*

1. Come, O Sab - bath day, and bring Peace and heal - ing
2. Earth - ly long - ings bid re - tire, Quench the pas - sions'
3. Wipe from ev - 'ry cheek the tear, Ban - ish care and

*mf*

on thy wing; And to ev - 'ry troub-led breast Speak of the di -
hurt - ful fire; To the way-ward, sin op-pressed, Bring Thou Thy di -
si - lence fear; All things working for the best, Teach us the di -

vine be - hest: Thou shalt rest, Thou shalt rest!
vine be - hest: Thou shalt rest, Thou shalt rest!
vine be - hest: Thou shalt rest, Thou shalt rest!

# Passover and Freedom

## When Israel, of the Lord Beloved

Sir Walter Scott

Jacob Beimel

*f Moderato*

1. When Is - ra - el, of the Lord be - lov - ed,
2. By day a - long the as - ton - ish'd lands The
3. Thus pres - ent still, though now un - seen, When
4. And oh, when stoops on Ju - dah's path, In

Out from the land of bond - age came, His fa - ther's God be -
cloud - y pil - lar glid - ed slow; By night Ar - a - bia's
bright - ly shines the pros - p'rous day, Be thoughts of Thee a
shade and storm, the fre - quent night, Be Thou, long - suf - f'ring,

fore him moved, An aw - ful guide in smoke and flame.
crim - soned sands Re - turn'd the fie - ry col - umn's glow.
cloud - y screen To tem - per the de - ceit - ful ray.
slow to wrath, A burn - ing and a shin - ing light.

# Passover and Freedom

May be used also for Chanukkah

**120**

## 'Twas Like a Dream

"Scottish" Version      PSALM 126      Robert Schumann

*mf Moderato*

*mf*

1. 'Twas like a dream, when by the Lord From
2. The na - tions owned that God had wrought Great
3. Who sow in tears, with joy shall reap; Though

bond - age Zi - on was re - stored; Our mouths were filled with
works, which joy to us had brought; As south - ern streams when
bear - ing pre - cious seed they weep While go - ing forth, yet

mirth and songs To God, to whom all praise be - longs.
filled with rain, He turned our cap - tive state a - gain.
shall they sing When, com - ing back, their sheaves they bring.

# Passover and Freedom

## True Freedom

**121**

James Russell Lowell

Based on Sephardic "Az Yasheer"

*f* Moderato

1. Men, whose boast it is, that ye  Come of fa-thers, brave and free,
2. Is  true free-dom not to break  Fet - ters for our own dear sake,
3. They are slaves, who fear to speak  For the fall - en and the meek;

*f*

If there breathe on earth a slave, Are ye tru - ly free and brave?
And with hea - then hearts for - get That we owe man-kind a debt?
They are slaves, who will not choose Ha - tred, scoff -ing and a - buse,

If you do not feel the chain When it works a broth-er's pain,
No; true free-dom is to share All the chains our broth-ers wear,
Rath-er than in si-lence shrink From the truth they needs must think;

Are ye not base slaves in-deed, Slaves un-wor-thy to be freed?
And with heart and hand to be Earn-est to make oth-ers free.
They are slaves, who dare not be In the right with two or three.

Are ye not base slaves in-deed, Slaves un-wor-thy to be freed?
And with heart and hand to be Earn-est to make oth-ers free.
They are slaves, who dare not be In the right with two or three.

# Passover and Freedom

May be used for Chanukkah

## 'Twas Like a Dream

PSALM 126

Adapted to a traditional
"Sheer Hamaalos" melody by A. W. B.

1. 'Twas like a dream, when by the Lord, From bond-age Zi - on was re-stored;

Our mouths were filled with mirth and songs To God, to whom all praise belongs.

2. The na-tions owned that God had wrought Great works, which joy to us had brought;

# 'Twas Like a Dream
## Continued

As southern streams when filled with rain, He turned our cap-tive state a- gain.

3. Who sow in tears, with joy shall reap, Though bear-ing pre-cious seed they weep;

While go-ing forth, yet shall they sing When, coming oack, their sheaves they bring.

# Passover and Freedom

May be used for Chanukkah or Purim

**123**

## If Our God had not Befriended

Edward Churton · PSALM 124 · Jacob Weinberg

*Allegretto*

1. If our God had not be-friend-ed, Now may grate-ful Is-rael say,
2. Then the tide of venge-ful slaugh-ters O'er us had been seen to roll,
3. Praise to God, whose mer-cy - to - ken Beam'd to still that rag-ing sea:

If the Lord had not de - fend - ed When with foes we stood at bay,
And their pride, like an-gry wa - ters, Had en-gulf'd our struggling soul,
Lo, the snare is rent and bro - ken, And our cap - tive souls are free.

Mad - ly rag - ing, mad-ly rag - ing, Deem-ing our sad lives their prey:
Those loud wa - ters, those loud wa - ters, Proud and spurn - ing all con - trol,
Lord of glo - ry, Lord of glo - ry, Help can come a-lone from Thee.

# Passover and Freedom
## From Heaven's Height

Harry H. Mayer
Tr. fr. the Ger. of L. Philippson

B. Jacobsohn

1. From heav - en's height  Soft, ver - nal breez - es blow;
2. From heav - en's height  God's man - date stern re - sounds,
3. From heav - en's height  God's prov - i - dence shines clear;
4. To heav - en's height  Look up with faith and trust;

God's glo - rious light  Its Au - thor's pow'r doth show,
To ty - rant's might,  Pro - claim - ing law - ful bounds;
Un - to our sight  His pur - pos - es ap - pear;
Ce - les - tial might  Pro - tect thee, child of dust;

With sun - ny hues,  Trans - fig - ur - ing the earth,
As long a - go,  God hum - bled E - gypt's pride,
His word di - vine  All life cre - ates, sus - tains;
Give thanks to God  For fields with ver - dure clad,

While spring - time woos The flow - ers back to earth.
God's will, e'en so,  May now not be de - fied.
His high de - sign  The des - pot's plans re - strains.
His good - ness laud,  And in His care be glad.

131

# Passover and Freedom

## God of Might

Composite

Traditional "Addeer Hu"

*f* *Andante con moto*

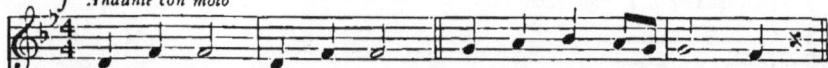

1. God of Might, God of Right, Thee we give all glo - ry;
2. Now as erst, when Thou first Mad'st the proc - la - ma - tion,
3. Be with all who in thrall To their task are driv - en;

Thine all praise in these days As in a - ges hoa - ry,
Warn - ing loud ev - 'ry proud, Ev - 'ry ty - rant na - tion,
In Thy power speed the hour When their chains are riv - en;

When we hear, year by year Freedom's won-drous sto - ry.
We, Thy fame still pro-claim, Bend in a - dor - a - tion.
Earth a-round will re-sound Glee - ful hymns to heav - en.

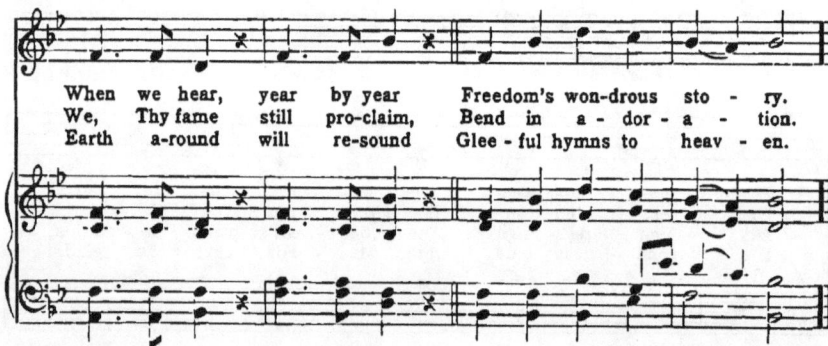

# Passover

## To Thee, Above All Creatures' Gaze

James K. Gutheim
Tr. fr. the Hamburg Temple Hymnal

Eugen Haile

*f  Andante*

1. To    Thee,   a - bove   all   crea-tures' gaze,   To   Thee whom earth and
2. Thou  didst   re - deem  the   cap - tive band,   Who   were en-slaved by
3. O     God,    Thy chil - dren   re - cog - nize   With   grate - ful hearts this

heaven do praise,  Whose  ev - er   watch - ful  Prov - i - dence  Proves
ty - rant's hand;  Their  cries were heard, their groans were stilled, Their
pre - cious prize, Thy  peo - ple    at    this   ho - ly shrine  Pro-

dai - ly Thine om - nip - o - tence— To  Thee  our  thanks in cho - rus  rise.
yearn-ing hopes at  last ful - filled,  And  free - dom dawned on Is - ra - el.
claim  a - loud Thy power di - vine: "The Lord will reign for ev - er - more!"

# Passover

## When Israel to the Wilderness

Max Meyerhardt

Jacob Beimel

*mf Andante moderato*

1. When Is - ra - el to the wil - der - ness
2. And, guid - ed by that heav'n - ly flame,
3. Yet, not a - lone in days of yore,
4. A lamp of ra - diant, glow - ing hue,
5. Oh, heav'n - ly lamp! Thy light shall shine

*mf*

Had fled from Pha - raoh's cru - el might,
That bea - con from the Lord's own hand,
Has God His won - drous mer - cy shown,
By Is - rael borne in ev' - ry clime,
'Till sin and hate from earth de - part,

Th' E - ter - nal sent to lead them on,
The cho - sen peo - ple safe - ly reached
For still He grants to all man - kind
Through fire and flood, through tears and blood,
'Till wrong shall fail and right pre - vail,

A cloud by day, a fire by night.
Their des - tined goal,— the Prom - ised Land.
A glo - rious light to lead them on.
With cour - age grand and faith sub - lime.
And jus - tice rule the hu - man heart.

134

# Passover and Booths
## Song of the Dew

**128**

Solomon Solis-Cohen, Tr. fr. Solomon Ibn Gabirol

Pinchos Jassinowsky
Based on Traditional "Tal" melody

*p Andante moderato*

1. O — rain — de - part with bless-ings, de - part with bless-ings, With
2. With psalm— and song I'll praise Him; With psalm I'll praise Him; My
3. His Name,— with glo - ry cov - ers, With glo - ry cov -ers His
4. Hasten, O God, Thy prom-ise, hast- en O God, Thy prom-ise, "I

blessings come, O dew; For Might-y to de - liv - er Is He that sends the dew,
words shall fall as dew, My Rock, my Strong Deliv'- rer Is He that sends the dew,
folk, as earth the dew; A - bun-dant in de-liv'-rance Is He that sends the dew,
will be Israel's dew," And might-y to de - liv - er, Let fall this day Thy dew!

*f*     *p*     *poco rit.*

For might - y to de - liv - er Is He that sends the dew.
My Rock, my strong De - liv'- rer Is He that sends the dew.
A - bun - dant in de - liv'-rance Is He that sends the dew.
And Might - y to de - liv - er, Let fall, this day, Thy dew!

135

# Passover or Spring

### Behold, it is the Spring-tide of the Year!

Alice Lucas                                   Traditional

*f Allegro con brio*

1. Be - hold, it is - the spring-tide of the year! O -
2. And in the spring, when all the earth and sky Re -
3. For as from out the house of bond - age went The
4. And still from ris - ing un - to set - ting sun Shall

ver and past is win - ter's gloom - y reign, The hap - py time of
joice to - geth - er, still from age to age Rings out the sol - emn
host of Is - rael, in their midst they bore The her - it - age of
this our her - it - age and watch - word be: "The Lord our God, the

sing - ing-birds is near, And clad in bud and bloom are hill and plain.
chant of days gone by, Pro - claim-ing Is - rael's sa - cred her - it - age.
law and free-dom, blent In ho - ly u - ni - ty for - ev - er-more.
Lord our God is One, His law a - lone it is that makes us free!"

# Passover

### Praise The Lord

Leopold Stein.  Translated by I. S. Moses          Traditional "Addeer Hu"

*f  Andante con moto*

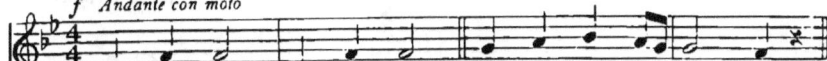

1. Praise the Lord! one ac - cord, Sound throughout cre - a - tion;
2. Lo! He frees all He sees Trust - ing in His pow - er;
3. God is here! Help is near In fierce storm and weath - er
4. Lo! the spring joy doth bring, Win - ter's frosts are end - ed;
5. Let Thy will guide us still, Let Thy love be o'er us,

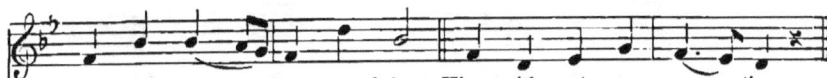

Laud and sing ...... hon - or bring Him with - out ces - sa - tion;
Doth im - part ...... to each heart Com - fort ev - 'ry hour; ——
Be but still! for His will Keeps us all to - geth - er;
Glad-ness reigns, life re-mains, With sweet pleas-ure blend - ed;
Let Thy light, in our night Show Thy path be - fore ... us!

And His fame loud pro-claim, Ev - 'ry land and na - tion.
Threat what may, He is aye Our de - fense and tow - er.
Trust in Him, Ser - a - phim Hov - er o'er us ev - er.
God doth bear what His care And His love de - fend - ed.
Ours Thy love, from a - bove And Thy light that leads us.

# Passover (7th Day)

## Sound the Loud Timbrel

Thomas Moore

Jacob Weinberg

*Allegro guerriero e marcatissimo*

1. Sound the loud tim-brel o'er Egypt's dark sea! The
2. Praise    to the Conqueror, praise to the Lord, His

Lord    hath  triumphed, His peo-ple are free!    Sound the loud    tim-brel o'er
word was our  ar - row,  His breath was our sword!    Praise to the    Con-que-ror,

E - gypt's dark sea!    The Lord    hath    tri-umph'd, His peo - ple are free.
praise to the Lord,    His word    was our ar - row,  His breath was our sword!

Sing, for the pride of the ty-rant is bro-ken, His char-iots, his horsemen, all
Who shall re-turn to tell E-gypt the sto-ry Of those she sent forth in the

splen-did and brave, How vain was their boasting, the Lord hath but spok-en, And
hour of her pride? For the Lord hath looked out from His pillar of glo-ry, And

char-iots and horsemen are sunk in the wave. Sound the loud tim-brel o'er
all her brave thousands are dashed in the tide. Sound the loud tim-brel o'er

Egypt's dark sea! The Lord hath triumphed, His peo-ple are free.
Egypt's dark sea! The Lord hath triumphed, His peo-ple are free.

# Passover, Pentecost, or Booths

**132**

## Fling Wide the Gates

PSALM 118

Composite

Melody of F. Halevy's "Min Hamaytsar", Adapted by A. W. B.

*f Con moto*

1. Fling wide the gates of right-eousness, And en-ter in the Lord to bless;
2. The stone the build-ers cast a-way Stands the chief cornerstone to-day:
3. The Lord a-lone is God: His light Shines thro' the darkness of our night.

This is the por-tal of the Lord; Flock here, all ye who love His word;
This work is from the Lord: to us How great it seems, how mar-vel-lous!
Thou art our God; we praise Thy name: Our God; we will ex-alt Thy fame.

Haste we to sing His glor-i-ous Name, From whom our strong salvation came.
This is the day the Lord hath made; Re-joice we in it and be glad.
Praise ye the Lord; for good is He And lov-ing to e-ter-ni-ty.

# Spring
## A Message Sweet

Florence Switton

Simon Hecht

133

*mf Andante*

1. A mes - sage sweet the breez - es bring, It
2. Both child and man de - light to hear The
3. 'Neath balm - y, south - ern skies, so clear, The
4. Wher - e'er we gaze God's glor - ies shine, His

is the soft clear voice of spring; To blades of grass and
ver - nal rain - drop's pat - ter clear; The ten - der blos - soms
birds the sea - son's mes - sage hear; Their songs of praise to
will con - trols each climb - ing vine, And with each sea - son's

sleep - ing seeds God's won - drous word it on - ward speeds.
gent - ly sway, Kissed by the zeph - yrs on their way.
God a - bove Pro - claim to all how great His love.
glad re - turn His mar - vel 'tis that we dis - cern.

# Spring

## "Hymn of Spring"

N. Lindsay Norden

*f* *Moderato*

1. When warm - er suns and blu - er skies Pro - claim the op - 'ning year,
2. Earth with her thou - sand voic - es sings Her song of glad-some praise,
3. The ear - ly flowers bloom bright and fair, Fair shines the morn-ing sky;
4. Like morn at spring-time, sweet and clear, That greets our gladdened eyes,

*mf*

What hap - py sounds of life a - rise, What love - ly scenes ap - pear!
And ev - 'ry blade of grass that springs, God's lov - ing law o - beys.
The birds make mu - sic in the air, The brook goes sing - ing by.
The spring of Heav'n's e - ter - nal year Shall bring new earth and skies.

# Israel

## Ten Thousand Martyrs

Max Meyerhardt

Jacob Weinberg

*p Andante*

1. Ten thou-sand mar-tyrs died for Israel's cause  With for-ti-tude sub-
2. Weep not, O  Is-rael, for thy martyred ones,  For though no monuments
3. Their names are  writ  on  hon-or's deathless page,  And  on the scroll of

lime  'mid smoke and flame;  And while the  cruel  foe stood mocking
rise ———  o'er their tomb,  Yet fame up-on  the sacred spot shall
glo-ry ———  grav-en  high,  And though earth's proud-est mon-u-ments de-

'round, They called  on  God  and blessed His  ho-ly  name.
shed  Her fair-est  gar-lands and her  fair-est  bloom.
cay,  Their deeds,  sub-lime, will  nev-er, nev-er  die.

## Israel

### Hear Us, Eternal King

Eve Davieson

Felice Giardini

*f*     *Andante maestoso*

1. Hear us, E - ter - nal King, Hear Thou the praise we bring,
2. Burst Thou the pris - on bars, Lift us to yon pure stars,
3. Let us a - rise and shine, Till the glad com - ing time

An - thems and song! Thou who didst part the deep, Thou wilt Thy
Giv - er of Light! Help us to dare and do, Till we, Thy
When na - tions all Know Thee as One a - lone, Make Thee in

first - born keep, Is - ra - el's arm is weak, Thy pur - pose strong.
chos - en few, Hal - low our mis - sion true, Guar-dian of Right.
peace their own, Till at Thy might - y throne Pros-trate they fall.

### There is a Mystic Tie

Max Meyerhardt

Joseph Achron
Based in part on a Jewish Folk Melody

*mf*    *Moderato* ( ♩=69-72)

1. There is a mys - tic tie that joins The chil-dren of the mar - tyr
2. For still in rev -'rent tones is heard The sac - red cry, always the

*mf*

# There is a Mystic Tie
## Continued

race, In bonds of sym - pa - thy and love That
same, "O Is - rael, hear, our God is One, Blest

time and change cannot ef - face. E'en though to - day the
be for aye His ho - ly name!" This is the mys - tic

Jews do dwell In ev - 'ry clime and ev - 'ry land,
tie that joins The child - ren of the an - cient race;

Yet, joined by that im-mort - al tie, A ho - ly bro-therhood they stand.
This is the grand and ho - ly bond That time and change can-not ef - face.

# Israel

**There is a Mystic Tie**

Max Meyerhardt
*mf Moderato*

Sephardic Tune, "Hallel"

*mf*

1. There is a mys - tic tie that joins The chil - dren
2. E'en though to - day the Jews do dwell In ev - 'ry
3. For still in rev - 'rent tones is heard The sa - cred
4. This is the mys - tic tie that joins The chil - dren

of the mar - tyr - race, In bonds of sym - pa -
clime and ev - 'ry land, Yet, joined by that im -
cry, al - ways the same, "O Is - rael, hear, Our
of the an - cient race; This is the grand and

thy and love That time and change can - not ef - face.
mor - tal tie, A ho - ly broth - er - hood they stand.
God is One, Blest be for aye His ho - ly name!"
ho - ly bond That time and change can - not ef - face.

# Israel

## Let Israel Trust in God Alone

James K. Gutheim
Tr. from the Hamburg Temple Hymnal

Wm. Lowenberg

*f Con spirito*

1. Let Is - rael trust in God a - lone And
2. Let Is - rael strive for truth a - lone, In

in His pow'r con - fide, For He is faith - ful to His word,
love to bless man - kind, And in the bonds of broth - er - hood

If we in Him a - bide; His coun - sels must for -
All na - tions soon to bind, So that they all with

ev - er stand, All na - tions bow to His com - mand.
one ac - cord, Ac - know - ledge and o - bey the Lord.

147

# Israel

## One God! One Lord!

Penina Moise

*mf Moderato*

G. A. Rossini

1. One God! One Lord! One might - y King! In u - ni -
2. Thee, Sover-eign of the u - ni - verse, Through a - ges,
3. To Thee a - lone, when life re - cedes, The dy - ing

*mf*

ty ....... will Ju - dah sing; Trans - mit - ting e'er from
'mid all climes di - verse, The Jew - ish child is
Is - rael - ite still pleads; In One all - gra - cious

sire to son The truth that God is on - ly One!
taught to praise, To lisp Thy name, to walk Thy ways.
God and Guide His fleet - ing spir - it doth con - fide.

## "Let There be Light"

Isaac M. Wise

*f Andante*

J. S. Mombach

1. 'Let there be light", at dawn of time, The Lord of Hosts pro - claimed,
2. And since that hour the light has grown In full-ness more and more;

*f*

"Let there be light," this call sub-lime Went forth when Ho-reb flamed,
It shall in-crease till all shall own One God and Him a - dore;

Then broke on Is-rael's mind a day, Il - lu-mined by a heaven-ly ray,
And strive to know His right-eous will And His com-mandments to ful-fill,

Then broke on Is-rael's mind a day, Il - lu-mined by a heaven-ly ray.
And strive to know His right-eous will And His com-mandments to ful-fill.

# Feast of Weeks

## From Heaven's Heights the Thunder Peals

Isaac M. Wise

Lewandowski's Shevuos
"Mee Chomocho," adapted by A. W. B.

*f Moderato*

1. From heaven's heights the thun-der peals, The trumpets sound with might;
2. The i - dols reel, their tem-ples shake, Des - pot - ic pow'rs re - bound;
3. Let Ju-dah's harp in - tone His praise, Our Fa-ther's glo - ry sing;

In storm and clouds the Lord re - veals The glo - ry of His light.
With awe the mountain sum-mits quake, Be - fore the aw - ful sound.
For Truth and light, for heav'nly grace, Re - veal'd by God, our King.

The Lord of Hosts proclaims His Word, To man He speaks, Cre - a - tion's Lord.
From Horeb's height descends the Word, To man He speaks, Cre - a - tion's Lord.
Ex - tol His name in one ac-cord, To man He speaks, Cre - a - tion's Lord.

# Feast of Weeks

## From Sinai's Height a Fountain Gushes

James K. Gutheim  
Tr. fr. Jacob Freund

Jacob Beimel  
Based on the "Akdamos" cantillation mode

*f* Moderato vigoroso

1. From Si-nai's height a foun-tain gushes, That pours its flood in cir - cles wide;
2. On Si-nai's crest a tree is grow-ing, A lof - ty tree, with widespread arms,
3. O'er Si-nai's sum-mit flames a beacon; Ce - les-tial splen-dor from it streams;
4. The wa-ters of this crystal fountain, The tree whose fruit such bliss doth yield,

Its crys-tal stream e'er on-ward rush-es, And fraught with blessings is its tide;
No words, how-ev - er strong and glowing, Can fit - ly paint its glorious charms;
Its brilliance time nor clouds can weaken; Undim'd still shine the an-cient beams;
The bea-con - light up-on the mountain, Are Si - nai's law, to us revealed;

Who from this stream re - stores his heart, Feels thro' his veins fresh vig-or start.
To all who gar - ner its increase, This tree yields hap-pi - ness and peace.
The eye il - lu-mined by its light Will ev - er find the path of right.
They who its pre-cepts know and guard From man have praise, from God reward.

# Feast of Weeks—Confirmation

## Lord, Into Thy Sacred Dwelling

Henry Berkowitz

Max Grauman

*f  Andante cantabile*

1. Lord, in - to Thy sa - cred dwell-ing En - ter we this ho - ly day;
2. Lord, con - firm in us, we pray Thee, Such un - falt-'ring faith and love;
3. Make us each a firm de - fen - der Of Thy To - rah, true and pure;

While our hearts with joy are swell-ing, At Thine al - tar flowers we lay.
As our fa-thers show'd be-fore Thee, When a - gainst their foes they strove.
That it al-ways may en - gen - der Love and hope, and faith se-cure.

## Lord, Into Thy Sacred Dwelling
### Continued

To-kens of the pledge we ren - der   To the laws our fa-thers   heard,

Wealth and life did they sur - ren - der,   For the treas - ure Thou didst   give;

May with-in us live   its spir - it,   Lead us on - ward in the   right;

When at   Si - nai   they did ten - der   Fe - al - ty un - to   Thy word.

O   may we too,   glad - ly   ten - der   Faith-ful ser-vice while   we live.

That the   na-tions may re-vere   it,   And all wrongs be   put   to flight.

# Confirmation

**145**     Our Father, We Beseech Thy Grace

Ida Goldstein          Heinrich Schalit

*Solenne*   *mf*

1. Our Fa - ther, we beseech Thy   grace, As   in   Thy pres-ence

2. To - day in rev'rent awe we   strew   Thy   al - tar with fresh

3. As blos-soms that in ston - y   ways, In   fra - grant clusters

rev' - rent - ly   In   this Thy ho - ly dwell - ing   place,   We

off' - rings sweet;   Not   as   of   yore our   fa - thers slew—   Thy

oft   are   found;   So   teach our lives to   show Thy   praise,   That

## Our Father We Beseech Thy Grace
### Continued

*f*

ded - i - cate our lives    to Thee.    Not    proud - ly   do   we   seek Thy
crea-tures dumb, and deemed  it  meet    To    shed their blood  in   sac - ri -
we   may sweet-en  life's  dull round:   To    toil  with faith through bus - y

*f*

face,        In    fond   hu - mil - i - ty    we    move
fice:        We    bear   in - stead these flow'rs new - blown,
years;       And   though dark  clouds ob - scure  the   sun,

*p*                                          *f*

Near - er Thy shrine and  nest - le    there,    To    ask   Thy   love.
That with their breath our pray'rs may  rise     Un - to    Thy   throne.
To   whis- per still through blind-ing  tears:   Thy   will   be    done!

*p*

*f*

# Confirmation

## Hark, the Voice of Children

S. H. Sonnenschein, St. 1 and 2
Louis Wolsey, St. 3

Harm. by Geo. H. Loud

*mf Con moto*

1. Hark, the voice of chil - dren Sound-ing forth with might,
2. Pray'rs and songs of glad - ness, In this sa - cred shrine,
3. Jud - dah, we thy chil - dren Pray for strength and love;

Ju-dah's sons and daugh-ters Vow to do the right. Is-rael's loft - y
Seal your con - firm - a - tion, Crown your faith di - vine! Nev-er cease to
Make us ban - ner bear - ers, True to God a - bove. Ga-ther us to -

ban - ner Leads them to suc - cess, God him - self pro - tects them,
love it, And for - sake it not, Wear its shield of hon - or
geth - er, 'Round thy To - rah's light, Bless thy sons and daugh - ters

### REFRAIN

He their vows will bless. On-ward, chil-dren, on - ward, Fear-less, firm and
With-out stain or blot.
Who thy laws re - cite.

true,  Keep your hearts up - lift - ed,  Peace and truth pur - sue.

## 147  See, O God, We Children Come

David Philipson
*mf Moderato*

Traditional

1. See,  O God, we chil-dren come,  At Thy shrine our place to take;
2. Hear,  O Fa - ther, hear our prayer,  From our hearts it soars to Thee;

*mf*

Ho - ly, ho - ly is this day,  Bless us for Thy great name's sake.
Teach us, God, our du - ties all,  Thee to seek, Thy love to see;

Now  to  Thee our pray'rs as - cend,  To  our  words in love at - tend.
True  to  be, and good and kind,  Pure in  heart and soul and mind.

157

# Confirmation

## Lord, What Off'ring Shall We Bring

John Taylor

Jacob Weinberg

mf Andante

1. Lord, what off - 'ring shall we bring,
2. Will - ing hands to lead the blind,
3. Teach us, O Thou heaven - ly King,

At Thine al - tars when we bow? Hearts, the pure un -
Heal the wound - ed, feed the poor; Love, em - brac - ing
Thus to show our grate - ful mind, This ac - cept - ed

sul - lied spring Whence the kind af - fec - tions flow.
all man - kind; Char - i - ty, with lib - 'ral store.
off - 'ring bring: Love to Thee and all man - kind.

# Confirmation

## Pledging Our Lives

Harry H. Mayer

A. Epstein

**149**

f Maestoso

1. Pledg - ing our lives and our strength to the cause,
2. Vow - ing to serve as God's priests from our youth—
3. Pa - tient and trust - ful the path we would tread,

Wrought for and fought for by he - roes of old,
Dan - gers af - fright not nor hard - ships ap - pall—
Lead - ing us God - ward, though steep be its slope;

Is - ra - el's ban - ner in - scribed with God's laws,
We would de - vote our - selves whol - ly to truth,
Is - ra - el's ban - ner un - furl'd o - ver - head,

Is - ra - el's ban - ner a - loft we would hold.
Loy - al and brave, we would heed du - ty's call.
Val - iant - ly striv - ing, in God we shall hope.

# Confirmation

## Father, See Thy Suppliant Children

Mrs. S. E. Munn    By permission of I. S. Moses

1. Fa - ther, see Thy suppliant chil - dren Trem-bling stand be- fore Thy throne, To con-firm the vow of Ho - reb, "We will serve the Lord a - lone."

2. Thy com-mand shall be en-grav - en On the tab - lets of our heart, Till the heart in death be brok - en, Till the cord of life shall part.

SOLO

When dark tempests, low -'ring gath - er, It will be our strength and stay,

# Father, See Thy Suppliant Children
## Continued

It will be our guardian an-gel Up - on life's la - bo - rious way.

3. As a shelt-'ring cloud at noon-tide, As a flam-ing fire by night,

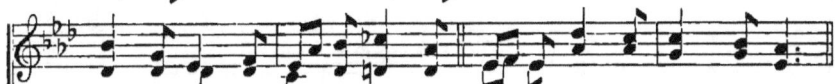

Thro' pros-per - i - ty and sor - row, It will guide our steps a - right.

4. Till we reach the land of prom - ise, When the toils of earth are past.

Till we sleep the sleep e - ter - nal In the realms of peace at last.

# Confirmation

**151**
## Father, See Thy Suppliant Children

Hamburg Temple Hymnal
Tr. by Felix Adler

A. Rubin

*mf Allegretto*

1. Fa - ther, see Thy sup-pli-ant chil-dren, Trembling stand be -fore Thy throne,
3. As    a shelt-'ring cloud at noon-tide, As    a flam - ing fire by night,

To  con-firm the  vow  of Ho - reb, "We will  serve the  Lord  a -lone."
Thro' pros-per - i - ty  and sor-row, It will  guide our  steps  a - right.

2. Thy com-mand shall be  en-grav - en    On  the  tab - lets  of  our heart,
4. Till  we reach the land  of prom-ise,  When the  toils  of  earth are past,

Till  the heart in  death be brok - en,  Till the  cord  of  life shall part.
Till  we sleep the  sleep e - ter - nal  In  the  realms of  peace at  last.

# Confirmation

## Father, See Thy Suppliant Children

Felix Adler

A. W. Binder

*mf  Andante con espressione*

*mf*

1. Fa - ther, see Thy sup - pliant chil - dren
2. Thy com - mand shall be en - grav - en
3. As a shelt - 'ring cloud at noon - tide,
4. Till we reach the land of prom - ise,

Trem - bling stand be - fore Thy throne, To con - firm the
On the tab - lets of our heart, Till the heart in
As a flam - ing fire by night, Thru pros - per - i -
When the toils of earth are past, Till we sleep the

vow of Ho - reb, "We will serve the Lord a - lone."
death be brok - en, Till the cord of life shall part.
ty and sor - row, It will guide our steps a - right.
sleep e - ter - nal In the realms of peace at last.

# Confirmation

### Blessed, Blessed

M. Jastrow.  St. 2 composite

A. W. Binder

Bless - ed, O bless - ed Mo - ment most ho - ly, Lead - ing the

low - ly Youth to the Lord. Sweet are the les - sons

Of this hour's sto - ry, Ne'er may its glo - ry Fade from our

minds. Come ye, all peo - ples, Bow down be - fore Him,

Hum - bly a - dore Him, Sing loud His praise.

# Confirmation

## Blessed, O Blessed

M. Jastrow. St. 2, 3, Composite.

Alois Kaiser

*mf Semplice*

1. Bless - ed, O bless-ed Mo - ment most ho - ly, Lead - ing the
3. Come ye, all peo - ples, Bow down be - fore Him, Humb - ly a -

*mf*

First time | Second time | Fine

low - ly Youth to the Lord.
dore Him, Sing loud His praise.

2. Sweet are the les - sons Of this hour's sto - ry,

D. C.

Ne'er may its glo - ry Fade from our minds.

# Summer

## Summer Suns are Glowing

Wm. Walsham How

A. W. Binder

*mf Animato*

1. Sum-mer suns are glow-ing O-ver land and sea; Hap-py light is
2. God's free mer-cy stream-eth O-ver all the world, And His ban-ner
3. Lord, up-on our blind-ness Thy pure ra-diance pour; For Thy lov-ing-
4. We will nev-er doubt Thee, Tho' Thou veil Thy light; Life is dark with-

*mf*

flow-ing, Boun-ti-ful and free. Ev-'ry-thing re-joic-es
gleam-eth, Ev-'ry-where un-furled. Broad and deep and glo-rious,
kind-ness Make us love Thee more. And when clouds are drift-ing,
out Thee, Death with Thee is bright. Light of light, shine o'er us.

In the mel-low rays; All earth's thousand voic-es Swell the psalm of praise.
As the heav'n a-bove, Shines in might vic-to-rious His e-ter-nal love.
Dark a-cross our sky, Then, the veil up-lift-ing, Fa-ther, be Thou nigh.
On our pil-grim way; Go Thou still be-fore us To the end-less day.

# New Year

## Into the Tomb of Ages

Penina Moise

James G. Heller

*Solemne*

1. In - to the tomb of a - ges past An - oth - er year has
2. With firm re-solves your spir - it nerve, The God of right a -
3. Peace to the house of Is - ra - el! May joy with - in it

now been cast; ...... Shall time un - heed - ed take its flight, Nor
lone to serve; Speech, tho't and act to re - gu - late, By
ev - er dwell! May sor - row on the op - 'ning year, For -

leave one ray of high - er light, That on man's pil - grim -
what His per - fect laws dic - tate; Nor from His ho - ly
get - ting its ac - cus - tomed tear, With smiles a - gain fond

age may shine And lead his soul to spheres di - vine?
pre - cepts stray, By world - ly i - dols lured a - way.
kin - dred meet, With hopes re - vived, the New Year greet!

167

# New Year

**157**

## Into the Tomb of Ages Past

Penina Moise

A. W. Binder
Trad. Rosh Hashanah
Adon Olam melody.

*mf Andante con espressione*

1. In - to the tomb of a - ges past An - oth - er year has now been
2. With firm re - solves your spir - it nerve, The God of right a - lone to
3. Peace to the house of Is - ra - el! May joy with - in it ev - er

cast; Shall time un - heed - ed take its flight, Nor leave one ray of high - er
serve; Speech, tho't and act to reg - u - late, By what His per - fect laws dic -
dwell! May sor - row on the op - 'ning year, For - get - ting its ac - cus - tomed

light, That on man's pil - grim - age may shine And lead his soul to spheres di - vine?
tate; Nor from His ho - ly precepts stray, By world - ly i - dols lured a - way.
tear, With smiles a - gain fond kindred meet, With hopes revived, the New Year greet!

168

# New Year

## Dawn

158

Moses ibn Ezra
Tr. by Alice Lucas

Jacob Beimel
Based on a traditional Rosh Hashanah chant

*mp Andante religioso*

1. Thou, O Al-might-y, know-est all The pas-sions that my heart en-thrall, Thy ma-ny mer-cies I re-call, And to Thy throne for re-fuge flee. No

2. prof-it un-to Thee it were That I Thy chast-en-ing rod should bear, Turn then, O Lord, and hear my prayer And par-don mine in-iq-ui-ty. To

3. Thee my hopes, my long-ings, rise, To Thee my soul for suc-cor flies, And I be-wail my sins with sighs, Like to the moan-ing of the sea. Thy

4. Name puts all my cares to flight, And ra-diates thro' my dark-est night, The thought of Thee is my de-light, And sweet as hon-ey - - - - - - comb to me.

*ten. mf*

*f*

I-II-III

Last verse

# New Year

## The Lord is King

(Adonoi Melech)
Translated by Solomon Solis-Cohen

A. W. Binder
Based on two traditional Rosh Hashanah modes

*f* *Andantino*

1. Ere space ex-ists, or earth, or sky, The Lord —— is King!
2. When earth He flings mid star-fill'd space, The Lord —— is King!

Ere sun or star shone forth on high, The Lord —— was King!
When liv-ing crea-ture there found place, The Lord —— was King!

When earth shall be a robe out-worn, And sky shall fade like mists of
When homeward from earth's cor-ners four, He calls the scat-tered folk once

morn, Still shall the Lord for-e'er be King! The Lord is King!
more, Then shall the Lord for-e'er be King! The Lord is King!

## The Lord is King
### Continued

The Lord was King! For - ev - er shall the Lord be King!
The Lord was King! For - ev - er shall the Lord be King!

**160**        Tent-like This Day

Israel Zangwill
Tr. fr. the Heb. of Eleazer Kalir

Edward Samuel

*mf*   *Molto moderato*

1. Tent - like this day the King stretched out the sky,
2. He girds Him - self with maj - es - ty and might,
3. For He who knows each ac - tion and its aim,
4. Mer - cy for all whose hopes in Thee do rest,

*mf*

His glo - ry and His love to tes - ti - fy; This day for
And earth and heav - en trem - ble in af - fright; But He who
Will mer - ci - ful - ly mod - er - ate our blame This day, when
Thy dev - o - tees in whom the world is blest; Let ben - e -

judg - ment all, both low and high, Must face their King.
fash - ions hearts will judge a - right, Our gra - cious King.
sol - emn trump - et - blasts pro - claim Our Lord the King.
dic - tions spring in ev - 'ry breast, E - ter - nal King.

171

# New Year and Day of Atonement

## On Mighty Wings

James K. Gutheim
Tr. fr. Hamburg Temple Hymnal

Max Grauman
Adapted to traditional Oveenu Malkaynu melody

*mf* *Andante*

1. On migh - ty wings rush swift - ly by The hours, —— the
2. We stand, O God, with awe and fears Be - fore —— Thy
3. We can - not hide our tres - pass - es, Can - not —— our

days, the year; We can - not stay how - e'er we try
ho - ly throne; Our thoughts, our deeds, our joys, our tears
deeds re - scind; With con - trite heart we must con - fess:

172

The flight of time's ca - reer. A fleet - ing shad - ow
To Thee, O Lord, are known. If an - gels e'en, so
"Our Fa - ther, we have sinned!" O God, Thy par - don

is our life, 'Tis as a pas - sing dream; Its
pure and bright, Can - not en - dure Thy test, How,
we im - plore, Thou know - est we are frail, Re -

la - bors seem but emp - ty strife, Its aims a flash, a gleam.
then, can we ap - proach Thy sight, Who are by sin, op - pressed.
fresh us from Thy mer - cy's store, Up - lift us when we fail.

# Day of Atonement and Penitence

## Despise Not, Lord

Alice Lucas
Tr. fr. the Heb. of Jehudah Ha-Levi

Russell King Miller

*mf* Moderato

1. De - spise not, Lord, my low - ly pen - i - tence,
2. A - far from Thee in midst of life I die,
3. The world is too much with me and its din
4. Bare of good deeds, scorch'd by temp - ta - tion's fire,

*mf*

Ere comes the day, when, dead - en'd ev - 'ry sense,
And life in death I find when Thou art nigh.
Pre - vents my search e - ter - nal peace to win.
Yet to Thy mer - cy dares my soul as - pire;

My limbs too fee - ble grown to bear my weight,
A - las! I know not how to seek Thy face,
How can I serve my Mak - er when my heart
But where - fore speech pro - long, since un - to Thee,

A bur - den to my - self, I jour - ney hence.
Nor how to serve and wor - ship Thee, most High.
Is pas - sion's cap - tive, is a slave to sin?
O Lord, is man - i - fest my heart's de - sire?

174

# Day of Atonement and Penitence

### Forgive Us Lord

Florence Montefiore

Samuel Alman
Based on a traditional Yom Kippur mode

*Largo Maestoso* (M. M. ♩ = 60)

1. For - give us Lord, we turn to Thee, Re - new our days, our grief is sore, Thy par - don and Thy mer - cy be, On us, O Lord, for ev - er more.
2. Thou giv - est on this day of days New birth to ev - 'ry strick - en soul, "Re - turn to me" Thy man - date says, "And I will heal thee, make thee whole."
3. We are Thy sheep with - in Thy fold, Re - mem - ber not our sin - ful past! Grant us re - mis - sion as of old, Ac - cept the off' - ring of our fast.
4. Un - to Thy sons, who pen - i - tent, With con - trite hearts be - fore Thee stand, Thou ev - er - more be - nef - i - cent, Thou stretch - est out Thy pard - 'ning hand.
5. For - give us, Lord! we would a - tone, - Save us, O save us! Lord most High! We have no help but Thee a - lone, And Is - rael calls — O, — — — — hear their cry!

D. C.

I II III IV Verses V *dim.* Last Verse

175

# Day of Atonement and Penitence

**164**

## Out of the Depths, O Lord

Alice Lucas

PSALM 130

A. W. Binder

*mf* *Andante espressivo*

1. — Out of the depths, O Lord, I
2. — If Thou shouldst close - ly mark in -
3. My soul waits for the Lord, com -
4. Let Is - ra - el hope in God, whose

*mf*

cry to Thee; O hear my voice this day, And
i - qui - ties, Could a - ny stand, O Lord! But
pas - sion - ate Un - to His peo - ple's need, More
mer - cies last Un - end - ing and su - preme; And

let Thine ear to me at - ten - tive be, Al - might - y, when I pray!
with Thee ev - er - more for - give-ness is, That men may fear Thy word.
than the watchmen for the morn - ing wait, Yea, more than they in - deed.
He from all transgressions of the past Shall Is - ra - el re - deem.

# Day of Atonement

## Our Fortress Strong

Mrs. Goulston

Ferdinand Dunkley

*mf Andante*

*mf*

1. Our fort - ress strong art Thou, O Lord, The
2. From eve to morn, from morn till night, We
3. Low at Thy feet we pros - trate kneel, Lord,
4. Ac - cept our fast, our tremb - ling prayer, This

Rock to which we cling; In Thee we trust with
fast, we hope, we pray; Oh, let Thy par - don
to im - plore Thine aid; In mer - cy Thou our
of - fer - ing we bring; Oh, shield us with Thy

one ac - cord, Our Fa - ther and our King.
give us light On this most sol - emn day.
fate wilt seal, Though we have dis - o - beyed.
love, Thy care, Our Fa - ther and our King.

# Day of Atonement

## To Thee We Give Ourselves

Gustav Gottheil · Based on the traditional Kee hinay kachomer melody

*mf Andantino*

1. To Thee we give our - selves to - day; For - get - ful of the
2. Who could en - dure, shouldst Thou, O God, As we de - serve, for

world out - side, We tar - ry in Thy house, O God! From
ev - er chide! We, there-fore, seek Thy par - don-ing grace From

e – ven - tide to e – ven - tide. From Thine all - search - ing,
e – ven - tide to e – ven - tide. O may we lay to

right - eous eye Our deep - est heart can noth - ing hide; It
heart how swift The years of life do on - ward glide; So

cri - eth up to Thee for peace, From e - ven - tide to e – ven-tide.
learn to live that we may see Thy light at our life's e - ven-tide.

# Day of Atonement

## Thy Faithful Servant, Lord, Doth Yearn

Addie Funk, tr. fr. the Heb. of Solomon Ibn Gabirol          Harry Rowe Shelley

*mf   Animato*

1. Thy faith-ful ser-vant, Lord, doth yearn For Thy con-sol-ing grace,
2. To Thy des-pond-ent ser-vant show The path of pen-i-tence;

Spread o-ver him its heal-ing wing, His guilt do Thou ef-face.
He striv-eth pain-ful-ly for words To tell, how he re-pents.

Were not Thy word: Turn back from sin And I will turn to Thee, —
Oh, let my pen-i-tence to-day My own soul's sure-ty be;

I, like a helms-man in the storm, Would, help-less, face the sea.
Con-trite I vow to serve Thee well; Be mer-ci-ful to me!

**168**     ## Yom Kippur Prayer

Isabella R. Hess        Jacob Weinberg

*p Lento e legato*

1. Hear my pray'r, O hear my pray'r! Lead me, that I go a-right!
2. Cleanse me, and I shall be clean, Thou a-lone canst make me pure!
3. Teach me how to serve Thee best, Thus would I re-pay Thy care!

On-ly by Thy guid-ing flame Safe my foot-steps in life's night!
Give me strength to walk life's road, On-ly thus can I en-dure!
Guide me, cleanse me, stay my feet, Thou, who art the Heart of Pray'r!

# Day of Atonement

### Hymn for Atonement Day

Judah ben Samuel Halevi
(Yah Sh'ma Evjonecha*)—Tr. by Solomon Solis-Cohen

Jacob Weinberg

*mf Andante*

1. Lord, Thine hum-ble serv-ants hear, Sup - pli-ant now be-fore Thee; Our
2. Lord, Thy peo - ple, sore oppressed, From the depths im-plore Thee; Our
3. Lord, blot out our e - vil pride, All our sins be-fore Thee; Our
4. Lord, no sac - ri - fice we bring, Pray'rs and tears im-plore Thee; Our
5. Lord, Thy par - don grant to all That in truth im-plore Thee; Our

Fa - ther, from Thy chil-dren's plea Turn not, we im-plore Thee!
Fa - ther, let us not, this day, Cry in vain be - fore Thee.
Fa - ther, for Thy mer - cy's sake, Par - don, we im - plore Thee.
Fa - ther, take the gift we lay, Con -trite hearts, be - fore Thee.
Fa - ther, let our even - ing pray'r Now find grace be - fore Thee.

\* This poem, uncertainly attributed to Halevi, is a Pizmon in the Minchah Service of Yom Kippur,
Sephardic Liturgy.

# Day of Atonement and Penitence

**170**

## Create in this Weak Form of Mine

PSALM 51

Lily Weitzman

Arr. by Arthur Lieber

*mf Andante religioso*

*mf*

1. Cre - ate in this weak form of mine A
2. Grant me, O Lord, a spir - it pure To
3. And from Thy ho - ly pres - ence, Lord, Cast
4. Oh, op - en Thou my seal - ed lips, My

true and trust - ful heart, That from Thy ho - ly
dwell for aye in me, That I may seek through
me not out, I pray, Re - mem - ber not my
droop - ing spir - its raise, And I will all my

laws, O Lord, I nev - er may de - part.
all my life Sweet joys that come from Thee.
err - ing youth, But wash my sins a - way.
days on earth, Thy lov - ing - kind - ness praise.

183

# Day of Atonement

## Why Art Thou Cast Down?

J. K. Gutheim
Fr. the Hamburg Temple Hymnal

A. W. Binder
Based on V'al kulom melody

*p Lento con espressione*

1. Why art thou cast down, my soul, Why dis - qui - et - ed
2. Why art thou cast down, my soul, Why dis - qui - et - ed

in me? Feel'st thou not the Fa - ther nigh,
in me? Was thy head in sor - row bowed

Him whose heart ... con - tains us all? Lives no God for
When death snatched a friend from sight? Was thy heart with

thee on high, Lov - - ing while His judg - ments fall?
an - guish rent 'Neath the dread - - ed reap - er's blight?

184

Look a - bove! ..... God is love! God is Love!
Have no fear! ...... God is near! God is near!

Why art thou cast down, my soul, To the skies turn thine eyes;
Soul, my soul, be strong in faith, Tears take flight; for in light —

Be thou not cast down, my soul; Ev - 'ry tear on
Be thou not cast down, my soul; Dwell our dead on

earth that flows, God, the world's great Rul - er knows.
heav - en's shore, Bless - ed, bless - ed ev - er - more.

185

# Day of Atonement

## Lo, as the Potter Moulds His Clay

Elsie Davis
Tr. fr. the Heb. of R. Meir b. Baruch of Rothenburg

Traditional "Kee hinnay kachomer"

*mf  Largo*

1. Lo, as the pot - ter molds his clay, Shap - ing and forming it from day to day, Thus in Thy hand, O Lord, are we, O Thou whose mer - cies nev - er pass a - way.

2. E'en as the ma - son hews the stone, one is carv'd and wrought, and shattered one, Thus in Thy hand, O Lord, are we, Thou who of life and death art Lord a - lone.

3. Lo, as a - midst the fier - y glow smith his i - ron forg - es blow on blow, Thus in Thy hand, O Lord, are we, O Thou who sav - est those by care laid low.

4. Lo, as the sil - ver seven times tried in the smelter's fur - nace pur - i - fied, Thus in Thy hand, O Lord, are we, O Thou who balm and heal - ing scatterest wide.

# Day of Atonement
## Dim Mine Eyes With Many Teardrops

173

Mrs. Isaac L. Rypins

Based on Sephardic "Bemotzoay"

1. Dim mine eyes with ma - ny tear - drops,
2. Strength - en Thou mine eyes, O Fa - ther,
3. Gird my limbs with trust and pa - tience,

Weak my wear - y limbs with pain,
With the pow'r Thy truth to see;
Let my soul from doubts be free;

Weak my soul with doubts and long - ings
Make me strong, O God and Fa - ther,
Make me strong, O God and Fa - ther,

How may I this life sus - tain?
With a firm - er faith in Thee.
With a firm - er faith in Thee.

187

# Day of Atonement

## The Lifting of Mine Hands

**174**

Nina Davis Salaman
Tr. fr. the Heb. of Mordecai b. Sabbattai

FOR CHOIR

Samuel Alman

1. The lifting of my hands, ac-cept of me As
2. In thy great mercy, hear and understand my words, my med-i-ta-tion;
3. God whom we have not found, whose might is whole, For

though it were pure eve-ning sac-ri-fice, And let my pray'r be
if I hold, Grace in Thy sight, O God, who from of old, Hast
them Thou mad'st Thine in a - - - - - ges gone, If man give much, or

in-cense of sweet spice, Ac-coun-ted right and per-fect un-to Thee.
been a dwell-ing place, Then from mine hand, Take Thou the gift I bring Thee,
lit-tle, 'tis all one, When he re-turns, Thou will ac-cept his soul,

And when I call Thee, hear; for day once more Sinks to the hour when
plead-ing here, With suppli-ca - - - tion when the hour
If but his heart be true, when he shall draw, Nigh with his off-'ring:

## The Lifting of Mine Hands
### Continued

Is - rael brought of yore. The ev'n - ing sac - ri - fice.
draws near, For ev'n - ing sac - ri - fice.
this is all the law Of ev'n - ing sac - ri - fice.

## 175     At Midnight, so the Sages Tell

A. S. Isaacs

From G. F. Händel

*f Con spirito*

*f*

1. At mid - night, so the sa - ges tell, When
2. Up sprang the roy - al bard, in - spir'd, His
3. At mid - night, when dark doubts as - sail, And
4. O bid me seize the harp of faith And

Da - vid slept pro - found, A harp sus-pend - ed o'er his couch
fin - gers touch'd the chord, And with strange gladness in his soul,
anx - ious fears sur - round, O soul of mine, a - mid the gloom
sing a ho - ly strain Un - til each day my life and thought

Gave forth a trem-bling sound, Gave forth a trem-bling sound.
In psalms he praised the Lord, In psalms he praised the Lord.
Give forth a joy - ous sound, Give forth a joy - ous sound.
Re - sound in glad re - frain, Re - sound in glad re - frain.

# Day of Atonement

## God, That Doest Wondrously

### "AYL NORA ALEELAH"*

Moses Ibn Ezra
Tr. by Solomon Solis-Cohen

Sephardic Melody
Arr. by A. W. Binder

1. God, that do - est won - drous - ly, God, that do - est
2. Souls in grief be - fore Thee pour'd, Ag - o - nize for
3. Mer - cy, grace, for these low - bowed But up - on th' op -

won - drous - ly, Par - don at Thy peo - ple's cry,
deed and word; "We have sinn'd; For - give!" they cry,
press - or proud, Judg - ment for his vic - tims' cry

As the clos - ing hour draws nigh! Few are Is - rael's
As the clos - ing hour draws nigh! Heal them! Let their
As the clos - ing hour draws nigh! For our fa - thers'

*Pizmon introductory to the N'eelah (concluding) Service of the Day of Atonement, Sephardic
Liturgy, attributed in some rituals to Moses ibn Ezra. (S.S-C)

## God, Thou Doest Wondrously
### Continued

sons, and weak;    Thee    in    pen - i - tence    they    seek.
trust    in    Thee    Turn    a - side    the    dread    de - cree;
right - eous-ness,    Save    us    now    in    our    dis - tress;

O,    re - gard their anguished cry,    As    the    clos - ing    hour draws nigh.
Doom them not, but heed their cry,    As    the    clos - ing    hour draws nigh.
Make us glad with freedom's cry,    As    the    clos - ing    hour draws nigh.

4. God that do - est won-drous - ly    God that do - est won-drous - ly

Par - don    at    Thy    peo - ple's cry,    As    the    clos - ing    hour draws nigh.

# Day of Atonement (N'eelah)

## On Parting

John Ellerton

Max Grauman
Based on a traditional N'eelah melody

*mf* *Andante religioso*

1. Fa - ther, a - gain to Thee our hearts we lift;
2. Grant us Thy peace up - on our home - ward way;
3. Grant us Thy peace, Lord, thro' the com - - ing night;
4. Grant us Thy peace through-out our earth - ly life,

We now be - seech Thee, grant Thy part - ing gift;
With Thee be - gan, —— with Thee shall end the day;
Turn Thou for us its dark - ness in - to light; From
Our balm in sor - row, and our stay in strife;

Stand - ing be - fore Thee ere our wor - ship cease,
Guard Thou the lips from sin, the heart from shame,
harm —— and dan - ger keep Thy chil - dren free,
Then, when Thy voice shall bid our con - flict cease,

We —— low - ly
That —— in this
For —— dark and
Call —— us, O

Organ

bend - ing, wait Thy word —— of peace.
house —— have call'd up - on Thy name.
light —— are both a - like to Thee.
Lord, —— to Thine e - ter - - nal peace.

# Day of Atonement

## N'eelah Hymn

Author unknown
Tr. by Alice Lucas

Sephardic Melody
Arr. by A. W. Binder

*Moderato*

1. Lord of Hosts, whom all a - dore, Grant us par - don,
2. Par - don Thou our sins this day, When we pen - i -
3. O re - new our days of old With Thy mer - cies

we im - plore, At the N' - ee - lah once more,
tent - ly pray, And our hearts to Thee out - pour,
man - i - fold, And our years as here - to - fore,

At the N' - ee - lah once more. We, the "few in
At the N' - ee - lah once more. Be our shield and
At the N' - ee - lah once more. We be - seech Thee

num - ber" named,   Sup - pli - cat - ing   and   a - shamed,
strong-hold still,   And   our   cup   with   glad - ness   fill,
by   Thy name,   Lord,   the   year   of   grace   pro - claim,

Seek Thy mer - cy's   plenteous store   At   the   N' - ee - lah once   more.
When  we  stand Thy   throne be-fore   At   the   N' - ee - lah once   more.
And  Thy  scat-tered   flock re-store   At   the   N' - ee - lah once   more.

4. Lord   of Hosts, whom all   a - dore  Grant us par - don   we   im - plore,

At   the   N' - ee - lah once more,   At   the   N' - ee - lah once more.

# Day of Atonement (N'eelah)

## The Sun Goes Down

Composite

Josef Stark
Based on the Traditional N'eelah melody

*mf  Andante*

1. The sun goes down, the sha-dows rise, The day of God is
2. While still in clouds the sun de-lays, We pray Thee, Lord of
3. And when our sun of life re-treats, When eve-ning sha-dows

near its close, The glow-ing orb now home-ward flies,
earth and heav'n, That love may shed its peace-ful rays,
'round us fall, Our rest-less heart no long-er beats,

A gen-tle breeze fore-tells re-pose. Lord, —— crown our work,
New hope un-to our souls be giv'n. Oh, may the part-ing hour, the
And grave-ward sinks our earth-ly pall, We shall be-hold,

crown our work be-fore the night: At ev-en-tide let there be light.
part-ing hour be bright: At ev-en-tide let there be light.
we shall be-hold a glo-ri-ous sight: At ev-en-tide there will be light.

# Feast of Booths
## The Lulav

Jessie E. Sampter

Jacob Beimel
Traditional Succos melody

1. In many a stone-bound ci - ty, Still roofed be-
2. And in those tab - er - na - cles, The wan - d'rer's
3. Who bring in want and sor - row The stran - ger's

neath the skies, The Lord of
bless - ed re - lief He turns our
fruit with psalms, Shall plant our in

bound-less pi - ty Lets lit - tle bow - ers a - rise.
hea - vy shack-les To strings of fruit and leaf.
joy to - mor - row Their ci - trons and their palms.

# Feast of Booths and Autumn

Once More the Liberal Year

John G. Whittier

James G. Heller

*ff Moderato*

1. Once more the lib'-ral year laughs out O'er
3. We shut our eyes, the flow'rs bloom on; We

rich-er stores than gems or gold; Once more, with har-vest
mur-mur, but the corn ears fill; We choose the sha-dow,

song and shout, Is na-ture's blood-less tri-umph told.
but the sun That casts it, shines be-hind us still.

2. O fa - vors ev - 'ry year made new! O
4. Now let these al - tars, wreath'd with bow'rs And

bless - ings with the sun - shine sent! The boun - ty o - ver -
piled with fruit, a - wake a - gain Thanks - giv - ing for the

runs our due, The ful - ness shames our dis - con - tent.
gold - en hours, The ear - ly and the lat - ter rain.

# Feast of Booths
## "Succoth Hymn"

Joseph Leiser

Pinchos Jassinowsky

*mf Moderato*

1. For gar - nered fields and mead - ows cropped, And
2. To Thee we come with hearts made glad, For
3. With face up - turned in sun and rain, And
4. That nev - er falt - 'ring, though our arms Were
5. We thank Thee, yea, for throbs of love That

or - chards plucked of peach and pear, Lord, what Thy hand has
wheat that is our staff and stay; For oats and rye that
stout re - solves to do our task, O Lord, who gives to
wea - ry and our spir - its spent; That brave - ly we en -
glo - ri - fy each earth - born soul And link all puls - ing

giv - en us, For this we bring our grate - ful prayer.
caught the glint Of sun - set on a sum - mer's day.
each his due, Thy bless - ings for these do we ask:
dured the toil And an - guish that the sea - sons sent.
hearts to Thee In one vast un - i - ver - sal whole.

# Feast of Booths

## Thy Praise, O Lord

Alice Lucas, Tr. fr. Heb. "A'ameer"                    N. Lindsay Norden

*f Maestoso marcato*

1. Thy praise, O Lord, will I pro-claim In hymns un-to Thy glorious name;
2. May'st Thou in mer-cy man-i-fold, Dear un-to Thee Thy peo-ple hold,
3. They o-ver-flow with pray'r and praise To Him who knows the fu-ture days,

O Thou, Re-deem-er, Lord and King, Re-demp-tion to Thy faith-ful bring!
When at Thy gate they bend the knee And wor-ship and ac-knowl-edge Thee.
Have mer-cy, Thou, and hear the pray'r Of those who palms and myr-tle bear.

Be-fore Thine al-tar they re-joice With branch of palm and myr-tle-stem;
Do Thou their heart's de-sire ful-fill, Re-joice with them in love this day,
Thee day and night, they sanc-ti-fy And in per-pet-ual song a-dore;

*rall.*

To Thee they raise the pray'r-ful voice, Have mer-cy, save and pros-per them.
For-give their sins and thoughts of ill, And their trans-gress-ions cast a-way.
Like to the heav'n-ly host, they cry: "Bless-ed art Thou for ev-er-more."

*rall.*

# Feast of Booths

## A Succoth Prayer

Isabella R. Hess

Pinchos Jassinowsky

1. For the gold - en sun and the dart - ing rain — That
2. For the sun - lit days and the nights, star clear, — That
3. For bless - ings in the gen - er - ous store — That

brought the gift of the yel - low grain, For the sing - ing winds
mark the course of the chang-ing year, For the low-hung skies
prove a fa - ther's kind - ness more, For —— all that marks

For the Golden Sun
Continued

and the crys - tal dew     That   make   the   earth
of —— som - ber gray      When a  rest - ful  spir - it
Thy —— lov - ing care,     Dear ———— God,   we

bloom with life a - new,   Dear  God,  we  of - fer grate-ful pray - er,
fills —— the —— day,      Dear  God,  we  of - fer grate-ful pray - er,
of - fer grate-ful pray'r,  Dear  God,  we  of - fer grate-ful pray - er,

Dear      God,     we    of - fer  grate - ful  pray - er.
Dear      God,     we    of - fer  grate - ful  pray - er.
Dear      God,     we    of - fer  grate - ful  pray - er.

203

# Feast of Booths

**185**    Hymn for Tabernacles

Alice Flowerdew        S. Alman

*f Maestoso*

1. Fath - er of mer - cies, God of love, Whose gifts all crea - tures
3. spring's sweet influ - ence, Lord, was Thine, The sea - sons knew Thy
5. ne'er may our for - get - ful hearts O'er - look Thy boun - teous

share, The roll - ing sea - sons as they move, Pro -
call; Thou mad'st the sum - mer sun to shine, The
care; But what Thy lov - ing hand im - parts, Ac -

Hymn for Tabernacles
Continued

claim Thy cons-tant care.    2. When in the bo-som of the earth
sum-mer dews to fall.    4. Thy gifts of mer-cy from a-bove
cept with praise, and share.

FINE

The sow-er hid the grain, Thy good—ness marked its
Ma-tured the swel-ling grain; And now the har-vest

D. C.

se-cret birth, And sent the ear-ly rain. The
crowns Thy love, And plen-ty fills the plain. O

# Feast of Booths

Harvest

Barbara Joan Singer

Jacob Singer

*mf Moderato*

All through the long bright days in June, The leaves grew green and fair, —

*mf*

And waved in hot mid-sum-mer's noon, Their soft and yel-low hair.

206

And now with Au-tumn's moon-lit eves, The har - vest - time has come.

We pluck a - way the frost - ed leaves, And bear the treas - ure home,

We pluck a - way the frost - ed leaves And bear the treas - ure home.

# Feast of Booths

## Take Unto You

Alice Lucas

Samuel Alman
Based on a trad. Succos melody

Largo (M. M. ♩=60)

1. "Take un - to you the boughs of good - ly trees,
2. Thus kept they har - vest in — the years gone by,

Organ or hum

Branch-es of palm, and wil - lows of the brook,
And blessed the Lord for all His bount - eous store,

And build you booths to dwell there-in with these."

And songs of praise and prayer a - rose on high,

So it was writ - ten in the sac - red book.

To Him whose mer - cies are for - ev - er - more.

# Feast of Booths and Autumn

## Hymn of the Harvest

John Hampden Gurney

C. Hugo Grimm

*f Con energia*

1. Lord of the har - vest, Thee we hail,
2. When spring doth wake the song of mirth, When
3. But chief - ly when Thy boun - teous hand
4. Lord of the har - vest, all is Thine, The

Thy dai - ly bless - - - ings do not fail; The
sum - mer warms the fruit - ful earth, When
New plen - ty scat - - - ters o'er the land, When
rains that fall, the suns that shine, The

vary - ing sea - sons have their round; With good - ness all our
win - ter sweeps the na - ked plain, When au - tumn yields its
sounds of mu - sic fill the air, As home - ward men earth's
seed once hid - den in the ground, The skill that makes our

years are crown'd; Our thanks we pay This ho - ly day.
ri - pen'd grain, We ev - er sing To Thee our King;
treas - ures bear, We, too, will raise Our hymn of praise,
fruits a - bound. New ev - 'ry year Thy gifts ap - pear;

O let our hearts ——— with praise re - sound.
Through all their chang - - - es Thou dost reign.
For we Thy com - - - mon boun - ties share.
New prais - es from ——— our lips shall sound.

# Feast of Conclusion

## 189 A Week Within the Sukko Green

### SH'MEENEE ATSERES

Isabella R. Hess

Heinrich Schalit

1. A week with-in the suk-ko green We've
2. A-gain we lift our voice in pray'r, O

sung Thy bound-less praise, Now end-ed is the
send Thy bless-ed rain, That when an-oth-er

au-tumn feast, The gold-en har-vest days.
har-vest comes We may re-joice a-gain!

# Feast of Conclusion

## A Week Within the Sukko Green

Isabella R. Hess  SH'MEENEE ATSERES  Jacob Weinberg

*mf* *Andantino con moto*

1. A week with-in the suk - ko green, We've sung Thy boundless praise,
2. A-gain we lift our voice in pray'r, O send thy bless-ed rain,

*mf*

Now end - ed is the aut - umn feast, The gold - en har - vest days.
That when an - oth - er har - vest comes We may re - joice a - gain!

*f*

213

# Feast of Conclusion

### or for Rejoicing of the Law

New Version        PSALM 119        Jacob Weinberg

1. Thy word is to my feet a lamp, The way of truth to show;
2. When I with griefs am so op-prest That I can bear no more,
3. O let my sac - ri - fice of praise With Thee ac - cep-tance find;
4. Thy tes - ti - mo - nies I have made My her - it - age and choice;

A cheer-ing light to mark the path Where - in I ought to go,
Ac - cord - ing to Thy word, do Thou My faint-ing soul re - store,
And in Thy right-eous judgments, Lord, In - struct my will - ing mind,
For they, when oth - er com - forts fail, My droop-ing heart re - joice,

A cheer-ing light to mark the path Where - in I ought to go.
Ac - cord - ing to Thy word, do Thou My faint-ing soul re - store.
And in Thy right-eous judgments, Lord, In - struct my will - ing mind.
For they, when oth - er com - forts fail, My droop-ing heart re - joice.

# Thankfulness

## In Answer to My Prayer

Harry H. Mayer

Jacob Singer
Based on Cantillation mode of "Song of Songs"

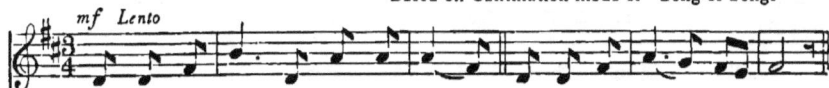

*mf Lento*

1. O God, my ev - er con-stant Friend, I owe all thanks to Thee,
2. How soon Thy ten - der voice re - sponds In an-swer to — my prayers,
3. Give me to know Thy near-ness, God, Thy wis-dom and Thy might,

*mf*

Whose nev - er fail-ing love and care Are watch-ing o - ver me.
When trust - ing Thy pro -tect - ing love, I bring to Thee my cares.
The bound-less meas-ure of Thy love Thro' all the day and night.

# Thankfulness
## We Thank Thee

George E. L. Cotton

Jacob Singer

f Con spirito

1. We thank Thee, Lord, for this fair earth, The
2. Thanks for the flowers that clothe the ground, The
3. Yet teach us still how far more fair, More

glitt'r - ing sky, the sil - ver sea, For all their beau - ty,
trees that wave their arms a - bove, The hills that gird our
glo - rious, Fa - ther, in Thy sight, Is one pure deed, one

all their worth, Their light and glo - ry come from Thee.
dwell - ings round, As Thou dost gird Thine own with love.
ho - ly prayer, One heart that owns Thy spir - it's might.

# Thankfulness

## O Render Thanks

### PSALM 106

A. W. Binder

*f* *Andante con moto*

1. O rend - er thanks to God a - bove, The
2. Who can His might - y deeds ex - press, Not
3. Hap - py are they, and on - ly they, Who

*f*

foun - tain of e - ter - nal love, Whose mer - cy firm through
on - ly vast, but num - ber - less? What mor - tal el - o -
from Thy judg-ments nev - er stray; Who know the truth, nor

*p*

a - ges past, Has stood, and shall for - ev - er last.
quence can raise, His tri - bute of im - mor - tal praise?
on - ly so, But al - ways prac - tise what they know.

# Thankfulness

## We Plough the Fields

Matthias Claudius
Tr. by Jane M. Campbell

C. Hugo Grimm

**195**

*f Risoluto*

1. We plough the fields, and scat - ter The good seed on the land,
2. He on - ly is the Mak - er Of all things near and far;
3. We thank Thee, then, O Fath - er, For all things bright and good,

But it is fed and wa - ter'd By God's al-might - y hand;
He paints the way-side flow - er, He lights the eve - ning star;
The seed-time and the har - vest, Our life, our health, our food;

He sends the snow in win - ter; The warmth to swell the grain;
The winds and waves o - bey Him, By Him the birds are fed;
Ac - cept the gifts we of - fer For all Thy love im - parts,

The breez - es, and the sun - shine, And soft re - fresh - ing rain:
Much more to us, His chil - dren, He gives our dai - ly bread.
And what Thou most de - sir - est, Our hum - ble, thank - ful hearts.

All good gifts a - round us. Are sent from Heav'n a - bove,

Then thank the Lord, O thank the Lord, For all —— His love.

# Thankfulnesss

## 196    O Lord! to Thee Who Dwell'st Above

George Jacobs                                        Alois Kaiser

*f Andante con moto*

1. O Lord! to Thee who dwell'st a - bove, We
2. To Thee, whose mer - cies nev - er end, Our
3. Then let our hearts and lips u - nite To

raise the sa - cred hymn of praise, For Thou hast blest us
o - ver - flow - ing thanks we pour; Whose light and truth through
chant our thanks in joy - ful lays, As we in grat - i -

with Thy love, And guid - ed us in all our ways.
earth ex - tend, Whose good - ness is for ev - er - more.
tude re - cite, O God, thy ev - er - last - ing praise.

# Charity

## Thy Brother

Theodore Chickering Williams

James G. Heller

1. When thy heart, with joy o'er-flow-ing, Sings a thank-ful prayer,
2. When the har-vest-sheaves in-gath-ered Fill thy barns with store,
3. If thy soul, with power up-lift-ed, Yearn for glo-rious deed,
4. Hast thou borne a se-cret sor-row In thy lone-ly breast?
5. Share with him thy bread of bless-ing, Sor-row's bur-den share;

In thy joy, O let thy broth-er With thee share.
To thy God and to thy broth-er Give the more.
Give thy strength to serve thy broth-er In his need.
Take to thee thy sor-rowing broth-er For a guest.
When thy heart en-folds a broth-er, God is there.

# Winter

## 'Tis Winter

Samuel Longfellow

James G. Heller

*Andantino*

1. 'Tis win - ter now; the fal - len snow Has left the
2. And though a - broad the sharp winds blow, And skies are

heav - ens all cold - ly clear; Through leaf - less boughs the sharp winds
chill, and frosts are keen, Home clos - er draws her cir - cle

blow, And all the earth lies dead and drear. And yet God's
now, And warm - er glows her light with - in. O God, who

love     is     not     with-drawn;   His   life   with - in   the
giv'st   the   win - ter's cold,   As   well   as   sum - mer's

keen   air breathes,   His   beau - ty   paints   the   crim - son
joy - ous rays,   Us   warm - ly   in   Thy   love   en -

dawn,   And   clothes   the   boughs   with   glit - ter - ing wreaths.
fold,   And   keep   us   through   life's   win - try   days.

# The Law

## This Feast of the Law

Israel Zangwill
Tr. fr. the Heb.

Jacob Beimel
Based on traditional Hakofos melody

*f  Moderato Vigoroso*

1. This Feast of the Law all your glad - ness dis - play,
2. My God I will praise in a ju - bi - lant lay,
3. My heart of Thy good - ness shall car - ol al - way,

To - day all your hom - a - ges ren - - - der.
My hope in Him nev - er sur - ren - - - der,
Thy prais - es I ev - er will ren - - - der.

What prof - it can lead one so pleas - ant a way,
His glo - ry pro - claim where His chos - en sons pray,
While breath is, my lips all Thy won - ders shall say,

# This Feast of the Law
## Continued

What jew - els can vie with its splen - - - dor?
My Rock all my trust shall en - gen - - - der.
Thy truth and Thy kind - ness so ten - - - der.

Then ex - ult in the Law on its fes - ti - val day,
Then ex - ult in the Law on its fes - ti - val day,
Then ex - ult in the Law on its fes - ti - val day,

The Law is our Light and De - fend - - - er.
The Law is our Light and De - fend - - - er.
The Law is our Light and De - fend - - - er.

# The Law
## Rejoicing of the Law

Abraham Ibn Ezra
Tr. by Alice Lucas

Jacob Beimel
Based on a Simchas Torah Melody

*f* *Moderato Vigoroso*

1. My faith shall be my rock of might, Its law my por - tion and my right, Its tes - ti - mo - nies my de - light, And day by day, my voice I raise In song and hymn to chant their praise.

2. How did th' an - gel - ic host la - ment When from their midst, by God's in - tent, The ho - ly law to earth was sent. "Woe that the pure and sanc - ti - fied Should now on sin - ful lips a - bide."

3. The peo - ple trem - bled when they saw Ap - proach - ing them the heav'n - ly law, Their voic - es rose in joy and awe: "Thy cov - e - nant, O Lord, ful - fill, De - clare it, we will do Thy will."

4. Great won - ders He on Si - nai wrought, When un - to us His law He taught, Where - fore to praise His name I sought; But what am I and what my words Be - fore th' Al - might - y Lord of lords?

5. Hear Thou Thy peo - ple's pray'r, O King, When like the heav'n - ly host they sing Thrice Ho - ly, Ho - ly — ut - ter - ing Sweet hymns and songs of pleas - antness With joy and awe Thy name to bless.

226

# The Law
## Come, Let us Praise

Florence Montefiore

C. Hugo Grimm

*Allegretto*

1. Come, let us praise our God and Lord, Who
2. Our shield it is, our help and stay, A
3. At Si - nai in the days of old Midst
4. And with the Law, the man - date came, Through
5. Fear ye the Lord, His name a - dore, O -

un - to Is - rael did ac - cord, The treas - ure of His
bea - con - light up - on our way, A guide to save us,
signs and won - ders man - i - fold, God bade all Is - ra -
end - less a - ges still the same "The Lord is One and
bey His word, His grace im - plore, And trust His mer - cy

ho - ly word, The treas - ure of the Law.
when we stray, Our shel - ter is the Law.
el be - hold The giv - ing of the Law.
One His name, And ho - ly is the Law."
ev - er - more, Who gave the hol - y Law.

# The Law

## 202

### Unveil Mine Eyes

#### PSALM 119

Scottish Version

F. Belmont

*mf Moderato*

1. Un - veil mine eyes that of Thy law The
2. I of the per - fect way of truth My
3. In lov - ing kind - ness let my prayer And
4. Great peace have they who love Thy law, Of -

won - ders I may see: — I am a wand - 'rer
choice have free - ly made, — Thy judg-ments, which most
cry be heard by Thee; — Ac - cord - ing to Thy
fence they shall have none; — I hope for Thy sal -

on this earth Hide not Thy face from me. —
right - eous are, Be - fore me I have laid. —
prom - ise, Lord, Re - vive and quick - en me. —
va - tion, Lord, When Thy com - mand I've done. —

# The Law
## "The Torah"

Max D. Klein

Pinchos Jassinowsky

*mf* Allegretto

1. All praise to Thee we bring, To Thee, our fa-thers' God, For
2. Our fa-thers loved Thy Word, They went through fire and flame; Thy
3. For pro-phet and for sage, Who led us on the way, And
4. To us the will im-part, That we as firm may be To
5. O Is-rael's Guide and Shield, Up-lift us through Thy Law; Un-

*mf*

all the teach-ing of Thy Law, The way all Is-ra-el trod.
Law they kept in life and death, And sanc - ti-fied Thy Name.
gave all Is-rael strength and light, We thank Thee, God, to-day.
live our lives, as they lived theirs, For Is-ra-el and for — Thee.
veil our eyes that we may see The won - ders which they saw.

# Feast of Lights

### Kindle the Taper

#### CHANUKKAH

Emma Lazarus

Jacob Singer

*f Maestoso*

1. Kin - dle the ta - per like the stead - fast star A -
2. Clash, Is - ra - el, the cym - bals, touch the lyre,
3. Still ours the dance, the feast, the glor - ious Psalm, The

blaze on —— eve - ning's fore-head o'er the earth; Send thro' the night its
Blow the loud trump - et and harsh-tongued horn; Chant psalms of vic - tory
mys - tic lights of em - blem and the Word. Where is our Ju - dah?

lus - ter till a - far, An eight-fold splen-dor shine a - bove thy hearth.
till the heart take fire, The Mac - ca - be - an spir - it leap new - born.
Where our five-branch'd palm? Where are the li - on war - riors of the Lord?

# Feast of Lights

## Kindle the Taper

Emma Lazarus

A. W. Binder

1. Kin - dle the ta - per, like the steadfast star   A - blaze on even-ing's
2. Clash, Is - ra - el the cymbals, touch the lyre,   Blow the loud trum-pet
3. Still ours the dance, the feast the glor-ious Psalm,   The mys - tic lights of

fore - head o'er the earth;   Send thru the night its lus - ter
and harsh-tongu - ed horn,   Chant psalms of vic-t'ry till the
em - blem and the Word.   Where is our Ju-dah? Where our

till a - - far An eight-fold splen - dor shine a-bove thy hearth.
heart takes fire, The Mac-ca - be-an spir-it leaps new - born.
five - branched palm? Where are the li -on war-riors of the Lord?

# Feast of Lights

## Before the Menorah

Elma Ehrlich Levinger

A. W. Binder

*mf Spiritoso*

1. In the can - dles' rays I see Love - ly pic - tures
2. Sol - diers all, they smiled in pride, Glad and un - a -

*mf*

beck - 'ning me! Ju - dah with his shield and sword,
fraid, they died. God of Is - rael, may I be A

# Before the Menorah
## Continued

Pledged   to   bat - tle   for   the   Lord;   El - e - a - zer
sol - dier   wor - thy   them   and   Thee.

steadfast, strong, 'Mid the   mock - ing   heath-en throng; Han -nah straight as

can - dle's flame,   Sons   who glor - i - fied her   name.

D. C. Al Fine

# Feast of Lights

**207**
## Rock of Ages

M. Jastrow, G. Gottheil
Ad. from the Ger. of Leopold Stein

Old synagogal melody Mooz Tsur

*ff Maestoso*

1. Rock of A - ges, let our song Praise Thy sav - ing pow - er;
2. Kind-ling new the ho - ly lamps, Priests approved in suf - fering,
3. Chil-dren of the mar - tyr-race, Whether free or fet - tered,

Thou, a - midst the rag - ing foes, Wast our shelt-'ring tow - er.
Pu - ri - fied the nation's shrine, Brought to God their of - fering.
Wake the ech - oes of the songs Where ye may be scat - tered.

# Rock of Ages
## Continued

Fu - rious, they as - sailed us, But Thine arm a - vail - ed us,
And His courts sur-round - ing Hear, in joy a - bound - ing,
Yours the mes - sage cheer - ing That the time is near - ing

And Thy word Broke their sword When our own strength failed us.
Hap - py throngs, Sing - ing songs With a might - y sound - ing.
Which will see All men free, Ty - rants dis - ap - pear - ing.

# Feast of Lights

**208**

### Fortress-Rock, my God, my Aid!

F. DeSola Mendes
Tr. fr. the Hebrew "Mooz Tsur"

Old Synagogal Melody Mooz Tsur

*f  Maestoso*

1. — For-tress-Rock, my God, my aid! To Thee my prais - es shall as-cend;
2. My soul is wea-ried by the woe The a - ges rained up - on my head;
3. 'Twas then Thou broughtest me at length To Zi - on's rock - y tem - ple-hill;
4. The Syr - ian last his an - ger spent Up - on my poor de-fense-less head.

Our Guar-dian in the days of yore, On Is - rael bid Thy grace descend.
From ear - ly days when E-gypt's hate Sustained me on "af - fliction's bread."
A - las, I was not faith - ful there, For oth - er gods I wor-shiped still!
My shrine de - filed, my Law proscribed, I - dol - a - try set up in-stead.

The truth our people's seers have known, All men, a - wak-'ning then shall own;
But from Thy great re-deem - ing Hand, The blow fell by the Red Sea's strand;
The bit - ter cup an ex - ile sees, I drained un - to its low - est lees,
Then brave a - rose the Mac - ca-bee Who foes beat off most glori-ous-ly,

Thy Law of Love, all laws a-bove, Our time-long sor - rows full shall end.
With pomp and boast, the Pharaoh's host Was hurled deep in - to o - cean's bed.
But hope-ful dreams by Babel's streams Came true in e - dicts of Thy will!
And these glad days at-test their praise Who for Thy truth so no - bly bled!

*Small notes omitted in first stanza.

# Feast of Lights
## Great Arbiter of Human Fate

209

Penina Moise
*f Moderato*

Edward Samuel

1. Great Ar - bi - ter of hu - man fate, Whose glo-ry ne'er de-cays,
2. A - mid the ru - ins of their land; (In Sa-lem's sad de-cline.)
3. Not long to vain re - grets they yield, But for their cher-ished fane,
4. 'Twas Thine, O ev - er - last-ing King And u - ni - ver - sal Lord!

To Thee a - lone we ded - i - cate The song and soul of praise.
Stood forth a brave but scant - y band To bat - tle for their shrine.
Nerved by true faith, they take the field, And vic - to - ry ob-tain.
Whose won-ders still Thy ser-vants sing, Whose mercies they re - cord.

Thy pres-ence Ju - dah's host in-spired, On dan-ger's post to rush;
In bit - ter - ness of soul they wept, With-out the Temple wall,
But whose the pow - er, whose the hand, Which thus to tri-umph led
Oh! thus shall Mer-cy's hand de - light To cleanse the blemished heart,

By Thee the Mac - ca - bee was fired, I - dol - a - try to crush.
For weeds a - round its court had crept, And foes its priests en - thrall.
The slend - er but he - ro - ic band, From which blasphem-ers fled?
Re - kind - le vir - tue's wan - ing light, And truth and peace im - part.

237

# Feast of Lights

## Where Judah's Faithful Sons are Found

Harry H. Mayer     (May be used for Purim)     Samuel Alman

*f*  *Maestoso* (M. M. ♩ = 104)

1. Where Ju-dah's faith-ful sons are found, Tho' few their num - ber be,
2. O    let our hymns to heav'n a - rise, In   strains of   love   and peace,

Though foes op-press, let songs re-sound, Our fath-ers' God, to Thee.
Brave souls yield not   to   tears and sighs, Their songs of   hope ne'er cease.

Hear, brothers mine, where-e'er   ye dwell, This truth our   pro-phets told:
Our   fathers' faith is   liv - ing still, In   spite of   fire and sword,

God will   your foemen's wrath dis-pel,   If   to   your faith   ye   hold.
Thy songs sub-lime our hearts shall thrill To   hope in   Is - rael's Lord.

238

# Laying the Cornerstone
## In Mercy Lord, Incline Thine Ear

**211**

Isaac M. Wise

A. W. Binder

1. In mer - cy, Lord, in - cline Thine ear To
2. Re - veal once more ce - - les - tial light O'er
3. To truth be laid this cor - ner - stone, Be
4. Pour down Thy grace in sun - ny rays, Let

Zi - on's faith - ful band; In love and grace our
Zi - on's ho - ly tents, Dis - pel the clouds and
reared these mas - sive walls; To Thee, Most High, and
Ju - dah's tem - ple be The house of praise to

plead - ings hear, Re - veal Thy might - y hand.
end the night, Let truth per - vade all lands.
on - - ly One, Be arched these sa - cred halls.
teach Thy ways, De - vo - ted, Lord, to Thee.

# Laying the Cornerstone

## Firm This Cornerstone be Laid

Penina Moise
1st stanza, composite

E. J. Stark

*f* Lento

1. Firm this cor-ner-stone be laid; Firm the walls a - bove it rise;
2. House of Ju-dah, bless the Lord, Let His praise be your de-light;
3. Joy-ful-ly your al-tars rear, Tho' with rough-est stones you build;
4. 'Round your loved and hal-lowed shrine An - gel vis - it - ants shall stand;

Shrines which lov-ing hands have made Zi - on's God will not de-spise.
On your hearts His law rec-ord, Walk ye in its per-fect light.
If your wor-ship be sin - cere, Faith's high pur-pose is ful-filled.
'Tis a Beth-el as di - vine As the Luz of Ho-ly Land.

# Dedication

## A New Shrine

Louis Marshall
*f* Allegro deciso

James G. Heller

1. A new shrine stands in beau - ty reared, Where sci - ons of a
2. Here shall the words of praise be sung, From days when yet the
3. Hence shall as - cend the fer - vent pray'rs Of thanks for joys, of
4. On this new al - tar there shall blaze Re - ful - gent - ly the
5. May jus - tice ev - er here pre-vail, May love for all man-

faith  re - vered  Re — new  their  vows  to  God;  To
world  was young,  Of  psalm - ist  and  of  seer;  Like
trust  when cares  And  sor - rows  rack  the  soul.  Here
Bi — ble's rays  Of  right - eous - ness  and  truth;  Here
kind  ne'er fail,  And  char - i - ty  ne'er  cease;  May

Him  this house they  ded - i - cate,  To  Him  their hearts they
tor - rent shall the  cho - rus run,  "The  Lord,  our  God, the
shall  the breast where  sin  has surged  By  the  a - tone-ment's
shall  the won - drous  tale  be told,  The  mir - a - cle of
God's She - ki - nah  here  e'er rest,  That  they who ga - ther

con - se - crate  Up — on  this  sa - cred  sod.
Lord  is  One,  Hear  thou,  O  Is - rael,  hear!"
fires  be  purged,  Here  ho - ly  thoughts con - sole.
Is - rael  old,  And  its  un - dy - ing  youth.
here  be  blest  With  con - cord  and  with  peace.

# Dedication and Anniversary

**214**

## To Worship God in Truth

Harry H. Mayer

Traditional "Askenazi Tune" from Lyra Anglo-Judaica

*mf  Con moto*

1. To wor-ship God in truth And in sin-cer-i-ty,
2. Lord, come and sanc-ti-fy This shrine that we have reared,
3. Then let us strive to be God's serv-ants tried and true,
4. Lord God, this shrine we built, In faith-ful-ness and love,

This house we ded-i-cate His dwelling-place to be:
And help us prove that here The one God is re-vered;
His priests while in these halls, His priests the whole world through;
Thy peace be ev-er here, Thy blessing from a-bove;

Our free-will gift it is, A joy-ous of-fer-ing,
What here we feel and speak Our lives will dem-on-strate
In trop-ic lands or froz-en, Wher-ev-er we may roam,
To wor-ship Thee in truth And in sin-cer-i-ty,

Which to His al-tar now, With grateful heart we bring.
When we our pi-ous vows In lov-ing deeds trans-late.
May we His presence feel As 'neath the tem-ple's dome.
This house we ded-i-cate Thy dwelling-place to be.

# Dedication or Anniversary

## Our Pious Fathers

F. De Sola Mendes—alt.

Max Grauman

*f Andante*

1. Our pi - ous fa - thers built their shrine A lad - der firm to be, —— To send a - loft their prayers, their joys, Their sor - rows, God, to Thee.

2. Our fa - ther's Guide, we hon - or Thee On this our fest - al day, —— For all the good - ness, help and care Thou didst to us dis - play.

3. Con - tin - ue un - to us Thy grace, To pros - per and pro - tect! —— Ac - cept each heart's pe - ti - tion here We to Thy throne di - rect.

# Anniversary

## O Thou, Whose Presence

**216**

John Haynes Holmes

James G. Heller

*f Maestoso*

1. O Thou, whose Pre - sence moved be - fore The
3. E - ter - nal God who blessed our sires, When
5. This tem - ple make an ark of grace, Where

dark - ly wan - d'ring tribes of yore, Whose stead - fast pur - pose,
here they lit their al - tar fires, And raised with them this
we may meet Thee face to face; This shrine an al - tar

like a star, Looked down on na - tions from a - far?
sac - red dome, Where now Thou mak - est still Thy home;
fair and tall, Whence sounds the thun - der of Thy call.

## O Thou, Whose Presence
### Continued

2. Thou God, whose liv - ing voice was heard In
4. To us, dear Lord, this lat - ter day, Send
6. And lo, Thy peo - ple, now as then, Will

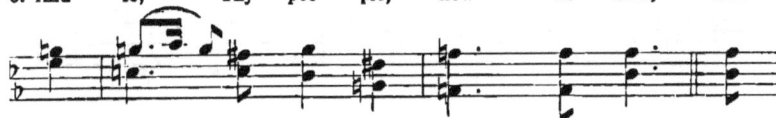

psalm - ist's song and pro - phet's word, Whose ho - ly will turned
out Thy light up - on our way; Lift high Thy spir - it's
seek Thy Prom - ised Land a - gain, And stay not, till in

kings to dust, And glo - ri - fied the mar - tyr's trust.
pil - lared fame A - bove our wild - er - ness of shame.
fields un - trod, Is built the King - dom of our God.

# Anniversary

## Come let us Sing in Sweet Accord

Louis Stern

Max Grauman

*f* Con moto

1. Come let us sing in sweet ac - cord Our
2. The pres - ent, rich with har - vests fair, The
3. The foun - ders and the lead - ers great, Gone
4. They build - ed wise - ly, worked and watched With

hap - py, glad - some lays, While mind and heart on
fut - ure bright and vast — O let us not for -
to e - ter - nal rest, We name them in our
high, un - self - ish aim, Proud mon - u - ments of

mem - 'ry's wings Re - vert to by - gone days.
get this truth — Are root - ed in the past.
hearts to - day And call their mem - 'ry blest.
lov - ing deeds Pro - claim their death - less fame.

# The Marriage

## All Wise, All Great

Austin Dobson

Jacob Singer

1. All - wise, All - great whose an - cient plan, Or -
2. Al - might - y Rul - er, in whose hand The
3. Through - out their life - long jour - ney still, Guide

dained the wom - an for the man, Look down, O Lord, on
mor - row and its is - sues stand, What - e'er the lot Thy
Thou these two in good and ill, And where - so - e'er the

these who now Be - fore Thy sa - cred al - tar bow.
will as - sign, We can but say our all is Thine.
way ex - tend, Be with them, Fa - ther, to the end.

# The Marriage

## Blest is the Bond

Penina Moise  St. 3 l. 3 alt.

James G. Heller

1. Blest is the bond of wed - ded love, —— When
2. They will sweet coun - sel in - ter - change, —— And
3. Blest are the vows of wed - ded life, —— When

they who at its al - tar bow - Re - mem - ber that the God a -
as each sea - son on-ward rolls, — Prove that no chance can e'er es -
they from righteous lips pro - ceed, — When, love en - no-bling man and

bove —— Is wit - ness to their ho - ly vow. ——
trange —— The feel - ing that u - nites — their souls. ——
wife —— Time hal - lows that which God — de - creed.

# The Funeral

## It Singeth Low

John W. Chadwick

C. Hugo Grimm

*p Molto Tranquillo*

1. It sing - eth low in ev - 'ry heart, We hear it, each and all,
2. 'Tis hard to take the bur - den up, When these have laid it down;
3. More home - like seems the vast unknown, Since they have en - tered there;

A song of those who ans - wer not, How - ev - er we may call.
They bright - ened all the joy of life, They soft - ened ev - 'ry frown;
To fol - low them were not so hard, Wher - ev - er they may fare.

They throng the si - lence of the breast, We see them as of yore—
But oh! 'tis good to think of them When we are troub - led sore;
They can - not be where God is not; On an - y sea or shore

The kind, the brave, the true, the sweet, Though they are here no more.
Thanks be to God that such have been, Though they are here no more.
What - e'er be - tides, Thy love a - bides, Our God for ev - er - more.

# The Funeral

## My Faith

Sophia Navra

(FOR CHOIR)

Boris Levenson

*p Moderato*

1. I leave the bur-dens of my life, And
2. God sent me here with pur-pose true, My
3. Full oft I stum-ble as I go, And
4. I can-not reach my life's i-deal, It
5. Some-times I feel a help-less child, A
6. The shad-ow val-ley, at the last, Where

all the wea-ri-ness and — strife, With
ig-no-rance and weak-ness knew, And
tears of sor-row quick-ly flow, But
tow-ers far a-bove the real, But
poor weed tossed on wa-ters wild. And
man-y loved of mine have passed, Seems

Him, who or-ders all my ways, And knows the lim-its
wheth-er light or dark-ness fall, His ten-der love is
He to whom my grief is known, Leaves me not long to
when I think of count-less years Of fu-ture life in
yet God's skies are o-ver me, And yet He rules the
but a step from night to day. For all the new and

## My Faith
### Continued

*mf*      *p*   *rit.*

| of | my | days, | And | so | I | rest, | And | so | I | rest. |
| o - | ver | all. | And | it | is | best, | And | it | is | best. |
| weep a - | lone. | He | send - | eth | peace, | He | send - | eth | peace. |
| un - known | spheres | My | mur - | murs | cease, | My | mur - | murs | cease. |
| wide, wide | sea. | I | need | not | fear, | I | need | not | fear. |
| shrouded | way | God | will | be | near, | God | will | be | near. |

*mf*     *p*   *rit.*

---

## 222     Whose Works, O Lord, Like Thine

Alice Lucas                           Ivor Warren

*mf Moderato*

| 1. | Whose | works, | O | Lord, | like | Thine | can | be, | Who | 'neath | Thy |
| 2. | There | are | the | sin - | less | spir - | its | bound | Up | in | the |
| 3. | Sweet | peace | and | calm | their | spir - | its | bless, | Who | reach | that |
| 4. | This | is | the | rest | for - | ev - | er | sure, | This | is | the |
| 5. | This | is | the | land | the | spir - | it | knows; | That | ev - | er - |

*mf*

| throne | of | grace, | For | those | pure | souls | from |
| bond | of | life, | The | wea - | ry | there | new |
| heav - | enly | home, | And | nev - | er | end - | ing |
| her - | it - | age, | Whose | good - | ness | and | whose |
| last - | ing - | ly | With | milk | and | hon - | ey |

| earth | set | free, | Hast | made | a | dwell - | ing - | place! |
| strength | have | found, | The | weak | have | rest | from | strife. |
| pleas - | ant - | ness | Such | is | the | world | to | come. |
| bliss | en - | dure | Un - changed | from | age | to | age. |
| o - | ver - | flows — | And | such | its | fruit | shall | be. |

251

# The Funeral

## Friend After Friend

J. Montgomery
St. 1, l. 5 and 6 alt.

C. Hugo Grimm

*p Andantino*

1. Friend af - ter friend de - parts, Who hath not lost a
2. Be - yond the flight of time, Be - yond this vale of

friend? There is no un - ion here of hearts That
death, There sure - ly is some bless - ed clime Where

finds not here an end; But be not sad nor vain - ly grieve
life is not a breath, Nor life's af - fec - tions, tran - sient fire,

## Friend After Friend
### Continued

When friends from earth must take their leave.  3. There is a world a-
Whose sparks fly up-ward and ex-pire.  4. Thus, star by star de-

bove, Where part - ing is un-known, A long e - ter - ni-
clines, Till all are passed a - way, As morn - ing high and

ty of love Be - fore God's glori-ous throne; And faith be-holds the
high - er shines To pure and per - fect day; Nor sink those stars in

dy - ing here Trans - la - ted to that hap - pier sphere.
emp - ty night, But hide them-selves in heaven's own light.

# The Funeral

**224**

## Of all the Thoughts of God

Elizabeth Barrett Browning

M. Deutsch

*mf  Andante*

1. Of all the thoughts of God that are Borne in - ward in - to souls a - far, A - long the psalm - ist's mu - sic deep, Now tell me if that a - ny is, For gift or grace sur - pass - ing this: "He giv - eth His be - lov - ed sleep? He giv - eth His be - lov - ed sleep?"

2. What would we give to our be - loved, The he - ro's heart to be un - moved, The po - et's star - tuned harp, to sweep, The pa - triot's voice, to teach and rouse, The mon - arch's crown, to light the brows? He giv - eth His be - lov - ed sleep? He giv - eth His be - lov - ed sleep.

3. "Sleep soft, be - loved!" we some - times say, Who have no tune to charm a - way Sad dreams that through the eye - lids creep; But nev - er dole - ful dream a - gain Shall break the hap - py slum - ber when He giv - eth His be - lov - ed sleep. He giv - eth His be - lov - ed sleep.

4. His dews drop mute - ly on the hill, His cloud a - bove it sail - eth still, Tho' on its slope men sow and reap; More soft - ly than the dew is shed, Or cloud is float - ed o - ver - head, He giv - eth His be - lov - ed sleep. He giv - eth His be - lov - ed sleep.

# Righteousness
## A Noble Life

A. S. Isaacs

C. Hugo Grimm

**225**

*mf* *Moderato*

1. A no - ble life, a sim - ple faith, An o - pen heart and hand,
2. These are the firm - knit bonds of grace, Though hid - den to the view,
3. The cries of clash - ing creeds are heard, On ev - 'ry side they sound,
4. A no - ble life, a sim - ple faith, An o - pen heart and hand,

These are the love - ly lit - a - nies Which all men un - der - stand.
Which bind in sac - red broth - er-hood All men the whole world through.
But no age is de - gen - e - rate In which such lives are found.
These are the love - ly lit - a - nies Which all men un - der - stand.

# Peace

## God of the Nations Near and Far

John Haynes Holmes

Peter C. Lutkin

*f Andante*

1. God of the nations, near and far,
2. The clash of arms still shakes the sky,
3. But clear-er far the friend-ly speech Of
4. And strong-er far the clasp-ed hands Of
5. O Fath-er! from the curse of war, We

Ru-ler of all man-kind, Bless Thou Thy peo-ple
King bat-tles still with king, Wild through the fright-ed
sci-en-tists and seers, The wise de-bate of
la-bor's teem-ing throngs Who in a hun-dred
pray Thee, give re-lease, And speed, O speed the

as they strive The paths of peace to find.
air of night The blood-y toc-sins ring.
states-men and The shouts of pi-o-neers.
tongues re-peat Their com-mon creeds and songs.
bless-ed day Of jus-tice, love and peace.

## Hail the Glorious Golden City

Felix Adler

Composer Unknown

*f Andante*

1. Hail the glo-rious Gold-en Cit-y, Pic-tured by the seers of old!
2. We are build-ers of that cit-y; All our joys and all our groans
3. And the work that we have build-ed, Oft with bleed-ing hands and tears,

# Hail the Glorious Golden City
## Continued

Ev - er - last - ing light shines o'er it, Wondrous tales of it are told:
Help to rear its shin-ing ram-parts; All our lives are build-ing stones:
And in er - ror and in an-guish, Will not per-ish with our years:

On - ly right- eous men and wo - men Dwell with - in its gleam-ing wall;
Wheth-er hum - ble or ex - alt - ed, All are called to task di - vine;
It will last and shine trans-fig - ured In the fin - al reign of Right;

Wrong is ban-ished from its bor - ders, Jus-tice reigns supreme o'er all,
All must aid a - like to car - ry For-ward one sub-lime de - sign,
It will merge in - to the splen-dors Of the Cit - y of the Light,

Wrong is ban-ished from its bor-ders, Jus-tice reigns su-preme o'er all.
All must aid a - like to car - ry For-ward one sub-lime de-sign.
It will merge in - to the splen-dors Of the Cit - y of the Light.

# Social Progress and Dedication

**228** Though Our Hearts Dwell Lovingly

Sadye Sternberg

*f Allegro Moderato*

Arr. from Jacques Blumenthal

1. Though our hearts dwell lov - ing - ly On God's wondrous care of old,
2. We are strong and we may hope To push on - ward with good cheer;
3. Rear a tem - ple, found - ed deep, Pil - lared strong with help-ful deeds,

And our glo - rious his - to - ry, Carved by Is - rael's fa - thers bold,
Shall we but in mem-ories grope When new du - ties claim our ear?
Broad - er views its win-dows sweep, Open - ed wide to pres - ent needs.

Let not ours the er - ror be With our past to be con - tent,
God's all-know - ing, pa - tient eye Sees the goal for us to win,
No - bler hymns we can - not raise To our pa - tri - archs re-vered,

Though the past held vic - to - ry Lo, the fu - ture is not spent.
E - ons swift are roll-ing by, Heav-en's call is heard with-in.
Than to build such shrines these days, Grand-er than of old ap-peared.

258

# Social Progress
## Not Alone for Mighty Empire

Wm. P. Merrill

W. A. Mozart

*Allegro moderato*

1. Not  a - lone for might - y  em - pire, Stretching far o'er land and  sea,
2. Not  for bat - tle-ship and for-tress, Not  for conquests of  the  sword,
3. For  the ar-mies of  the  faith-ful, Lives that passed and left  no  name;
4. God  of jus-tice, save the  peo-ple From the war of race and  creed,

Not  a - lone for bount-eous harvests, Lift  we up  our hearts to Thee;
But  for con-quests of  the  spir-it, Give  we thanks to Thee, O Lord;
For  the glo - ry that  il - lu-mines Pa - triot souls of death-less fame;
From  the strife of class and  fac-tion— Make our na - tion free in-deed;

Stand - ing in the  liv - ing pres-ent, Mem - o - ry and hope be - tween,
For  the her - it - age  of  freedom, For  the al - tar, home and  school,
For  the peo-ple's proph - et - lead-ers, Loy - al  to Thy liv - ing  word —
Keep  her faith in sim - ple manhood, Strong as when her life  be - gan,

Lord,  we would with deep thanksgiv - ing Praise Thee more for things un-seen.
For  the o - pen door  to manhood In  a  land the peo - ple rule.
For  all he - roes of  the  spir - it, Give  we thanks to Thee, O Lord.
Till  it find its full  fru - i - tion In  the Broth-er-hood of Man!

# Social Progress

## Onward Brothers, March Still Onward

Havelock Ellis

Ludwig van Beethoven
Theme from Ninth Symphony

*f Allegro moderato con spirito*

1. On - ward broth - ers, march still on - ward, Side by side and
2. Old - en sag - es saw it dim - ly, And their joy to
3. Still brave deeds and kind are need - ed, No - ble thoughts and

*f*

hand in hand; We are bound for man's true king - dom,
mad - ness wrought; Liv - ing men have gazed up - on it,
feel - ing fair; We, too, must be strong and suf - fer,

We are an in - creas - ing band. Tho' the way seems
Stand - ing on the hills of thought. All the past has
We, too, have to do and dare. On - ward, broth - ers,

oft - en doubt - ful, Hard the toil which we en - dure,
done and suf - fered, All the dar - ing and the strife,
march still on - ward, March still on - ward, hand in hand,

Tho' at times our cour-age fal - ter, Yet the prom-ised land is sure.
All has helped to mould the fu - ture, Make man mas - ter of his life.
'Till we see at last God's kingdom, 'Till we reach the Prom-ised Land.

# Social Progress

## Believe Not Those

Anne Bronte

Samuel Alman
Based on a traditional melody

*mf Largo* (M. M. ♩ = 52)

1. Be - lieve not those who say, The up - ward path is smooth,
2. It is the on - ly road, Un - to the realms of joy;
3. To la - bor and to love, To par - don and en - dure,
4. Be this thy con - stant aim, Thy hope, thy chief de - light;
5. If but thy God ap - prove, And if, with - in thy breast,

Be - lieve not those who say, The up - ward path is smooth,
It is the on - ly road, Un - to the realms of joy;
To la - bor and to love, To par - don and en - dure,
Be this thy con'-stant aim, Thy hope, thy chief de - light;
If but thy God ap - prove, And if, with - in thy breast,

*Un poco piu mosso*

*rall.*

Lest thou shouldst stumble in the way, And faint — be - fore the truth.
But he who seeks that blest a - bode, Must all — his powers employ.
To lift thy heart to God a - bove, And keep — thy conscience pure.
What matter who should whis-per blame, Or who — should scorn or slight.
Thou feel the com - fort of His love, The ear — nest of His rest.

*rall.*

262

# Social Progress

## Let There be Light

William Merrell Vories

Jacob Singer

*f* *Maestoso*

1. Let there be light, Lord God of Hosts! Let there be wis-dom on the earth!
3. Give us the peace of vi - sion clear To see our broth-ers, good our own,

Let broad hu-ma - ni - ty have birth! Let there be deeds, in-stead of boast!
To joy and suff-er not a - lone: The love that cast-eth out all fear!

2. With - in our passion'd hearts in - still The calm that end - eth strain and strife;
4. Let woe and waste of war-fare cease, That use - ful la - bor yet may build

Make us Thy min - is - ters of life; Purge us from lusts that curse and kill!
Its homes with love and laugh- ter fill'd! God, give Thy way-ward child-ren peace!

# Social Progress
## God! Send us Men

F. J. Gillman alt.

Boris Levenson

*mf Allegro energico*

*mf*

1. God! Send us men whose aim shall be,
2. God! Send us men a - lert and quick
3. God! Send us men of stead - fast will,
4. God! Send us men with hearts a - blaze,

Less to de - fend some an - cient creed, Than to live out the
Thy loft - y pre - cepts to trans - late, Un - til the laws of
Pa - tient, cour - a - geous, strong and true; With vi - sion clear and
All truth to love, all wrong to hate; These are the pa - triots

*poco rit.*

laws of Right, In ev - 'ry thought and word and deed.
Right be - come The laws and hab - it of the state.
mind e - quipped, Thy will to learn, Thy work to do.
na - tions need, These are the bul - warks of the state.

*poco rit.*

# Social Progress

## The God that to the Fathers

Minot J. Savage

Lewis M. Isaacs

*mf  Andante con moto*

1. The God that to the fa - thers Re-vealed His ho - ly will
2. 'Twas but far off, in vi - sion, The fa-thers' eyes could see
3. We trust in God's free spir - it, The ev - er broad'ning ray

Has not the world for - sak - en; He's with the chil-dren still.
The glo - ry of the king - dom, The bet - ter time to be;
Of truth, that shines to guide us A - long our for - ward way,

Then en - vy not the twi - light That glimmered on their way;
To - day, we see ful - fill - ing The dream they dreamt of yore,
Let us to - day be faith - ful, As were the pi - o - neers,

Look up and see the dawn - ing That broad-ens in - to day.
While near - er draws and near - er, The Gold - en Age in store.
Till lo, their work complet - ed, The Gold - en Age ap - pears.

# Social Progress

## 'Tis not the Large, the Huge, the Vast

Abraham Cronbach

James G. Heller

*ff Maestoso*

1. 'Tis not the large, the huge, the vast Im-
2. Yea, pro - gress is the weak made strong; The
3. Sweet pa - tience with all err - ing ones And

men - si - ties and show of power Where-in doth gra - cious
sick made whole, the joy - less glad. Fair pro - gress reigns when
tol - er - ance and sym - pa - thy; What-e'er en - lar - ges

pro - gress dower The pres - ent bet - ter than the past.
groan - ings sad Give way to hope's ex - ult - ant song.
lib - er - ty, And love that all op - press - ion shuns:

'Tis not the Large, the Huge, the Vast
Continued

In growth of things no pro-gress lies; Nay,
When, peace pre-vail-ing o-ver strife, All
More beau-teous lives and fair-er souls, Be -

pro-gress is the growth of men Who pass from out their
na-tions si-lence, hate o'er-come, The rum-blings cruel of
hold 'tis these true pro-gress are! 'Tis these a-lone shall

nar-row ken To vis-ions bound-less as the skies.
mar-tial drum And cher-ish each the oth-er's life.
lift the bar That keeps us from the shin-ing goals.

# Social Progress

## Hymn for the Golden Age

David Levy

J. Beimel

*f Moderato*

1. Now up-on the earth de-scending, Peace is like a prayer,
2. Now the clouds of war re-treat-ing, Van-ish with the years,
3. Hail the Gold-en Age ad-vanc-ing, With its vi-sion clear,
4. God, to Thee our prais-es sing-ing, We Thine aid im-plore,

Truth and peace their voi-ces blend-ing, Ech-o far and near.
Swords to plow-shares men are beat-ing, Hope of Is-rael's seers.
Faith and hope each soul en-tranc-ing Thru' the cer-tain year.
Speed the hope the years are bring-ing, Knowledge more and more.

Free-dom from its chain is break-ing, Jus-tice to new life is wak-ing,
Men in broth-er-hood are meet-ing, Faith and love each oth-er greet-ing,
Conscience its straight path con-tend-ing, Free-dom long its course de-fend-ing,
Soon may all Thy reign pro-fes-sing, Love and truth their hearts pos-sess-ing,

All the world its sin for-sak-ing, God's new day is here.
Wrong and hat-red e'er de-feat-ing, Big-ot-ry and fears.
'Round the earth the mes-sage send-ing, "Lo, the day draws near."
And Thy ho-ly name con-fess-ing, Thee a-lone a-dore.

# Social Progress
## These Things Shall be

**237**

J. Addington Symonds

Boris Levenson

*f Moderato*

1. These things shall be! A loftier race Than e'er the world hath known shall rise, With flame of freedom in their souls And light of knowledge in their eyes.

2. They shall be gentle, brave, and strong, To spill no drop of blood, but dare All that may plant man's lordship firm On earth and fire and sea and air.

3. Nation with nation, land with land, Unarmed shall live as comrades free; In every heart and brain shall throb The pulse of one fraternity.

4. New arts shall bloom, of loftier mould, And mightier music thrill the skies; And every life shall be a song, When all the earth is paradise.

# Social Progress

## The Voice of God is Calling

John Haynes Holmes

Boris Levenson

*f Moderato*

1. The voice of God is call-ing Its sum-mons un-to men;
3. I hear my peo-ple cry-ing In cot and mine and slum;
5. We heed, O Lord, Thy sum-mons; And an-swer: "Here are we,"

*f*

As once He spake in Zi-on, So now He speaks a-gain.
No field or mart is si-lent, No cit-y street is dumb.
Send us up-on Thine er-rand, Let us Thy serv-ants be.

# The Voice of God is Calling
## Continued

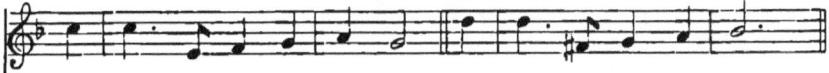

2. Whom shall I send to suc - cor. My peo - ple in their need?

4. I see my peo - ple fall - ing, In dark - ness and de - spair;

6. Our strength is dust and ash - es, Our years a pass - ing hour,

Whom shall I send to loos - en The bonds of shame and greed?

Whom shall I send to shat - ter The fet - ters which they bear?

But Thou canst use our weak - ness To mag - ni - fy Thy power.

271

# Social Progress

## Think Gently of the Erring One

Julia Fletcher Carney

Ellacombe

*f Maestoso*

1. Think gent - ly of the err - ing one And let us not for - get,
2. Speak gent - ly to the err - ing one, Thou yet may'st lead him back,

How - ev - er dark - ly stained by sin, He is our broth - er yet.

With ho - ly words and tones of love, From mis-ery's thorn - y track.

# Think Gently of the Erring Ones
## Continued

Heir of the same in - her - it -ance, Child of the self-same God;

For - get not, Thou hast of - ten sinned, And sin - ful yet must be:

He has but stumbled in the path We have in weak-ness trod.

Deal gent - ly with the err - ing one As God has dealt with thee.

# Blessing the Child

## This Child We Dedicate

From the German
Trans. by Sam Gilman

Jacob Singer

*mf* Andante

1. This child we ded - i - cate to Thee, O God of grace and pu - ri - ty. Shield it from sin and threaten-ing wrong, And let Thy love its life pro - long.

2. O may Thy spir - it gent - ly draw Its will - ing soul to keep Thy law, May vir - tue, pi - e - ty and truth Dawn e - ven with its dawn - ing youth.

# Children's Hymns

## Morning Prayer

Isabella R. Hess

Pinchos Jassinowsky

*mf* *Allegretto*

1. Fa - ther, as the day I greet, With a prayer the day I meet!
2. Give me grace the path to see What this day my way should be!

*mf*

Let me feel that Thou art near, That my soul may know no fear!
Ea - ger be my step or slow, Help me in that way to go!

# Children's Hymns
## We Thank Thee

Author Unknown

James H. Rogers

*mf Andante*

1. For moth-er-love and fa-ther-care, For bro-thers strong and
2. For this new morn-ing with its light, For rest and shel-ter
3. For flowers that bloom a-bout our feet, For ten-der grass, so
4. For blue of stream and blue of sky, For pleas-ant shade of

sis-ters fair, For love at home and here each day, For
of the night, For health and food, for love and friends, For
fresh, so sweet, For song of bird and hum of bee, For
branch-es high, For fra-grant air and cool-ing breeze, For

*slower*

guid-ance lest we go a-stray, Fa-ther in Heav'n, we thank Thee.
ev-'ry-thing Thy goodness sends, Fa-ther in Heav'n, we thank Thee.
all things fair we hear or see, Fa-ther in Heav'n, we thank Thee.
beau-ty of the bloom-ing trees, Fa-ther in Heav'n, we thank Thee.

*slower*

# Children's Hymns

## Evening Prayer

Jessie E. Sampter

A. W. Binder

*p Lento espressivo*

1. Great Lord of Life who lives in me, And lives in all I know,
2. I hope to wake this com-ing morn More strong and brave and bright,

With hap-py thoughts I go to sleep, And while I sleep I grow.
While Thou shalt stay both night and day With all I love to-night.

# Children's Hymns

## Child's Evening Prayer

244

Isidor Wise

Gershon Ephros

*p* Andante con moto

1. Through - out the night, O God a - bove Pro-
2. My life, with - in Thy lov - ing hands. With
3. Bless them that watch my wel - fare here, That

tect me in my sleep; — Let an - gels of Thy
trust - ful - ness I place; — O guard it with Thy
care for me on earth; — Bless fa - ther, broth - ers,

ho - ly love A - round me vig - il keep. —
an - gel hands In Thine un - bound - ed grace. —
sis - ters, dear, Bless her that gave me birth. —

# Children's Hymns

## The Stars Watch You

Max Grauman

1. When the stars at set of sun   Watch   you   from on high
2. All   you do   and   all   you say,   He   can   see and hear;
3. All   your joys and griefs He knows,   Counts   each   fall - ing tear;
4. What we   do   as   in   His sight,   We   can   do   with ease;

When   the morn - ing   is   be - gun,   Think   the   Lord   is   nigh.
When   you work   and   when   you play,   Think   the   Lord   is   near.
When   to Him   you   tell   your woes,   Think   the   Lord will   hear.
Ev - 'ry task   be - comes   more light,   When   we   think He   sees.

279

# Children's Hymns

## The Wise May Bring Their Learning

J. H. Rogers

*f* *Moderato*

1. The wise may bring their learn - ing, The rich may bring their wealth,
2. We'll bring Him hearts that love Him, We'll bring Him thank - ful praise,
3. We'll bring the lit - tle du - ties, We have to do each day,

*f*

And some may bring their great - ness, And some bring strength and health:
And young souls meek - ly striv - ing To walk in ho - ly ways.
We'll try our best to please Him At home, at school, at play.

We too would bring our treas-ures, To of - fer to our King;
And these shall be the treas-ures, We of - fer to our King,
And bet - ter are these treas-ures, To of - fer to our King,

We have no wealth or learn - ing, What shall the chil - dren bring?
And these are gifts that ev - er The poor - est child may bring.
Than rich - est gifts with - out them, Yet these a child may bring.

# 247
## Who Taught the Bird

A. W. Binder

1. Who taught the bird    to build her nest   Of   wool and hay and    moss?
2. Who taught the bus - y bee   to   fly    A - mong the sweet-est   flowers,
3. Who taught the lit - tle ant   the way    Its   nar-row hole   to   bore,
4. 'Twas God who taught them all   the way,   And   gave their lit - tle   skill;

Who taught her how    to weave it best,   And   lay the twigs   a - cross?
And   lay her store   of hon - ey   by    To   last in win - ter's hours?
And   thru the pleas - ant sum-mer day    To   ga - ther up   its   store?
He   teach-es chil - dren when they pray   To   do His ho - ly   will.

# Children's Hymns

## Lo! the Earth Rejoices

A. W. Binder

*f Animato*

1. Lo! the earth re - joic - es At the dawn of day,
2. See the red sun flam - ing In the east - ern skies,
3. Cool the morn - ing breez - es, Keen and fresh they blow;
4. Hark! the birds are sing - ing; What a mer - ry throng:
5. Yes, the earth re - joic - es At the dawn of day;

Chil - dren, lift your voic - es, Sing to God, and pray.
To the world pro - claim - ing It is time to rise.
Bring - ing, as God pleas - es, Warmth, or rain, or snow.
Woods and fields are ring - ing With the joy - ful song.
We will raise our voic - es, Sing to God, and pray.

# Children's Hymns
## Thankful Hearts

J. H. Rogers

*mf Leggiere*

1. Lit - tle chil - dren, Lord, are we, Child - ish words our
2. Thou hast given us life and light, Hap - py days and
3. Give us then, O Lord, we pray, Yet an - oth - er
4. All those oth - er gifts of Thine Come un - asked through
5. But a thank - ful heart must we Ask in prayer, O

*mf*

prayers must be; Yet we know that Thou wilt hear; Thou, O God, art
rest at night; Sun-shine, spring, and flow-ers fair, Lov - ing friends, whose
gift to-day; Give us thank-ful hearts that still Seek to do Thy
love di - vine; All the joy that child-hood knows, All the peace thru
Lord, of Thee; This, of all Thy gifts the best, Comes to hal - low

*softly*

al - ways near, Hold - ing all Thy chil - dren dear.
ten - der care, Guides and guards us ev - 'ry - where.
ho - ly will, Thy com - mand - ments to ful - fill.
life that flows, Ere we ask, Thy hand be - stows.
all the rest, Ev - er bless - ing, ev - er blest!

*softly*

## 250
### "Giver of All"

John Haynes Holmes

N. Lindsay Norden

**𝑝 Andante**

1. O Fath - er, Thou who giv - est all The
2. We thank Thee for the gift of home, For
3. For faith to con - quer doubt and fear, For

boun - ty of Thy per - fect love, We thank thee that up -
moth - er's love and fath - er's care; For friends and teach - ers, —
love to an - swer ev - 'ry call, For strength to do, and

on us fall Such ten - der bless - ings from a - bove.
all who come Our joys and hopes and fears to share.
will to dare, We thank thee, O Thou Lord of all.

# Children's Hymns

## A Little Kingdom I Possess

Louisa M. Alcott                                          J. H. Rogers

*mf Leggiere*

1. A lit - tle king - dom I poss - ess, Where thoughts and feel-ings dwell,
2. How can I learn to rule my - self, To be the child I should,
3. Dear Fa - ther, help me with the love That cast - eth out my fear!
4. I do not ask for an - y crown But that which all may win;

*mf*

And ver - y hard I find the task Of gov - ern - ing it well.
—— Hon - est and brave, nor ev - er tire Of try - ing to be good?
Teach me to lean on Thee and feel That Thou art ver - y near.
Nor try to con - quer an - y world Ex - cept the one with - in.

# A Little Kingdom I Possess
## Continued

For    pas - sion tempts and trou - bles me,   A    way - ward will mis - leads,
How    can   I   keep   a   sun - ny soul   To   shine a - long life's way?
That    no   temp - ta - tion   is   un - seen,   No   child - ish grief too small,
Be    Thou my guide un - til   I   find,   Led   by   a   ten - der hand,

And    self - ish - ness its   sha - dow casts On   all   my   will and deeds.
How    can   I   tune my   lit - tle heart, To   sweet - ly   sing all   day?
Since   Thou, with pa - tience in - fi - nite, Dost soothe and com - fort   all.
Thy    hap - py king - dom in   my - self And   dare   to take com - mand.

# Religious School

## All Things Bright and Beautiful

Cecil Frances Alexander

Harry Rowe Shelley

*f* *Con moto*

1. — All things bright and beau - ti - ful, All crea-tures great and small,
2. The pur - ple-head - ed moun - tain, The riv - er run - ning by,
3. The tall trees in the green - wood, The mead-ows where we play,

— All things wise and won - der - ful, The Lord God made them all.
The sun - sets and the morn - ing, That bright-en up the sky.
The rush - es by the wa - ter, We gath - er ev - 'ry day.

## All Things Bright and Beautiful
### Continued

Each lit - tle flow'r that o - pens, Each lit - tle bird that sings,
The cold wind in the win - ter, The pleas-ant sum - mer sun,
He gave us eyes to see them, And lips that we might tell,

He made their glow - ing col - ors, He made their ti - ny wings.
The ripe fruits in the gar - den, He made them ev - 'ry one.
How great is God Al - might - y, Who hath done all things well.

**253**

## Happy Who in Early Youth

The Hamburg Temple Hymnal
Tr. by James K. Gutheim

Arr. from Louis M. Gottschalk

*mf Andante con moto*

1. Hap - py who in ear - ly youth, While yet
2. Hap - py who in ten - der years Leans on
3. Guide, O guide this hope - ful band, Fa - ther,
4. Thine, O God, these souls are Thine, Un - de -

pure and in - no - cent, Stores his mind with
God for his sup - port; Who life's bark in
in Thy truth and light! May these chil - dren
filed they came to Thee; Guide them in Thy

heav'n - ly truth— Life's un - fad - ing or - na - ment.
vir - tue steers, That it reach sal - va - tion's port.
ev - er stand Firm in vir - tue and in right.
love di - vine— Heirs of im - mor - tal - i - ty.

# The Religious School

## We Build our School on Thee

Sebastian W. Mayer

James H. Rogers

*f Andante maestoso*

1. We build our school on Thee, O Lord, To
2. We work to-geth-er in Thy sight, We
3. Hold Thou each hand to keep it just, Touch

*f*

Thee we bring our com-mon need; The lov-ing heart, the
live to-geth-er in Thy love; Guide Thou our falt-'ring
Thou our lips and make them pure; If Thou art with us,

help-ful word, The ten-der thought, the kind-ly deed.
steps a-right, And lift our thought to heaven a-bove.
Lord, we must Be faith-ful friends and com-rades sure.

# The Religious School

## We Meet Again in Gladness

Anonymous

Simon Hecht

1. We meet a-gain in glad - ness, And thank-ful voic - es raise;
2. We thank Him for the knowl- edge To us im - part - ed here,
3. We thank Him for our coun - try The land our fa - thers trod;

To God, our heav'n -ly Fa - ther, We tune our grate-ful praise.

For pre - cept and ex - am - ple Laid to our hearts so near.

For lib - er - ty of con - science, And right to wor-ship God.

## We Meet Again in Gladness
### Continued

His own kind hand has kept —— us Through all the changing years,
For par - ents dear and lov - ing, Our joy and our de - light,
O Lord our heaven-ly Fa - ther Ac - cept the praise we bring,

His love it is that brings us A - gain to wor-ship here.
And for our faith-ful teach - ers, Who make our path-way bright.
And tune our hearts and voi - ces Thy glo-rious name to sing.

# Religious School

## "The Torch of Israel"

256

Adeline R. Rosewater

Joseph Achron
*Based on a Jewish Folk-Melody*

1. We hear the call of Is-rael's chil-dren 'Tis sound-ed down from age to age; Lift up the torch your fa-thers left you, It is your pre-cious her-it-age.

2. Hold high the torch your fa-thers left you, And keep it burn-ing bright and clear, 'Twill light the way that lies be-fore you, That you may trav-el with-out fear.

3. And when the light of the life is fail-ing, Pass on the torch to oth-ers near That they in turn may keep it burn-ing, The faith that they shall e'er hold dear.

## The Torch of Israel
### Continued

Your watch - word long as life is run; "The
Your prayer shall be from sun to sun: "The
Your clos - ing words ere life is done: "The

Lord our God, The Lord is One" Your watch - word
Lord our God, The Lord is One" Your prayer shall
Lord our God, The Lord is One" Your clos - ing

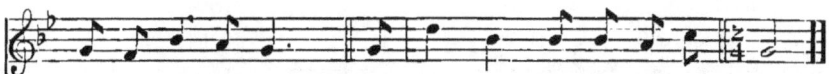

long as life is run; "The Lord our God, the Lord is One."
be from sun to sun: "The Lord our God, the Lord is One."
words ere life is done: "The Lord our God, the Lord is One."

# The Religious School

## Opening Song

Adeline R. Rosewater

James G. Heller

**257**

Dear Fa-ther, here Thy children come Thy pre-cepts all to learn;

To Is-ra-el and the To-rah blest To-day our thoughts we turn.

O give to us, we hum-bly pray An un-der-stand-ing mind,

## Opening Song
### Continued

That in the les - son of to - day Thy wis-dom we may find.

May we e'er fol - low in the path Our fa - thers trod be - fore,

That Is - rael's faith may nev - er die, But live for ev - er - more.

# Religious School
## Duties of Today

258

Nicholas Douty

A. W. Binder,
Based on a Sephardic melody

*mf  Andante con moto*

1. To - day    while the    sun    shines    Work    with a    will;
2. To - day    scat - ter    bright - ness;    Wher - ever you    go,

*mf*

To - day    all    your dut - ies    with    pa - tience ful - fill.
— Gladness comes with the giv - ing;    Waves grow    as they    flow.

To - day    love    the    good - ness    That's bet - ter    than    gold,
To - day    is    ours    on - ly;    Work, work    while you    may;

And the truth    seek whose val - ue    Can    nev - er    be    told.
There    will    be a to - mor - row, But guard well    to - day.

298

# Motherhood

## Rejoice and Offer Thanks to God

Harry H. Mayer                                         Jacob Singer

*Andante*

1. Re-joice, and of - fer thanks to God   For moth -ers whose de - vo - ted love
2. Her fond de - vo - tion to her child   Sur - pas - ses all that words can tell,

Through all   the chang-ing years has been   As   faith - ful   as   the stars   a-bove.
And   no   re-ward she asks but this   That we, her chil - dren, love her well.

Our   vir - tues are   our moth-er's pride,   Our wel - fare   is   her   hope and dream;
We   of - fer thanks and praise to God   That He   or-dained such moth-er - love

Her lov - ing hand still rests   in ours,   How- ev - er great our faults may seem.
To pour   its light   a-round   us here   And lead our hearts to   God   a-bove.

# Motherhood

## Hymn to Mothers

Harry H. Mayer

A. W. Binder

*f Allegretto spiritoso*

1. Re - joice, and of - fer thanks to God, For
3. Her fond de - vo - tion to her child Sur -

moth-ers whose de -vot - ed love Thro' all the chang-ing years has
pass - es all that words can tell, And no re-ward she asks but

been, As faith-ful as the stars a - bove. As faith - ful as the
this That we her chil-dren love her well. We of - fer thanks and

stars a - bove. Our vir - tues are our Moth - er's pride, Our
praise to God That He or - dained such Moth - er - love To

wel - fare is her hope and dream; Her lov - ing hand still rests in ours,
pour its light a-round us here And lead our hearts to God a - bove,

How - ev - er great our faults may seem, Our faults may seem.
And lead our hearts to God a - bove, To God a - bove.

# The Nation

261

## Uplift the Song of Praise

F. L. Hosmer

J. H. Rogers

1. Up - lift the song of praise To Him, our fa - thers' God!
2. Lift high the song of praise, O Na - tion grown in pow'r!
3. Up - lift the song of praise! His love and wis - dom own,
4. Lift high the song of praise, And bless His ho - ly name!

Who led them o'er the wa - t'ry ways To lands un - trod:
Hold fast through good and e - vil days Thy glo - rious dower:
Who lead - eth still in un - seen ways, By paths un - known.
Whose care a - bove the pass - ing days A - bides the same.

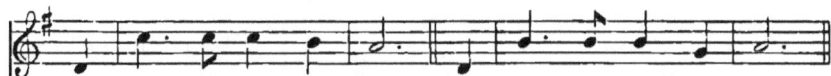

Seed    of    a race    to    be,    Up - on    His new - world shore,
The    age - long hope    ful - fil,    New - quick - ened    at    thy birth;
His    pur - po - ses    of    old    And prom - i - ses    en - dure,
Our    fa - thers' con - fi - dence    Thro' all    their pil - grim - age;

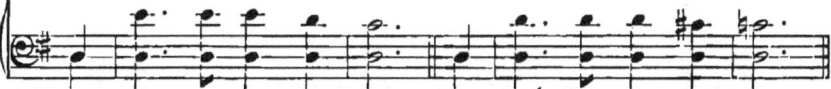

The    home    of Law    and    Lib - er - ty    For    ev - er - more.
Thy strength    thy God, whose right - eous will    Rules heav'n and    earth.
And through    the cir - cling years    un - fold,    For    ev - er    sure.
Our    dwell - ing - place    and    our    de - fence,    From age    to    age.

# The Nation

## O Beautiful for Spacious Skies

Katherine Lee Bates

Samuel Augustus Ward

*f Allegretto*

1. O beau - ti - ful for spa-cious skies, For am - ber waves of grain,
2. O beau - ti - ful for pil - grim feet, Whose stern, im-passioned stress,
3. O beau - ti - ful for he -roes proved In lib - er - a - ting strife,
4. O beau - ti - ful for pa - triot dream That sees be-yond the years,

For pur - ple moun-tain maj - es - ties A - bove the fruit-ed plain!
A thor -ough-fare for free - dom beat A - cross the wil - der - ness!
Who more than self their coun - try loved, And mer - cy more than life!
Thine al - a - bas - ter cit - ies gleam, Un-dimmed by hu - man tears!

## O Beautiful for Spacious Skies
### Continued

A - mer - i - ca! A - mer - i - ca! God shed his grace on thee,
A - mer - i - ca! A - mer - i - ca! God mend thine ev - 'ry flaw,
A - mer - i - ca! A - mer - i - ca! May God thy gold re - fine
A - mer - i - ca! A - mer - i - ca! God shed his grace on thee,

And crown thy good with broth - er-hood From sea to shin - ing sea.
Con - firm thy soul in self - con - trol, Thy lib - er - ty in law!
Till all suc-cess be no - ble-ness, And ev - 'ry gain di - vine!
And crown thy good with broth - er-hood From sea to shin - ing sea.

# The Nation

## God of Our Fathers

Daniel C. Roberts                                          George W. Warren

*Allegro maestoso*

*Trumpets, before each verse*

1. God of our fa - thers, Whose al - migh - ty
2. Thy love di - vine hath led us in the
3. From war's a - larms, from dead - ly pes - ti -
4. Re - fresh Thy peo - ple on their toil - some

hand          Leads forth in beau - ty all the star - ry band
past,         In this free land by Thee our lot is cast;
lence,        Be Thy strong arm our ev - er sure de - fense;
way,          Lead us from night to nev - er - end - ing day;

Of    shin - ing worlds in splen - dor through the skies,
Be    Thou our rul - er, guard - ian, guide and stay,
Thy   true re - lig - ion in our hearts in - crease,
Fill  all our lives with love and grace di - vine,

Our   grate - ful songs be - fore Thy throne a - rise.
Thy   word our law, Thy paths our cho - sen way.
Thy   boun - teous good - ness nour - ish us in peace.
And   glo - ry, laud and praise be ev - er Thine.

# The Nation

## America

Samuel F. Smith

Henry Carey (1743)

*ff Andante maestoso*

1. My coun - try, 'tis of thee, Sweet land of lib - er - ty,
2. My na - tive coun - try, thee, Land of the no - ble free,
3. Let mu - sic swell the breeze, And ring from all the trees
4. Our fa - thers' God to Thee, Au - thor of lib - er - ty,

Of thee I sing; Land where my fa - thers died, Land of the
Thy name I love; I love thy rocks and rills, Thy woods and
Sweet free-dom's song; Let mor - tal tongues a - wake; Let all that
To Thee we sing; Long may our land be bright With free-dom's

pil - grims' pride, From ev - 'ry moun - tain-side Let free - dom ring.
templ - ed hills; My heart with rap - ture thrills Like that a - bove.
breathe par-take; Let rocks their si - lence break, The sound pro - long.
ho - ly light; Pro- - tect us by Thy might, Great God, our King.

# The Nation

## The Star Spangled Banner

Francis Scott Key

1. O    say, can you    see    by the dawn's ear - ly    light, What so
2. On the shore dim - ly    seen    thro' the mists of    the    deep, Where the
3. And    where is that band    who so    vaunt - ing - ly    swore That the

proud - ly    we    hailed    at the    twi - light's last gleam - ing, Whose broad
foe's might - y    host    in dread    si - lence re - pos - es,    What    is
hav - oc    of    war    and the    bat - tle's con - fu - sion    A

stripes and bright    stars    thro' the    per - il - ous    fight,    O'er the
that which the    breeze    o'er the    tow - er - ing    steep,    As    it
home and    a    coun - try shall leave us    no    more?    Their

ram - parts we watch'd were so    gal - lant - ly streaming! And    the
fit - ful - ly    blows, half con - ceals, half dis - clos - es:    Now    it
blood has washed out    their    foul    foot steps' pol - lu - tion,    No

308

## The Star Spangled Banner
### Continued

rock - et's red glare, The bombs burst - ing in air, Gave
catch - es the gleam Of the morn - ing's first beam, In full
ref - uge could save, The hire - ling and slave, From the

proof thro' the night that our flag was still there!
glo - ry re - flect - ed, now shines on the stream.
ter - ror of flight, or the gloom of the grave.

**CHORUS**

O say, does the star - span - gled ban - ner still wave
'Tis the star - span - gled ban - ner! O long may it wave,
And the star - span - gled ban - ner in tri - umph doth wave,

O'er the land of the free, and the home of the brave?
O'er the land of the free, and the home of the brave.
O'er the land of the free, and the home of the brave.

# The Nation

265 B

### God the All-Merciful!

Henry F. Chorley
John Ellerton

Alexis T. Lwoff

1. God the All-mer-ci-ful! earth hath for-sak-en
2. God the All-right-eous One! man hath de-fied Thee;
3. God the All-wise! by the fire of Thy chasten-ing,
4. So shall Thy chil-dren in thank-ful de-vo-tion

Thy ways of bless-ed-ness, slight-ed Thy word;
Yet to e-ter-ni-ty stand-eth Thy word;
Earth shall to free-dom and truth be re-stored;
Laud Him who saved them from per-il ab-horred,

Bid not Thy wrath in its ter-rors a-wak-en;
False-hood and wrong shall not ta-ry be-side Thee:
Through the thick dark-ness Thy king-dom is hasten-ing:
Sing-ing in cho-rus from o-cean to o-cean,

Give to us peace in our time, O Lord.
Give to us peace in our time, O Lord.
Thou wilt give peace in Thy time, O Lord.
Peace to the na-tions and praise to the Lord.

310

# The Nation
## Hatikvo

N. H. Imber

*ff* *Andante maestoso*

1. Kol od ba - lay - vov p'nee - mo ne - fesh y' -
2. Kol od d' - mo - os may-ay-nay - nu yiz - lu k' -
3. Kol od may ha yar-dayn b'go - on m'lo g'
4. Kol od sho - mo a'lay d'ro-cha - yim sha - ar
5. Kol od d' - mo - os t'-ho - ros may - ayn

*ff*

hu - dee ho - mee - yo Ul - fa - a - say miz - roch
ge - shem n'do - vos r' - vo - vos mib' - nay
do - sov yi - zo - lu u-l' - yom Ki - ne - res
yu - kas sh'ee - yoh u' - vayn chor - vos y' -
bas a - mee noz' - los v' - liv - kos l'tzee-yon b'rosh

ko - dee - mo a - yin l' - tsee - yon tso - fee - yo.
a - may - nu od ho - l'-cheem al kiv' - ray o - vos.
ru-sho-la - yim od bas Tsee - yon bo - chee - yoh.
ash - mo - ros od to - kum ba - cha - tsee ha-lay - los.

311

Od  lo  ov - do  sik - vo - say - nu  Ha - tik - vo

ha - no - sho - no  lo - shuv  l' - e - retz  a - vo -

say - nu  lo - eer  bo  Do - vid  cho - no.  no.

Marcato

# SPECIAL HYMNS

# Evening Service for the Sabbath

## Ayn Kay-Lo-Hay-Nu

Louis Lewandowski

Ayn  kay - lo - hay - nu,  Ayn  ka - do - nay - nu,

Ayn  k' - mal - kay - nu,  Ayn  k' mo - shee - ay - nu,

# Ayn Kay-Lo-Hay-Nu

## Continued

Mee - chay - lo - hay - nu  Mee —— cha - do - nay - nu,

Mee  ch' - mal - kay - nu,  Mee  ch' - mo - shee - ay - nu.

No - de lay - lo - hay - nu,    No - de la - do - nay - nu,

No - de l'mal - kay - nu,    No - de l' - mo - shee - ay - nu.

Bo - ruch E - lo - hay - nu,    Bo - ruch A - do - nay - nu,

## Ayn Kay-Lo-Hay-Nu
### Continued

Bo - ruch Mal - kay - nu, Bo - ruch Mo - shee - ay - nu.

At - to hu E - lo - hay - nu, At - to hu A - do - nay - nu,

At - to hu Mal - kay - nu, At - to hu Mo - shee - ay - nu.

# Evening Service for the Sabbath

## Adon Olom

Eliezer Gerovitch

1. A - don  o - lom  a' - sher  mo - lach,  b' - te - rem  kol  y' - tseer  niv - ro,  l' - ays  na - a' - so  v' - chef - tso  kol,  a - zai  Me - lech  sh' - mo  nik - ro.

2. V' - a - cha - ray  kich - los  ha - kol,  l' - va - do  yim - loch  no - ro;  v' - hu  ho - yo  v' - hu  ho - veh,  v' - hu  yi - h' - yeh  b' - sif - o - ro.

3. V' - hu  e - chod  v' - ayn  shay - nee,  l' - ham - shil  lo  l' - hach - bee - ro;  b' - lee  ray - shees,  b' - lee  sach - lees,  v' - lo  ho - oz  v' - ha - mis - ro.

4. V' - hu  Ay - lee  v' - chai  go - a' - lee,  v' - tsur  chev - lee  b' - ays  tso - ro;  v' - hu  ni - see  u - mo - nos  lee,  m' - nos  ko - see  b' - yom  ek - ro.

5. B' - yo - do  af - keed  ru - chee,  b' - ays  ee - shan  v' - o - ee - ro;  v' - im  ru - chee  g' - vee - yo - see,  A - do - noy  lee  v' - lo  ee - ro.

# Evening Service for the Sabbath

## Yigdal

Leoni. Arr. by A. W. Binder

*Andante*  SOLO  *mf*

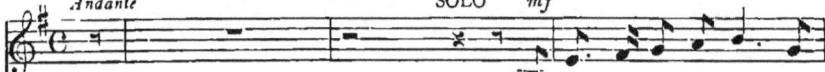

1. Yig - dal  E - lo-heem chai  v' -
2. Ayn  lo  d'-mus ha - guf  v' -
3. Hi - no  A-don  o - lom  l' -
4. Lo kom  b'-yis - ro - ayl,  k' -
5. Lo  ya - cha-leef ho - ayl  v' -
6. Go-mayl  l'-eesh che - sed  k -
7. Cha-yay  o - lom no - ta  b' -

yish  ta - bach,  nim - tso  v' - ayn  ays  el  m'-tsee - u - so
ay - no  guf,  lo  na - a - roch ay-lov  k'  du - sho - so,
chol  no - tsor,  yo - reh  g' - du-lo - so  u - mal - chu - so;
mo - she  od  no - vee  u - ma - beet  es  t' mu - no - so;
lo yomeer do-so,  l' - o - lo - meem  l'-zu - lo - so;
mif - o - lo,  no - sayn  l' - ro-sho ra  k'rish - o - so;
so - chay-nu;  bo - ruch  a - day  ad  shaym  t' - hi - lo - so.

*f* CHOIR and CONGREGATION

E - chod  v' - ayn  yo - cheed  k - yi - chu - do  ne -
Kad - mon  l' - chol  do - vor  a - sher  niv - ro,  ri -
She - fa  n' - vu - o - so  n' - so - no  el
To - ras  e - mes  no - san  l' - a - mo Ayl,  al
Tso - feh  v' - yo - day - a  s' - so - ray - nu,  ma -
Yish - lach  l' - kayts  yo - meen,  p' - dus  o - lom  kol -
Cha - yay  o - lom  no - ta,  b' - so - chay - nu;  bo -

329

Yigdal
Continued

| | | | | | | |
|---|---|---|---|---|---|---|
| lom | v' - gam | ayn | sof ——— | l' - | ach - | du - so. |
| shon | v' - ayn | ray - shees ——— | | l' - | ray - | shee - so. |
| an - | shay | s' | gu - lo - so | v' - | sif - | ar - to. |
| yad | n' - vee | - | o ——— | ne - | man | bay - so; |
| beet | l' - sof | do - vor ——— | | b' - | kad - | mo - so; |
| chai | v'-yaysh | ya - keer | ad, ——— | shaym | t'hi - | lo - so. |

# Morning Service for the Sabbath

Ayn Kay-lo-hay-nu

Julius Freudenthal

1. Ayn kay - lo - hay - nu, Ayn ka - do - nay - nu,
3. No - de lay - lo - hay - nu, No - de la - do - nay - nu,

Ayn k'- mal - kay - nu, Ayn k'mo-shee - ay - nu; 2. Mee chay - lo -
No - de l'- mal - kay - nu, No - de l'mo-shee-ay - nu; 4. Bo-ruch E - lo -

hay - nu, Mee cha - do - nay - nu, Mee ch'- mal - kay - nu,
hay - nu, Bo - ruch A - do - nay - nu, Bo - ruch Mal - kay - nu,

345

Mee ch'mo - shee - ay - nu. 5. At - to hu E - lo -

Bo - ruch Mo - shee - ay - nu.

hay - nu, At - to hu A - do - nay - nu, At -

to hu Mal - kay - nu, at - to hu Mo - shee - ay - nu.

# UNION HYMNAL

## PART II

## MUSICAL SERVICES

The Musical Services Are Published in a Separate Volume

# SERVICES FOR THE RELIGIOUS SCHOOL

## I

**Hymn**

**Responsive Reading (from Psalms xix, viii):**

The heavens declare the glory of God.  The skies show forth His wondrous works.
Day uttereth its speech unto day, and night unto night revealeth knowledge;
There is no speech, there are no words, neither is their voice heard,
Yet their line extends over all the earth and their words to the end of the world.
O Lord, our God, how glorious is Thy name in all the earth.
Thy majesty is rehearsed above the heavens.
When I behold Thy heavens, the work of Thy hands,
The moon and the stars which Thou hast established,
What is man that Thou art mindful of him,
And the son of man that Thou thinkest of him?
Yet Thou hast crowned him with glory and honor
And given him dominion over the works of Thy hands.
Thou hast put all things under his feet
Sheep and oxen, all of them, and also the beasts of the field,
The fowl of the air, the fish of the sea,
Whatever passeth through the paths of the sea.

**Together:**

O Lord our God, how glorious is Thy name in all the earth.

**Reader:**

Praise ye the Lord, to whom all praise is due.
Bor'-chu es A-do-noy ha-m'-voroch.

**Congregation:**

Praised be the Lord, to whom all praise is due forever and ever.

All Singing:

S. Sulzer

Bo - ruch A - do - noy ha - m' vo - roch l'o - lom vo - ed.

**Reader:**

We praise Thee, O Lord our God, Ruler of the world. In Thy love Thou causest light to shine over the earth and its inhabitants. Each morning brings Thy great command: Let there be light.

All things on earth are Thine and are created by Thy will. Without number are Thy works. In wisdom hast Thou made them all. Light and darkness, joy and sorrow come from Thee, who bringest harmony into nature and peace to the heart of man.

*(Congregation standing)*

**All Reading:**

Hear, O Israel: The Lord our God, the Lord is One.
Sh'ma Yis-ro-ayl A-do-noy E-lo-hay-nu, A-do-noy e-chod.

**All Singing:**

Sh'ma Yis - ro - ayl A - do - noy E - lo - hay - nu A - do - noy e - chod.

**Reader:**

Praised be His name whose glorious kingdom is forever and ever.
Bo-ruch shaym k'-vod mal-chu-so l'-o-lom vo-ed.

433

**All Singing:**

Bo - ruch shaym k' - vod mal - chu - so l' - o - lom vo - ed.

*(Congregation seated)*

**Responsive Reading:**

Thou shalt love the Lord thy God, with all thy heart, with all thy soul
and with all thy might;

And these words which I command thee this day shall be upon thy heart.

Eternal truth it is that Thou art God and there is none else;

Wonders without number hast Thou wrought for us and hast pro-
tected us to this day.

O God, who art our refuge and our help, we glorify Thy name now, as did
our fathers in ancient days.

Who is like Thee among the mighty, O God? Who is like Thee, glorious
in holiness, extolled in praises, working wonders?

**All Singing:**

S. Sulzer

Mee cho - mo - cho bo - ay - leem A - do - noy;

mee ko - mo - cho ne - dor ba - ko - desh,

434

no - ro s'hil - los o - say fe - lay.

**Reader:**

God reigneth for ever and ever.

**All Singing:**

A - do - noy yim - loch l'o - lom vo - ed.

**Prayer:**

Divine Creator of heaven and earth, Thy hand has made all nature beautiful. On every side we see the splendor of Thy work. The earth's green cloak of grass, the sturdy trees, the warm gold of the sunlight, and the calm beauty of moon and stars, all speak to our listening hearts and teach us the story of beauty and growth.

For all this wondrous beauty, we thank Thee. For all that brings us joy, we raise our voice in songs of praise. Teach us, O God, to obey Thy law. May we do our best with every task; may every word we speak be true, and every thought within our heart be clean and good. Because Thy world, O God, is beautiful, let our lives be noble too. Amen.

**Silent Devotion**

**All Singing:**

Alois Kaiser

May the words of my mouth and the med - i - ta - tions

435

of my heart be ac-cept-a-ble in Thy sight, O Lord, my Strength and my Re-deem-er. A-men.

**Address or Scriptural Reading**

**Hymn**

**Benediction:**

Creator of heaven and earth, bless our life with the beauty of holiness. Amen.

# II

**Hymn**

**Responsive Reading:**

### PSALM CXXI

I will lift up mine eyes unto the hills, whence shall my help come?
   My help cometh from God who made heaven and earth.
Thy footsteps will not stumble for He that guardeth thee will not slumber.
   He that guardeth Israel will not slumber nor sleep.
The Lord is thy Protector.
   The Lord is thy shade at thy right hand.
The sun shall not smite thee by day nor the moon by night.
   The Lord shall keep thee from all harm,
He shall keep thy soul.
   The Lord shall guard thy going out and thy coming in, now and forever.

# JOSHUA I

As I was with Moses so I will be with thee
  I will not fail thee nor forsake thee;
Only be strong and very courageous
  To observe the law which Moses My servant commanded thee.
Turn not from it to the right hand or to the left,
  That thou mayest have good success wherever thou goest.
This book of the law shall not depart out of thy mouth,
  But thou shalt meditate therein day and night,
For then thou shalt make thy way prosperous
  And then thou shalt have good success.
Have I not commanded thee?  Be strong and of good courage;
  Be not affrighted, neither be thou dismayed;

**Together:**

For the Lord thy God is with thee wherever thou goest.

**Reader:**

Praise ye the Lord, to whom all praise is due.
Bor'-chu es A-do-noy ha-m'voroch.

**Congregation:**

Praised be the Lord, to whom all praise is due forever and ever.

**All Singing:**

S. Sulzer

Bo - ruch A - do - noy    ha - m' vo - roch    l'o - lom    vo - ed.

**Reader:**

With great love hast Thou loved us, O our God.  Great has been Thy kindness to our fathers.  They believed and trusted Thee; therefore didst Thou teach them the laws of life, and show them the way of wisdom.  We, too, would learn to obey Thy will and to walk in Thy paths.  O, make us gladly obedient to Thy commandments, and fill our hearts with love and reverence for Thee.  We put our trust in Thee and joyfully raise our voices to proclaim Thy unity:

**All Reading:**

Hear, O Israel: The Lord our God, the Lord is One.
Sh'ma Yis-ro-ayl A-do-noy E-lo-hay-nu, A-do-noy e-chod.

**All Singing:**

Traditional

Sh'ma Yis-ro-ayl A-do-noy E-lo-hay - nu A-do-noy e-chod.

**Reader:**

Praised be His name whose glorious kingdom is forever and ever.
Bo-ruch shaym k'vod mal-chu-so l'-o-lom vo-ed.

**All Singing:**

Traditional

Bo - ruch shaym k'- vod mal - chu - so l'- o-lom vo - ed.

*(Congregation seated)*

**All Reading:**

Thou shalt love the Lord thy God, with all thy heart, and with all thy soul, and with all thy might. And these words, which I command thee this day, shall be upon thy heart. Thou shalt teach them diligently unto thy

children, and shalt speak of them when thou sittest in thy house, when thou walkest by the way, when thou liest down, and when thou risest up. And thou shalt bind them for a sign upon thy hand, and they shall be for frontlets between thine eyes. And thou shalt write them upon the doorposts of thy house, and upon thy gates:

To the end that ye may remember and do all My commandments, and be holy unto your God.

**Reader:**

Praised be Thou, O Lord our God, God of our fathers, Abraham, Isaac and Jacob. Thou art our Helper and Protector. As the heavens declare Thy glory, so would we praise Thy name on earth, and in the words of the prophet say: Holy, Holy, Holy is the Lord of Hosts, the whole earth is full of His glory.

**All Singing:**

S. Sulzer

Ko - dosh ko - dosh ko - dosh A - do - noy ts' - vo - os m'lo chol ho - o - retz k'-vo - - - do.

**Reader:**

In all places of Thy dominion, Thy name is praised and glorified.

439

**All Singing:**

S. Sulzer

Bo - ruch k' - vod A - do - noy mi - m' - ko - mo.

**Reader:**

The Lord will reign forever, thy God, O Zion, from generation to generation.

**All Singing:**

S. Sulzer

*Moderato*

Yim - loch A - do - noy l' - o - lom E - lo - ha - yich Tsee -

yon l' - dor vo - dor ha - l' - lu - yo.

**Prayer:**

Lord of all the ages, Guardian of Israel, we pray for Thy guidance and protection. New tasks and new duties await us in the years that are to

come. Great is the knowledge which we must still acquire. Many are the problems we must still learn to solve. Our bodies must grow in strength, and our minds develop in wisdom, and we lift up our eyes to Thee from whom comes our help.

Each day a new path extends before us. We shall not stumble, for we trust in Thee. With all our hearts we rely upon Thine aid. As difficult duties arise, give us the strength and wisdom to perform them well. When obstacles confront us, grant us the courage to surmount them bravely. May we grow in knowledge and in patience, in confidence and in joy, to be worthy of Thine everlasting love. O, send Thou Thy light and Thy truth to lead us in all our ways. Amen.

**Silent Devotion**

**All Singing:**

Alois Kaiser

*p* *Moderato*

May the words of my mouth and the med - i - ta - tions of my heart be ac - cept - a - ble in Thy sight, O Lord, my Strength and my Re - deem - er. A - men.

**Address or Scripture Reading**

**Hymn**

May the Lord guard our going out and our coming in, from this day forth, even forever.   Amen.

# III

**Hymn**

**Responsive Reading (Psalm cxxxix):**

O Lord, Thou hast searched me and known me.
  Thou understandest my thoughts from afar,
Thou measurest my walking and my resting.
  Thou art acquainted with all my ways,
For there is not a word on my tongue
  Which Thou knowest not, O Lord, altogether.
Whither shall I go from Thy spirit?
  Whither shall I flee from Thy presence?
If I ascend unto heaven, Thou art there.
  If I descend into the deep, Thou art there.
If I take the wings of the morning
  And dwell in the farthest seas
Even there would Thy hand lead me.
  And if I say the darkness shall enfold me  .
Even the darkness is not too dark for Thee.
  But the night shineth as the day,
The darkness gleams as the light.

**Together:**

Search me, O God, and know my heart.
Try me and know my thoughts.
See if I follow a path that is wicked,
And lead me in the way everlasting.

**Reader:**

Praise ye the Lord, to whom all praise is due.
Bor'-chu es A-do-noy ha-m'-voroch.

**Congregation:**

Praised be the Lord, to whom all praise is due forever and ever.

442

**All Singing:**

S. Sulzer

Bo - ruch A - do - noy ha - m' vo - roch l'o - lom vo - ed.

**Reader:**

We thank thee, O Lord, for making the light to shine over the earth and all its inhabitants. Wonderful are Thy works, O Lord. In wisdom hast Thou made them all.

With great love hast Thou loved us and our fathers. As Thou didst teach them the laws of life, so teach us to love and honor Thee. We delight in Thy help, and joyfully lift up our voices to proclaim:

*(Congregation standing)*

**Together:**

Hear, O Israel: The Lord our God, the Lord is One.
Sh'ma Yis-ro-ayl A-do-noy E-lo-hay-nu, A-do-noy e-chod.

**All Singing:**

Traditional

Sh'ma Yis-ro - ayl A-do - noy E - lo -hay - nu A - do - noy e - chod.

**Reader:**

Praised be His name whose glorious kingdom is forever and ever.
Bo-ruch shaym k'-vod mal-chu-so l'-o-lom vo-ed.

443

Traditional

*f* Andante Maestoso

Bo - ruch shaym k' - vod mal - chu - so l' - o - lom vo - ed.

*(Congregation seated)*

**Responsive Reading:**

Truth eternal and unchanging is Thy word which Thou hast spoken through Thy prophets,

Thou art the living God, Thy words bring life and light to the soul.

Thou hast been the help of our fathers in time of trouble and art our refuge in all generations,

O God, who art our refuge and our hope, we glorify Thy name now, as did our fathers in ancient days:

**All Singing:**

S. Sulzer

Mee cho - mo - cho bo - ay - leem A - do - noy;

mee ko - mo - cho ne - dor ba - ko - desh,

no - ro s'hil - los o - say fe - lay.

**Reader:**

God reigneth forever and ever.

**All Singing:**

A - do - noy yim - loch l'o - lom vo - ed.

*(Congregation standing)*

**Reader:**

Let us adore the ever-living God, who spread out the heavens and established the earth, whose glory is revealed in the heavens above and whose greatness is seen throughout the world. He is our God. There is none else. We bow the head and bend the knee and praise the blessed King of kings.

**All Singing:**
S. Sulzer

Va - a - nach-nu ko - r'-eem u-mish - ta - cha-veem u - mo-deem

lif - nay Me - lech mal-chay ham - lo-cheem ha - ko-dosh bo-ruch hu.

445

*(Congregation seated)*

**Reader:**

We pray that soon the day may come, when ignorance and superstition will disappear and all the inhabitants of the earth will worship Thee alone. May the time not be distant when all people will understand that they are brethren, so that as brethren they may be united forever before Thee. Then will Thy kingdom be established on earth.

**Prayer:**

Almighty Master of the world! The Universe is Thy dwelling place. In the highest heavens and the lowest depths, in fields and forests, in cities and deserts, and in the hearts of Thy children everywhere, is Thy glory found. For the opportunities of joy and goodness with which Thou dost fill our lives, we praise Thy holy name.

O help us to realize that Thou art ever near us and that we are always standing before Thee. Since Thou art Truth, may we never speak falsehood. Since Thou art Love, may we never be hateful to any of Thy children. May we open our hearts unto Thee with every word and deed, and by each unspoken thought make them temples worthy of Thy habitation. Amen.

**Silent Devotion**

**All Singing:**

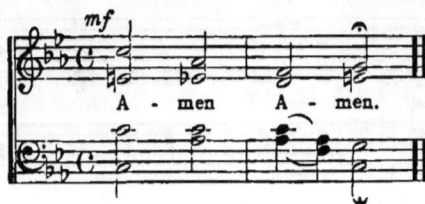

A - men     A - men.

**Address or Scriptural Reading**

**Hymn**

**Benediction:**

Lord, give strength unto Thy people. Teach all Thy children to live in friendship and peace. Amen.

446

# IV

**Responsive Reading (Psalm xxiv):**

The earth is the Lord's and the fullness thereof;
 The world and they that dwell therein,
For He hath founded it upon the seas
 And established it upon the floods.
Who shall ascend the mountain of the Lord?
 Who shall stand in His holy place?
He that hath clean hands and a pure heart,
 Who hath not taken My name in vain,
And hath not sworn deceitfully.

**Together:**

He shall receive a blessing from the Lord
And righteousness from the God of salvation.
Such is the generation of them that seek Thee,
That seek Thy presence, O God of Jacob.

*Or the following Psalm (xv):*

Lord, who shall live in Thy tabernacle?
 Who shall dwell upon Thy holy mountain?
He that walketh uprightly and worketh righteousness,
 And speaketh truth in his heart;
That hath no slander upon his tongue,
 Nor doeth evil to his fellow-man,
Nor taketh up a reproach against his neighbor,
 He that sweareth to his own hurt and changeth not;
He that putteth not out his money on usury,
 Nor taketh a bribe against the innocent,
In whose eyes vileness is despised,
 But he honoreth them that fear the Lord.

**Together:**

He that doeth these things shall never be moved.

**Reader:**

Praise ye the Lord, to whom all praise is due.
Bor'-chu es A-do-noy ha-m'-voroch.

**Congregation:**

Praised be the Lord, to whom all praise is due forever and ever.

**All Singing:**

S. Sulzer

Bo - ruch A - do - noy ha - m' vo - roch l'o - lom vo - ed.

**Reader:**

We praise Thee, O Lord our God, Ruler of the world. In Thy love Thou causest light to shine over the earth and its inhabitants. Each morning renews Thy great command: Let there be light.

All things on earth are Thine and are created by Thy will. Without number are Thy works. In wisdom hast Thou made them all. Light and darkness, joy and sorrow come from Thee, who bringest harmony into nature and peace to the heart of man.

*(Congregation standing)*

Hear, O Israel: The Lord our God, the Lord is One.
Sh'ma Yis-ro-ayl A-do-noy E-lo-hay-nu, A-do-noy e-chod.

**All Singing:**

Traditional

Sh'ma Yis - ro - ayl A - do - noy E - lo - hay - nu A - do - noy e - chod.

**Reader:**

Praised be His name whose glorious kingdom is forever and ever.

448

**All Singing:**

Traditional

Bo - ruch shaym k' - vod mal - chu - so l' - o - lom vo - ed.

*(Congregation seated)*

**Responsive Reading:**

Thou shalt love the Lord thy God with all thy heart, with all thy soul
and with all thy might.

These words which I command thee this day shall be upon thy heart.

Eternal truth it is that Thou alone art God, there is none beside Thee.

O God, who art our refuge and our help, we glorify Thy name now, as
did our fathers in ancient days.

**All Singing:**

S. Sulzer

Mee cho - mo - cho bo - ay - leem A - do - noy;

mee ko - mo - cho ne - dor ba - ko - desh,

no - ro s'hil - los o - say fe - lay.

449

**Reader:**

God reigneth forever and ever.

**All Singing:**

A - do - noy yim - loch l'o - lom vo - ed.

**Reader:**

Praised be Thou, O Lord our God, God of our fathers, Abraham, Isaac and Jacob. Thou bestowest loving-kindness upon all Thy children and art our Helper and Protector.

Thou art mighty forever, O Lord. In Thy mercy Thou upholdest the falling, healest the sick, and freest the enslaved. Blessed art Thou who hast implanted within us immortal life.

As the heavens declare Thy glory, so do we hallow Thy name on earth, and say in the words of the prophet: Holy, Holy, Holy is the Lord of Hosts, the whole earth is full of His glory.

*(Congregation standing)*

**All Singing:**

S. Sulzer

Ko - dosh ko - dosh ko - dosh A - do - noy ts' - vo - os m'lo chol ho - o - retz k'vo - - do.

450

In all places of Thy dominion, Thy name is praised and glorified.

**All Singing:**

S. Sulzer

Bo - ruch    k' - vod    A - do - noy    mi - m' - ko - mo.

**Reader:**

The Lord will reign forever, thy God, O Zion, from generation to generation. Hallelujah!

**All Singing:**

S. Sulzer

Yim - loch    A - do - noy    l' - o - lom    E - lo - ha - yich    Tsee -

yon    l' - dor    vo - dor    ha - l' - lu - yo.

*(Congregation seated)*

451

**Prayer:**

Heavenly Father, perfect in justice and holiness, Thou art the source of all goodness. It is Thy will that we strive to be holy as Thou art holy. Therefore, dost Thou require of us to do justice, to love mercy and to walk humbly before Thee. Our highest homage of Thee is our service to Thy children.

Teach us to understand that not alone in synagog and school should we revere Thy holy name. Our daily life must make clear our reverence of Thee. May our prayers here, and the lessons we learn in Thy house, inspire us to lead worthy and holy lives.

With all our strength may we strive to be worthy of Thy presence. O be Thou with us at all times, so that every noble thought may become a prayer, every word we utter a hymn of praise, and every worthy deed an act of homage to Thee, our Guide and Father. Amen.

**Silent Devotion**

**All Singing:**

Alois Kaiser

May the words of my mouth and the med-i-ta-tions of my heart be ac-cept-a-ble in Thy sight, O Lord, my Strength and my Re-deem-er. A-men.

**Address or Scripture Reading**

**Hymn**

**Benediction:**

Plant virtue in every soul and may the love of Thee, hallow every home and every heart.   Amen.

# SERVICES FOR YOUNGER CHILDREN
## I

**Hymn**

**Responsive Reading (Psalm xxiii):**

The Lord is my shepherd; I shall not want.
He maketh me to lie down in green pastures:
He leadeth me beside still waters,
He restoreth my soul:
He guideth me in straight paths for His name's sake.
Yea, though I walk through the valley of the shadow of death,
I will fear no evil, for Thou art with me;
Thy rod and Thy staff, they comfort me;
Surely, goodness and mercy shall follow me all the days of my life;
And I shall dwell in the house of the Lord forever.

**Reader:**

Praise ye the Lord, to whom all praise is due.
Bor'-chu es A-do-noy ha-m'-voroch.

**Congregation:**

Praised be the Lord, to whom all praise is due forever and ever.

**All Singing:**

S. Sulzer

Bo - ruch A - do - noy ha - m' vo - roch l'o - lom vo - ed.

**Reader:**

We praise Thee, Lord our God, Ruler of the world, for sending the sunlight to shine over the earth. With great love dost Thou teach us to live a good and pure life. Help us to understand and to do what Thou dost ask of us; and fill our hearts with love for Thee.

454

*Or the following version of the prayer:*

We praise Thee, King of all the world,
    Thy word in gladness all obey;
The stars grow dim, the sun appears,
    And evening changes into day.

Last night the world was tired and worn
    And praised Thee for the restful night;
Now birds and flowers and sons of man
    Rise in new strength to greet Thy light.

In wisdom hast Thou made them all,
    The sun to shine on yonder hill,
The stars to march across the sky,
    And us in joy to do Thy will.

*(All standing)*

Hear, O Israel: The Lord our God, the Lord is One.
Sh'ma Yis-ro-ayl A-do-noy E-lo-hay-nu, A-do-noy e-chod.

**All Singing:**

*(All seated)*

**Prayer (Together):**

We love the Lord with all our heart, with all our soul and all our might.
We will never forget the words of God which we are learning here. We
will think of them at home and in school; we will speak of them at work,
and at play. God's love for us will fill our thought, when we lie down to
restful sleep, and when we are awakened again by the light of day.

**Reader:**

As the heavens declare Thy glory, so do we praise Thy name on earth. In the words of the prophet we say: Holy, holy, holy is the Lord of hosts, the whole earth is full of His glory.

**All Singing:**

Ko - dosh ko - dosh ko - dosh A - do - noy ts' - vo - os m'lo chol ho - o - retz k'vo - - - do.

**Reader:**

In all places of Thy dominion, Thy name is praised and glorified.

**All Singing:**

Bo - ruch k' - vod A - do - noy mi - m' - ko - mo.

**Reader:**

The Lord will reign forever, thy God, O Zion, from generation to generation. Hallelujah!

**All Singing:**

S. Sulzer

Yim - loch  A - do - noy  l' - o - lom  E - lo - ha - yich Tsee -

yon  l' - dor  vo - dor  ha - l' - lu - yo.

**Prayer (Together):**

Kind Father of the world, we thank Thee every day, for all Thy goodness to Thy children. For health and home, for food and loving parents, we sing our grateful praise to Thee.

Teach us to be kind to all; to do no harm to any living thing. Inspire us to do our work well and to enjoy our play. As Thou dost give us happiness, may we bring joy to all who love us. Amen.

**Hymn**

**Benediction:**

Bless us and guard us, O Father. Let Thy light shine upon us and be gracious unto us, and grant us peace. Amen.

**Hymn**

**Responsive Reading (Psalm cxlv):**

I will honor Thee my God, O King,
  I will bless Thy name forever and ever,
Every day will I bless Thee
  And I will praise Thy name forever and ever.
Men shall speak of Thy mighty acts
  And I will tell of Thy greatness.
The Lord is good to all;
  His tender mercies are over all His works.
The Lord upholdeth all that fall
  And raiseth up those who are bowed down;
The Lord is near to all who call upon Him,
  To all that call upon Him in truth.

**Reader:**

Praise ye the Lord, to whom all praise is due.
Bor'-chu es A-do-noy ha-m'-voroch.

**All Singing:**

S. Sulzer

Bo - ruch A - do - noy ha - m' vo - roch l'o - lom vo - ed.

**Reader:**

We praise Thee, O Lord our God, Ruler of the world, earth and sky, that speak of Thy great goodness. The changing seasons, the growing trees and flowers tell us of Thee. We thank Thee for this new day which brings us joy and love, work and play. Teach us how to serve Thee every day in all that we think and do.

*(Congregation standing)*

**Reader:**

Hear, O Israel: The Lord, our God, the Lord is One.
Sh'ma Yis-ro-ayl A-do-noy E-lo-hay-nu, A-do-noy e-chod.

**All Singing:**

Traditional

Sh'ma Yis-ro-ayl A-do-noy E-lo-hay-nu A-do-noy e-chod.

*(Congregation seated)*

**Prayer (Together):**

Praised be Thou, Lord our God, God of our fathers, Abraham, Isaac and Jacob. Thou art kind to all Thy children. In love, Thou upholdest the falling, healest the sick, and givest life unto all.

**Reader:**

As the heavens declare Thy glory, so do we praise Thy name on earth. In the words of the prophet we say: Holy, holy, holy is the Lord of hosts; the whole earth is full of His glory.

**All Singing:**

S. Sulzer

Ko - dosh ko - dosh ko - dosh A - do - noy ts' - vo -

459

os      m'lo chol ho - o - retz k'-vo - - - do.

**Prayer (Together):**

Mighty Creator of heaven and earth, to Thee we speak our words of praise. We thank Thee for life with its joys, for parents who protect us, for friends who play and learn with us, and those who teach us the wonders of Thy world.

Help us to learn that which is beautiful and good. May every passing day deepen our mind, increase our strength, and bring us nearer in love to Thee. Amen.

**Hymn**

**Benediction:**

Give strength, O Lord, to all Thy children. Grant us the blessing of peace. Amen.

# FOR SABBATH

**Hymn**

**Responsive Reading:**

How goodly are thy tents, O Jacob, thy dwellings, O Israel!

Through Thy great mercy, O God, I come to Thy house and bow down in Thy holy temple to worship Thee.

O Lord, I love the place of Thy house and the abode in which Thy glory dwelleth.

I bow down and adore Thee, O God, my Maker.

May my prayer be offered in an acceptable time;

Mayest Thou, in the greatness of Thy mercy, answer me according to Thy faithfulness.

**Reader:**

My God, the soul which Thou hast given unto me came pure from Thee. Thou hast created it within me, that I may live and do the work that is pleasing in Thy sight. Help me, O God, to keep this soul clean and true. May no act of mine stain its purity or mar its beauty. While Thy spirit lives in me, I will worship Thee, Master of the world and Creator of all souls. Praised be Thou, O Lord, in whose hands are the souls of all the living and the spirits of all flesh.

*(Congregation standing)*

**Reader:**

Praise ye the Lord, to whom all praise is due.

Bor'-chu es A-do-noy ha-m'-voroch.

**Congregation:**

Praised be the Lord, to whom all praise is due forever and ever.

**All Singing:**

Bo - ruch A - do - noy  ha - m' vo - roch  l'o - lom  vo - ed.

*(Congregation seated)*

**Reader:**

We praise Thee, O Lord, who art the Creator and Ruler of the world. The earth is full of Thy possessions. The heavens declare Thy glory. Day by day, we behold the wonders of Thy creation. Light and darkness, sunshine and rain, joy and sorrow, come from Thee. In wisdom and love hast Thou made them all. Thou bringest harmony into nature and peace to the heart of man.

**Responsive Reading:**

With great love hast Thou loved us, O our God.
>Our fathers believed in Thee, and Thou didst teach them the laws of life, and show them the way of wisdom.

May we ever trust in Thee, and learn to know and fulfill all the teachings of Thy word.

Fill our hearts with love and reverence for Thee.

Help us to love all Thy creatures, even as Thou lovest us, O Father of all men.

Teach us to understand that, as Thou art One, all Thy children are one, united by a holy bond of brotherhood.

*(Congregation standing)*

**Reader:**

Hear, O Israel: The Lord our God, the Lord is One.
Sh'ma Yis-ro-ayl A-do-noy E-lo-hay-nu, A-do-noy e-chod.

**All Singing:**

Traditional

*f  Andante Maestoso*

Sh'ma Yis-ro-ayl A-do-noy E-lo-hay-nu A-do-noy e-chod.

**Reader:**

Praised be His name whose glorious kingdom is forever and ever.
Bo-ruch shaym k'-vod mal-chu-so l'o-lom vo-ed.

**All Singing:**

*f Andante Maestoso*

Bo - ruch shaym k' - vod mal - chu - so l' - o - lom vo - ed.

*(Congregation seated)*

**All Reading:**

Thou shalt love the Lord thy God, with all thy heart, and with all thy soul, and with all thy might. And these words, which I command thee this day, shall be upon thy heart. Thou shalt teach them diligently unto thy children, and shalt speak of them when thou sittest in thy house, when thou walkest by the way, when thou liest down, and when thou risest up. And thou shalt bind them for a sign upon thy hand, and they shall be for frontlets between thine eyes. And thou shalt write them upon the doorposts of thy house and upon thy gates:

To the end that ye may remember and do all My commandments and be holy unto your God. I am the Lord your God.

**Reader:**

Who is like unto Thee among the mighty, O Lord? Who is like unto Thee, glorious in holiness, extolled in praises, working wonders?

**All Singing:**

S. Sulzer

*p*

Mee cho - mo - cho bo - ay - leem A - do - noy;

mee ko - mo - cho ne - dor ba - ko - desh,

463

no - ro s'hil - los o - say fe - lay.

**Reader:**

The Lord reigneth forever and ever.

**All Singing:**

A - do - noy yim - loch l'o - lom vo - ed.

**Responsive Reading:**

We praise Thee, O Lord our God and God of our fathers, Abraham, Isaac
   and Jacob.
   Thou bestowest loving-kindness upon all Thy creatures,
Thou sustainest the living; Thou upholdest the falling.
   Thou healest the sick; Thou loosest the bound.
Thou rememberest the goodness of the fathers.
   Thou deliverest the oppressed and the persecuted.
Thou art the source of our life, and art our eternal hope.
   We praise Thee for the immortal life Thou hast implanted within us.

*(Congregation standing)*

**Reader:**

From generation to generation we declare Thy greatness, and throughout
all ages we proclaim Thy holiness; and in the words of the prophet we say:
Holy, holy, holy is the Lord of hosts; the whole earth is full of His glory.

464

S. Sulzer

Ko - dosh    ko - dosh    ko - dosh    A - do - noy    ts' - vo -
os    m'lo    chol    ho - o - retz    k'-vo - - - do.

**Reader:**

In all places of Thy dominion, Thy name is praised and glorified.

**All Singing:**

S. Sulzer

Bo - ruch    k' - vod    A - do - noy    mi - m' - ko - mo.

**Reader:**

The Lord will reign forever, thy God, O Zion, from generation to generation. Hallelujah!

**All Singing:**

S. Sulzer

Yim - loch A - do - noy l' - o - lom E - lo - ha - yich Tsee -

yon l' - dor vo - dor ha - l' - lu - yo.

*(Congregation seated)*

**All Reading:**

Our God and God of our fathers, grant that our rest on this Sabbath be acceptable to Thee. May we, sanctified through Thy commandments, become sharers in the blessings of Thy word. Teach us to be satisfied with the gifts of Thy goodness and gratefully to rejoice in all Thy mercies. Purify our hearts that we may serve Thee in truth. O help us to preserve the Sabbath as Israel's heritage from generation to generation, that it may ever bring rest and joy, peace and comfort to the dwellings of our brethren, and through it, Thy name be hallowed in all the earth. Praised be Thou, O Lord, who sanctifiest the Sabbath.

**Reader:**

Look with favor, O Lord, upon Israel, Thy people, and in Thy love at all times accept our worship. Praised be Thou, O God, whom alone we serve in reverence.

466

## All Reading:

We gratefully acknowledge, O Lord our God, that Thou art our Creator and Preserver, the Rock of our life and the Shield of our help. We render thanks unto Thee for our lives which are in Thy hand, for our souls which are ever in Thy keeping, for Thy wondrous providence and for Thy continuous goodness, which Thou bestowest upon us day by day. Truly, Thy mercies never fail and Thy loving-kindness never ceases. Therefore in Thee do we forever put our trust.

## Reader:

Grant us peace, Thy most precious gift, O Thou eternal source of peace, and enable Israel to be a messenger of peace unto the peoples of the earth. Bless our country that it may ever be a stronghold of peace, and the advocate of peace in the council of nations. May contentment reign within its borders, health and happiness within its homes. Strengthen the inhabitants of our land. Plant virtue in every soul, and may the love of Thy name hallow every home and every heart. Praised be Thou, O Lord, Giver of peace.

## Silent Devotion:

O God, keep my tongue from evil and my lips from speaking guile. Be my support when grief silences my voice, and my comfort when woe bends my spirit. Plant humility in my soul, and strengthen my heart with perfect faith in Thee. Help me to be strong in trial and temptation and to be meek when others wrong me, that I may readily forgive them. Guide me by the light of Thy counsel, and let me ever find rest in Thee, who art my Rock and my Redeemer. Amen.

## All Singing:

Alois Kaiser

May the words of my mouth and the med - i - ta - tions of my heart be ac - cept - a - ble in Thy sight, O Lord,

my Strength and my Re - deem - er. A - men.

# READING OF SCRIPTURE

**Responsive Reading:**

> Who shall ascend into the mountain of the Lord and who shall stand in
>     His holy place?
>     He that hath clean hands, and a pure heart; who hath not taken My
>     name in vain, and hath not sworn deceitfully.
> He shall receive a blessing from the Lord, and righteousness from the
>     God of his salvation.
>     Such is the generation of them that seek Thee; that seek Thy presence,
>     O God of Jacob.

**All Singing:**

G. Froelich

S'u sh'o - reem ro - shay - - - chem . . . u - s'-
u pis-chay o - lom, v' yo - vo me - lech hak - ko - vod, hak-

ko - vod. Mee hu zeh me - lech, hak - ko - - vod;

A - do - noy ... ts'vo - os, ... hu me - lech ha - ko - vod, se - lo.

*(Congregation standing)*

(The Scroll is taken from the Ark)

**Reader:**

Happy are they who are upright in the way; who walk in the law of the Lord.

**Together:**

Hear, O Israel: The Lord our God, the Lord is One.

Sh'ma Yis-ro-ayl A-do-noy E-lo-hay-nu, A-do-noy e-chod.

**All Singing:**

Alois Kaiser

L' - cho A - do - noy hag'-dul - lo v'hag-'vu - ro, ... v' - hat - tif -

e - res v'han - ne - tsach v'ha - hod. Kee-chol bash-sho - ma - yim

469

u - vo - o - rets. L' - cho A - do - noy ham -

mam - lo - cho V' - ham - mis - nas - say... l' - chol l' - rosh.

*(Congregation seated)*

### READING FROM THE TORAH

**All Reading:**

Thou who art the source of all good gifts, bless this congregation and be with all its members, their families and their households; prosper them in their various callings and occupations, help them in their needs, and guide them in their difficulties. Hear Thou the prayers of all who worship here this morning, comfort the sorrowing and cheer the silent sufferers. Bless those who guide and who serve this congregation, and those who contribute to its support. Reward with the joy of goodness the charitable and the merciful who aid the poor, care for the sick, teach the ignorant, and extend a helping hand to those who have lost their way in the world.

Fervently we invoke Thy blessing upon our country and our nation. Guard them, O God, from calamity and injury; suffer not their adversaries to triumph over them, and let the glories of a just, righteous and God-fearing people increase from age to age. Enlighten with Thy wisdom and sustain with Thy power those whom the people have set in authority: the President, his counselors, and advisors, the judges, law-givers and executives, and all those who are intrusted with our safety and with the guardianship of our rights and our liberties. May peace and good-will obtain among all the inhabitants of our land; may religion spread its blessings among us and exalt our nation in righteousness. Amen.

### RETURNING THE SCROLL TO THE ARK

*(Congregation standing)*

**Reader:**

O magnify the Lord with me, and let us exalt His Name together.

All Singing:

S. Sulzer

Ho - do al e - rets v'-sho - mo - yim Va - yo - rem
ke - ren l'am - - mo. T' - hil - loh l' - chol... cha -
see - - - dov, Li - v'-nay Yis - ro - ayl am k' - ro -
vo. Ha - l' - lu - yo, ha - l' - lu - yo.

**Reader:**

It is a tree of life to them that lay hold of it, and the supporters thereof are happy. Its ways are ways of pleasantness, and all its paths are peace.

S. Sulzer

Aytz cha-yeem hee la-ma-cha-zee-keem bo v'-som-che-ho v'-som'-che-ho m'-u-shor, d'ro-che-ho dar-chay no-am dar-chay no-am v'-chol n'-see-vo-se-ho sho-lom.

*(Congregation seated)*

**Hymn**
**Sermon**
**Hymn**

# Adoration

*(Congregation standing)*

## All Reading:

Let us adore the ever-living God, and render praise unto Him, who spread out the heavens and established the earth, whose glory is revealed in the heavens above, and whose greatness is manifest throughout the world. He is our God; there is none else.

We bow the head and bend the knee and magnify the King of kings, the Holy One, praised be He.

## All Singing:

S. Sulzer

Va - a - nach-nu  ko - r'-eem  u-mish - ta - cha-veem u - mo-deem

lif - nay Me - lech  mal-chay ham - lo-cheem  ha - ko-dosh  bo-ruch  hu.

*(Congregation seated)*

## Reader:

May the time not be distant, O God, when Thy name shall be worshiped in all the earth, when unbelief shall disappear and error be no more. We fervently pray that the day may come when all men shall invoke Thy name, when corruption and evil shall give way to purity and goodness, when

superstition shall no longer enslave the mind, nor idolatry blind the eye, when all inhabitants of the earth shall know that to Thee alone every knee must bend, and every tongue give homage. O may all, created in Thine image, recognize that they are brethren, so that, one in spirit and one in fellowship, they may be forever united before Thee. Then shall Thy kingdom be established on earth and the word of Thine ancient seer be fulfilled: The Lord will reign forever and ever.

**All Reading:**

On that day the Lord shall be One and His name shall be One.

**Hymn**

**Benediction**

## FOR PASSOVER

**Reader:**

God of Israel, Father of mankind, on this festival of the Passover our thoughts turn back to the days of Egypt, when Israel dwelt in bondage. The lash of the taskmaster was upon his shoulders, and the cruelty of the Pharaohs made his life bitter. But Thou didst raise up a deliverer, even Moses, who came out of his refuge in the desert, bearing Thy message: "Let my people go, that they may serve Me!" Right triumphed over might, and justice over oppression. With a strong hand and an outstretched arm didst Thou lead Thy people forth, and bear them as on eagle's wings. The rod of the oppressor Thou didst break, and the bars of iron Thou didst burst asunder. O Father, how great are Thy justice and mercy, unto the thousandth generation of those who love Thee and keep Thy commandments. We thank Thee, O Lord our God, for this season of the Passover, which recalls to our minds the great deliverance Thou didst work for Israel. Slaves were our forefathers in Egypt. Cause the memory of that slavery to abide within our souls, so that we may never oppress other men, nor act with haughty pride toward the weak and defenseless. Each year may we learn to dedicate ourselves anew to the cause of human freedom. May the memory of the Passover never depart from among the people of Israel. May it ever bring us courage and faith! Amen.

**Reader:**

Praise ye the Lord, to whom all praise is due.

Bor'-chu es A-do-noy ha-m'-voroch.

**Congregation:**

Praised be the Lord, to whom all praise is due forever and ever.

**All Singing:**

S. Sulzer

Bo - ruch A - do - noy ha - m' vo - roch l'o - lom vo - ed.

475

**Responsive Reading:**

Thou, O Lord, hast been the help of our fathers from everlasting.
  A Shield and a Savior hast Thou been unto them and their children throughout all generations.
Thou art the first and the last, and besides Thee we have no ruler, redeemer, nor savior.
  Thou didst redeem us, O Lord our God, from Egypt and didst deliver us from the house of bondage.
Thou castest down the proud and exaltest the humble.
  Thou deliverest the prisoners, redeemest the meek and aidest the poor.
Thou answerest Thy people Israel when they cry unto Thee in their distress.
  Who is like unto Thee, O Lord, among the mighty?
Who is like Thee, glorious in holiness, extolled in praises, working wonders?
  The Lord will reign forever and ever.

*(Congregation standing)*

**Together:**

Hear, O Israel: The Lord our God, the Lord is One.
Sh'ma Yis-ro-ayl A-do-noy E-lo-hay-nu, A-do-noy e-chod.

**All Singing:**

S. Sulzer

*f  Andante Maestoso*

Sh'ma Yis-ro-ayl A-do-noy E-lo-hay-nu A-do-noy e-chod.

**Reader:**

Praised be His name whose glorious kingdom is forever and ever.
Bo-ruch shaym k'-vod mal-chu-so l'-o-lom vo-ed.

**All Singing:**

S. Sulzer

Bo - ruch shaym k' - vod mal - chu - so l' - o - lom vo - ed.

*(Congregation seated)*

**Antiphonal Reading and Singing (adapted from Psalm cxxxvi):**

**Reader:**

O give thanks unto the Lord, for He is good, for His mercy endureth forever.

**All Singing:**

Kee - - - l' - o - lom chas - - - - - do.

**Reader.**

To Him who alone doeth great wonders:

**All Singing:** Kee l'olom chasdo

**Reader:**

To Him who made great lights, the sun to rule by day, the moon and the stars to rule by night:

477

**All Singing:**

Kee l'olom chasdo

**Reader:**

To Him who smote the Egyptians, and brought out Israel from among them:

**All Singing:**

Kee l'olom chasdo

**Reader:**

To Him who divided the Red Sea asunder and made Israel to pass through the midst of it:

**All Singing:**

Kee l'olom chasdo

**Reader:**

To Him who smote great kings and slew mighty rulers:

**All Singing:**

Kee l'olom chasdo

**Reader:**

Who remembered us in our low estate, and delivered us from our enemies:

**All Singing:**

Kee l'olom chasdo

**Reader:**

He giveth food to all flesh; O give thanks unto the God of heaven:

**All Singing:**

Kee l'olom chasdo

**All Read Together:**

With everlasting love hast Thou loved us, O Lord our God. And with great mercy hast Thou had compassion upon us, O our Father and King, for the sake of Thy great name. Because our fathers trusted in Thee, Thou didst teach them the laws of life, that they might do Thy will with a perfect heart. Enlighten our eyes through Thy law. Hasten the day when blessed peace shall descend upon the four corners of the earth, when oppression and persecution shall cease forever. Strike the yoke from all shoulders, and the chains from all limbs. Send liberty to all those who languish in bondage, and light to those who walk in darkness. Grant that the promised day may come, when justice shall flow like water and righteousness like a mighty stream; when men shall beat their swords into plowshares and their spears into pruning hooks. Blessed art Thou, O Lord our God, King of the universe, who sanctifiest Israel and the holy festivals. Amen.

**Reader:**

Who is like unto Thee, O God, among the mighty? Who is like unto Thee, glorious in holiness. extolled in praises, working wonders?

**All Singing:**

Arr. by Louis Lewandowski

Mee cho mo - cho bo - ay leem A - do - - - - - noy,

mee ko - mo - cho ne - e - dor ba - ko - desh,

no - ro s'hil - los o - - - say .... fe - lay?

**Reader:**

Mal-chus'cho ro-u vo-ne-cho: ze Ayli o-nu v'om'ru:
When Thy children beheld Thy sovereign power, they exclaimed: This
is my God; and they said: The Lord shall reign forever and ever.

**All Singing:**

Ado - noy    yim - loch    l'o - lom    vo - - ed.

**Reader:**

Praised be Thou, O Lord our God, God of our fathers Abraham, Isaac,
and Jacob. Thou art our Helper and Protector. As the heavens declare
Thy glory, so do we praise Thy name on earth. In the words of the prophet
we say: Holy, holy, holy is the Lord of Hosts, the whole earth is full of
His glory.

**All Singing:**

S. Sulzer

Andante

Ko - dosh    ko - dosh    ko - dosh    A - do - noy    ts' - vo -

os     m'lo chol ho - o - retz k'-vo - - - do.

## READING THE SCRIPTURE

**Reader:**

Thou hadst delivered Thy people Israel out of Egypt, O Lord. Thou didst lead them through the wilderness by the hand of Thy servant Moses. Many were their hardships, and many were their murmurings. At last, at Sinai, while the lightnings played about the summit of the mount, Thou didst reveal Thyself to them and give them Thy Law. The slavery of the people was not ended when they departed from Egypt. Not until Thy Law of justice and mercy had been implanted in their hearts did they truly become free men. We thank Thee, O Father, that through the ages Thou hast revealed Thyself to man, and that in every age Thou awakenest within him wisdom and understanding, and the knowledge of Thee. We thank Thee for Thy never-ending revelation of truth and goodness to our fathers and to all the races and generations of men.

*(Congregation standing)*

**All Singing:**                                      G. Froelich

*Maestoso*

S'u    sh'o - reem      ro - shay - - -     chem . . . u - s'-

u    pis-chay   o - lom,     v' yo - vo me - lech hak - ko - vod, hak-

481

SOLI

*p*

ko - vod.  Mee hu zeh me - lech, hak - ko - - vod;

*f* ALL  *rit.*

A - do - noy ... ts'vo - os, ... hu  me - lech ha - ko - vod, se - lo.

(The Scroll is taken from the Ark)

**Reader:**

Happy are they who are upright in the way; who walk in the Law of the Lord.

**Together:**

Hear, O Israel: The Lord our God, the Lord is One.
Sh'ma Yis-ro-ayl A-do-noy E-lo-hay-nu, A-do-noy e-chod.

**All Singing:**

*f* *Allegro maestoso*

L' - cho A - do - noy hag'-dul - lo v'hag-'vu - ro, ...  v' - hat - tif -

e - res v'han - ne - tsach v'ha - hod. Kee-chol bash-sho - ma - yim u - vo - o - rets. L' - cho A - do - noy ham - mam - lo - cho V'-ham - mis - nas - say... l' - chol l' - rosh.

*(Congregation seated)*

**Scriptural Reading (Exodus xii, 37-42; xiii, 3-10)**

RETURNING THE SCROLL TO THE ARK

*(Congregation standing)*

**Reader:**

O magnify the Lord with me and let us exalt His name together.

(The Scroll is replaced in the Ark)

**Reader:**

It is a tree of life to them that lay hold of it, and the supporters thereof are happy. Its ways are ways of pleasantness and all its paths are peace.

**All Singing:**

S. Sulzer

Aytz cha-yeem hee la-ma-cha-zee-keem bo v'-som-che-ho v'-som'-che-ho m'-u-shor, . d'ro-che-ho dar-chay no-am dar-chay no-am v'-chol n'-see-vo-se-ho sho-lom.

*(Congregation seated)*

Four Children ascend the platform and read the following:

**First Child:**

Heavenly Father, in Thy wisdom which is past our searching out, Thou didst send our fathers into the bondage of Egypt. Thou didst try their souls with hard labor and cruel servitude. In our observance of this festival of the Passover, we use the Maror, the bitter herb. It stands for the bitterness Israel endured in Egypt. We have also the Charoseth, the mortar our ancestors used for the bricks with which in toil and pain, they reared the great structures Pharaoh forced them to build.

**Second Child:**

But Thou, O Father, didst hearken to the cry of Thy people. Thou didst send them Moses, the deliverer. With the courage of a prophet, he faced Pharaoh, who sat upon his throne in royal power and glory, and gave to the monarch the command of the Lord: "Let My people go, that they may serve Me!" At last the gates were opened and the slaves went forth. On the eve of their freedom, they sacrificed a lamb to Thee, the paschal lamb, in token of which we still place a lamb bone upon our Seder table.

**Third Child:**

Thus Israel went forth out of Egypt. But the way of the wilderness was long. In haste did they go forth. Still during this week do we partake of the Matzoh, the bread of affliction, the unleavened bread which our fathers baked in the sun as they marched from Egypt to the Red Sea. The unleavened bread reminds us of the long years of their wandering and suffering, and all the trials and tribulations they had to endure before they reached the Promised Land, and before freedom and security fell to their lot.

**Fourth Child:**

For all this, O God of Israel, we give thanks unto Thee. Thy justice is from everlasting to everlasting and fails not. Tyrants must bow before Thee, and injustice and oppression flee away. Thou rulest the world in Thy wisdom and givest unto all men their due. From of old didst Thou summon Israel, even from the days of Abraham, Isaac, and Jacob. Thou didst redeem us from the yoke of Egypt, and bring us near unto Thee, to serve Thee and to carry the knowledge of Thee to all the sons and daughters of men. Therefore, O Lord, do we praise Thee and glorify Thy name!

All rise and join in singing the traditional Pesach Hymn, No. 125 or 130.

**Sermon**

**Hymn**

485

*(Congregation standing)*

**Together:**

Let us adore the ever-living God, and render praise unto Him who spread out the heavens and established the earth, whose glory is revealed in the heavens above and whose greatness is manifest throughout the world. He is our God; there is none else.

We bow the head and bend the knee and magnify the King of kings, the Holy One, praised be He.

**All Singing:**

S. Sulzer

Va - a - nach-nu    ko - r'-eem    u-mish - ta - cha-veem u - mo-deem

lif - nay Me - lech    mal-chay ham - lo-cheem    ha - ko-dosh  bo-ruch hu.

*(Congregation seated)*

**Reader:**

Not only our fathers didst Thou deliver from Egypt, but all of the sons of Israel unto this day as it is said: "And thou shalt tell thy son in that day, saying: it is because of that which the Lord did for me when I came forth out of Egypt." Our fathers cried unto Thee in their trouble, and Thou didst deliver them out of their distress. Thou didst rescue those that sat in darkness and the shadow of death, being bound in affliction and in fetters of iron. Thou didst save them and burst their bonds asunder.

486

Not unto us, O Lord, not unto us, but unto Thy name we give glory, for Thy mercy, and for Thy truth's sake. For Thou hast delivered our soul from death, our eyes from tears, and our feet from stumbling.

May we, whose fathers went forth from slavery to freedom, never forget this day. May its message live in our hearts, that we may carry it to all the children of men. May it herald the dawn of the day of universal liberty, when slavery and oppression shall be no more, when all men shall have gone through their wilderness and found their Sinai of truth and faith.

Bestow upon us, O Lord our God, the blessing of this festival, the blessing of life, joy and peace. Sanctify us with Thy commandments, and ordain that our portion be in Thy Law. Sanctify us with Thy goodness. Let our souls rejoice in Thy salvation. And purify our hearts to serve Thee in truth. Blessed art Thou, O Lord our God, the deliverer of Israel, who sendest freedom and truth unto all men. Amen.

**Hymn**

**Benediction**

# FOR PENTECOST

**Together:**

We come into Thy presence, O God and Father, on this Thy holy festival. In the days of yore Israel brought to the sanctuary the first fruits of the fields. The rains had fallen and made the land fertile. The sun had smiled upon the soil and sent the warmth of life to seed and to root. Thy blessing had rested upon the labor of the people. In token of their gratitude they gathered the fruits that gleamed russet or golden upon the trees of the orchard, and the first jewels the soil had sent forth, to gladden their hearts and to give assurance of a year of plenty and prosperity.

Yet another gathering of the first fruits did the festival of Sh'vuos come to signify—the first fruits of the Law, the covenant Israel concluded with Thee. Then was it written that Thou wouldst be his God, and he would be Thy people, a kingdom of priests and a holy nation. Throughout his history, Israel looked back with reverence to the time when the words of justice, righteousness and mercy first rang in his soul, and when he first set forth upon the pathway of Thy Law.

Grant, O God of truth and justice, that this day may still wake its echo in our hearts. As we grow in years, may we grow in knowledge of Thee and of Thy Law. May we learn to read the book of the past and to find in it, the inspiration of wisdom and the beauty of holiness. Amen.

**Reader:**

Praise ye the Lord, to whom all praise is due.

Bor-chu es A-do-noy ha-m'voroch.

**Congregation:**

Praised be the Lord to whom all praise is due forever and ever.

**All Singing:**

S. Sulzer

Bo - ruch  A-do - noy  ha - m' vo - roch  l'o - lom  vo - ed.

488

**Responsive Reading:** (Adapted from the Azharoth of Gabirol):

**Reader:**

Guard thy speech, O my heart, learn humility, fear God, and understand the justice of His words.

**Children:**

For it is He who pardons guilt, increases strength, and makes wise the simple.

I shall declare Thine ordinances, which are sweet to the taste, and shall show the way to those who travel the path of life.

Serve the Lord, and love Him with thy whole heart; cleave unto Him, and walk in His ways.

Carry His rods in thy heart like a healing balm, both in thy heart and on thy lips; write them on the doorposts of thy house and on thy gates.

Give honor and reverence to those who study the Law, which is the delight of the soul.

Learn the Law thyself and teach it to others; honor thy parents and be merciful to the poor.

On thy festivals cause the fatherless, the widow and the stranger to rejoice with thee.

The commandments of the Lord give life to those that observe them; and he that teacheth others shall shine with the brightness of the sun.

Those that obey them shall win a great reward, and the upright shall be crowned with the light of goodness.

*(Congregation standing)*

**Congregation:**

Hear, O Israel: The Lord our God, the Lord is One.
Sh'ma Yis-ro-ayl A-do-noy E-lo-hay-nu, A-do-noy e-chod.

**All Singing:**

Traditional

*f Andante Maestoso*

Sh'ma Yis-ro-ayl A-do-noy E-lo-hay - nu A-do-noy e-chod.

489

**Reader:**

Praised be His name whose glorious kingdom is forever and ever.
Bo-ruch shaym k'-vod mal-chu-so l'-o-lom vo-ed.

**All Singing:**

*(Congregation seated)*

**Responsive Reading (Psalm i):**

Happy is the man that hath not walked in the counsel of the wicked.
  Nor stood in the way of sinners, nor sat in the seat of the scornful.
But his delight is in the law of the Lord; and in His law doth he meditate
    day and night.
  And he shall be like a tree planted by streams of water, that bringeth
    forth its fruit in its season,
And whose leaf doth not wither; and in whatsoever he doeth he shall
    prosper.
  Not so the wicked; but they are like chaff which the wind driveth away.
Therefore the wicked shall not stand in the judgment, nor sinners in the
    congregation of the righteous.
  For the Lord regardeth the way of the righteous; but the way of the
    wicked shall perish.

**Together:**

Thou shalt love the Lord thy God with all thy heart, and with all thy
soul and with all thy might. And these words, which I command thee this
day, shall be upon thy heart. Thou shalt speak of them when thou sittest
in thy house, when thou walkest by the way, when thou liest down, and
when thou risest up. And thou shalt bind them for a sign upon thy hand,
and they shall be for frontlets between thine eyes. And thou shalt write
them upon the doorposts of thy house and upon thy gates. To the end that
ye may remember and do all My commandments and be holy unto your
God. I am the Lord, your God.
  And the Lord spoke unto Moses, saying: Speak unto all the congregation

of the children of Israel, and say unto them: Ye shall be holy; for I, the Lord your God, am holy.

It hath been told thee, O man, what is good, and what the Lord doth require of thee: only to do justice, and to love mercy, and to walk humbly with thy God. And thou shalt love thy neighbor as thyself; I am the Lord.

**Reader:**

Who is like unto Thee, O God, among the mighty? Who is like unto Thee, glorious in holiness, extolled in praises, working wonders?

**All Singing:** Arr. by Louis Lewandowski

Mee cho mo - cho bo - ay leem A - do - - - - noy,

mee ko - mo - cho ne - e - dor ba - ko - desh,

no - ro s'hil - los o - - - say . . . . fe - lay?

**Reader:**

Mal-chus'cho ro-'u vo-ne-cho: ze Aylee o-nu v'-om'ru:
When Thy children beheld Thy sovereign power, they exclaimed: This is my God: and they said:

**Together:**

The Lord shall reign forever and ever.

**All Singing:**

Alois Kaiser

Ado - noy    yim - loch    l'o - lom    vo - - ed.

## READING OF SCRIPTURE

**Reader:**

And it shall come to pass in the end of days, that the mountain of the Lord's house shall be established as the top of the mountains, and shall be exalted above the hills; and all nations shall flow unto it. And many peoples shall go and say: Come ye, and let us go up to the mountain of the Lord, to the house of the God of Jacob; and He will teach us of His ways, and we will walk in His paths. For out of Zion shall go forth the law, and the word of the Lord from Jerusalem.

Behold the days come, saith the Lord, that I will make a new covenant with the house of Israel. I will put My law in their inward parts, and in their heart will I write it; and I will be their God, and they shall be My people; and they shall teach no more every man his neighbor, and every man his brother, saying: Know the Lord; for they shall all know Me, from the least of them unto the greatest of them, saith the Lord.

*(Congregation standing)*

G. Froelich

*Maestoso*

S'u sh'o - reem ro - shay - - - chem . . . u - s'-

u pis-chay o - lom, v' yo - vo me - lech hak - ko - vod, hak -

SOLI

ko - vod. Mee hu zeh me - lech, hak - ko - - - vod;

*rit.*

ALL

A - do - noy . . . ts'vo - os; . . . hu me - lech ha - ko - vod, se - lo.

(The Scroll is taken from the Ark)

**Reader:**

Happy are they who are upright in the way; who walk in the Law of the Lord.

**Together:**

Hear, O Israel: The Lord our God, the Lord is One.
Sh'ma Yis-ro-ayl A-do-noy E-lo-hay-nu, A-do-noy e-chod.

All Singing:

Traditional

Sh'ma Yis-ro-ayl A-do-noy E-lo-hay-nu A-do-noy e-chod.

Alois Kaiser

L'-cho A-do-noy hag'-dul-lo v'hag-'vu-ro,... v'-hat-tif-

e-res v'han-ne-tsach v'ha-hod. Kee-chol bash-sho-ma-yim

u-vo-o-rets. L'-cho A-do-noy ham-

494

*(Congregation seated)*

**Scriptural Reading (Exodus 19:1-8):**

RETURNING THE SCROLL

*(Congregation standing)*

**Reader:**

O magnify the Lord with me and let us exalt His name together.

The Scroll is replaced in the Ark

**Reader:**

It is a tree of life to them that lay hold of it, and the supporters thereof are happy. Its ways are ways of pleasantness and all its paths are peace.

**All Singing:**

S. Sulzer

Aytz cha-yeem hee la - ma-cha-zee-keem bo v' - som - che - ho v'-

som'-che - ho m' - u - shor, d'ro - che - ho dar-chay no - am

495

dar - chay no - am   v'-chol   n'-see - vo - se - ho   sho - lom.

*(Congregation seated)*

Eleven Children ascend the platform and read the following:

**First Child:**

On this festival of Sh'vuos we remember the giving of the Law, the rules of wisdom and goodness which God inspired in the soul of Israel. They have been to us a pillar of cloud by day, and a pillar of fire by night. Through centuries of martyrdom, they have guided us and strengthened us. We give thanks unto Thee, O Lord, for the glory of this heritage which is ours. May we truly make it our own, so that it may enlighten our eyes and rejoice our hearts. In token of our loyalty to this Law, we repeat the words of the Ten Commandments, the loftiest expression of Israel's words of truth and justice:

**Second Child:**

I am the Lord, thy God, who brought thee out of the land of Egypt, out of the house of bondage.

**Third Child:**

Thou shalt have no other gods before Me. Thou shalt not make unto thee a graven image, nor any manner of likeness, of anything that is in heaven above or that is in the earth beneath, or that is in the water under the earth; thou shalt not bow down unto them, nor serve them; for I, the Lord thy God, am a jealous God, visiting the iniquity of the fathers upon the children unto the third and fourth generation of them that hate Me, and showing mercy unto the thousandth generation of them that love Me and keep My commandments.

**Fourth Child:**

Thou shalt not take the name of the Lord thy God in vain; for the Lord will not hold him guiltless that taketh His name in vain.

**Fifth Child:**

Remember the sabbath day, to keep it holy. Six days shalt thou labor, and do all thy work; but the seventh day is a sabbath unto the Lord, thy God; in it thou shalt not do any manner of work; thou, nor thy son, nor thy daughter, nor thy manservant, nor thy maidservant, nor thy cattle, nor thy stranger that is within thy gates; for in six days the Lord made heaven and earth, the sea and all that in them is, and rested on the seventh day; wherefore the Lord blessed the sabbath day, and hallowed it.

**Sixth Child:**

Honor thy father and thy mother, that thy days may be long upon the land which the Lord thy God giveth thee.

**Seventh Child:**

Thou shalt not murder.

**Eighth Child:**

Thou shalt not commit adultery.

**Ninth Child:**

Thou shalt not steal.

**Tenth Child:**

Thou shalt not bear false witness against thy neighbor.

**Eleventh Child:**

Thou shalt not covet thy neighbor's house; thou shalt not covet thy neighbor's wife, nor his manservant, nor his maidservant, nor his ox, nor his ass, nor anything that is thy neighbor's.

**Hymn**

Children rise and join in singing Sh'vuos hymn, No. 142 or 143 (or see Index "Law, The")

**Sermon**

**Hymn**

*(Congregation standing)*

**Reading Together:**

Let us adore the ever-living God, and render praise unto Him who spread out the heavens and established the earth, whose glory is revealed in the heavens above and whose greatness is manifest throughout the world. He is our God; there is none else.

We bow the head and bend the knee and magnify the King of kings, the Holy One, praised be He.

S. Sulzer

*mf* Andante

Va - a - nach-nu    ko - r'-eem    u-mish - ta - cha-veem u - mo-deem

lif-nay Me - lech    mal-chay ham - lo-cheem    ha - ko-dosh    bo-ruch hu.

*(Congregation seated)*

**Reader:**

Before we return to our homes, we lift up our hearts to Thee, O King and Father. We pray unto Thee to be with us as Thou wast with our fathers. Give us of Thy spirit; lead us and guide us. Make us know that when we seek Thee, we shall find Thee. May we come to know Thee as Thou dost dwell in our hearts and in the hearts of our fellow men. Implant righteousness in our souls. Show us the path of goodness, that we may follow it with clearer vision and firmer step. Teach us to love our neighbor as ourselves, and to be holy as Thou art holy. Grant that we may ever grow in knowledge and in wisdom, in reverence and in love.

May Israel's past be to us as a book in which we love to read, and from which we may learn noble lessons. May the law which guided our forefathers' footsteps direct us, too. May their spirit live within us. On this holy festival we dedicate ourselves to truth, to justice, and to mercy, which are Thy revelation to man. Amen.

**Hymn**

**Benediction**

# FOR TABERNACLES

**Reader:**

Our God and God of our fathers, on this day of Thy festival we rejoice to come into Thy presence, and to give thanks unto Thee for the bounty with which Thou hast blessed field, orchard, and vineyard. In this season of the year, our fathers built their booths and dwelt in them. Within our cities we lift grateful hearts unto Thee. Thou art the Creator of the world, the Giver of all good. Thou hast sent the rain in its season, and poured out Thy light upon the earth. Since the coming of the spring, the fields have been green with living plants and gay with flowers. Out of the flowers have come the fruit, out of the grasses, the grain. Summer and autumn have followed upon the footsteps of the spring, and the harvest time is here. Let all the children of men praise Thee, O God, for Thy wonderful goodness to all. Cause us, O Father, to cherish the heritage of Thy holy festival, and grant that all Israel, who sanctify Thy name, may rejoice thereon with songs and words of thanksgiving. Blessed art Thou, O Lord our God, who sanctifiest Israel and the festivals. Amen.

**Reader:**

Praise ye the Lord, to whom all praise is due.
Bor'-chu es A-do-noy ha-m'-voroch.

**Congregation:**

Praised be the Lord to whom all praise is due forever and ever.

**All Singing:**

S. Sulzer

Bo - ruch A - do - noy ha - m' vo - roch l'o - lom vo - ed.

499

**Responsive Reading:**

Blessed art Thou, O Lord our God, King of the universe, who hast created the world according to Thy will.

Blessed art Thou, O Lord our God, King of the universe, who commanded, "Let there be light!" and there was light.

Blessed art Thou, O Lord our God, King of the universe, who caused the dry land to appear, and life to grow in the waters and upon the earth.

Blessed art Thou, O Lord our God, King of the universe, who didst make the round of summer and winter, of spring and autumn.

Blessed art Thou, O Lord our God, King of the universe, who dost clothe the earth with life, as with a coat of many colors.

Blessed art Thou, O Lord our God, King of the universe, who waterest the ridges of the earth, making it soft with showers.

Blessed art Thou, O Lord our God, King of the universe, who hast blessed the growth thereof, and crowned the year with Thy goodness.

Blessed art Thou, O Lord our God, King of the universe, who hast clothed the meadows with flocks and covered the valleys with corn.

Blessed art Thou, O Lord our God, King of the universe, who providest for all our wants, in Thy goodness and mercy.

Blessed art Thou, O Lord our God, King of the universe, who hast granted us life, sustained us, and permitted us to celebrate this holy festival.

*(Congregation standing)*

**Reader:**

Hear, O Israel: The Lord our God, the Lord is One.
Sh'ma Yis-ro-ayl A-do-noy E-lo-hay-nu, A-do-noy e-chod.

**All Singing:**

Sh'ma Yïs-ro-ayl A-do-noy E-lo-hay-nu A-do-noy e-chod.

**Reader:**

Praised be His name whose glorious kingdom is forever and ever.
Bo-ruch shaym k'-vod mal-chu-so l'-o-lom vo-ed.

**All Singing:**

*(Congregation seated)*

**Responsive Reading (selected from I Chronicles xvi):**

**Reader:**

O give thanks unto the Lord, call upon His name; make known His
doings among the peoples.

**Congregation:**

Sing unto Him, sing praises unto Him; speak ye of all His marvelous
works.
Glory ye in His holy name; let the heart of them rejoice that seek the Lord.
Seek ye the Lord and His strength; seek His face continually.
Sing unto the Lord, all the earth; proclaim His salvation from day to day.
Declare His glory among the nations, His marvelous works among all
the peoples.
Honor and majesty are before Him; strength and gladness are in His place.
Let the heavens be glad, and let the earth rejoice; and let them say
among the nations: "The Lord reigneth."
Let the sea roar, and the fulness thereof; let the fields exult, and all that is
therein.
Then shall the trees of the wood sing for joy, before the Lord, for He
is come to judge the earth.
O give thanks unto the Lord; for He is good; for His mercy endureth
forever.

**All Singing:**

Ho - du la - do - noy kee - tov kee l' - o - lom chas - do.

**Reader:**

Though our mouths were filled with song as is the sea, and hymns were upon our tongues as is the number of its waves, we could not sing praises enough unto Thee, O God. Though our eyes were bright as the sun and moon, our hands outspread like the eagle's wings, and our feet swift as the deer's, we would still be unable to thank Thee enough, O Lord our God, for all the bounties Thou hast showered upon us and upon our fathers. Thou, O Lord our God, didst redeem us from Egypt, and didst release us from the house of bondage. Thy tender mercy has supported us, and Thy kindness has not forsaken us. Therefore every mouth shall adore Thee; every tongue shall praise Thee; and every knee shall bend before Thee. Blessed art Thou, O Lord and King, great and adored in praises, the God of thanksgiving, the Lord of wonders. Amen.

**Together:**

Who is like unto Thee, O God, among the mighty? Who is like unto Thee, glorious in holiness, extolled in praises, working wonders?

**All Singing:**

Mee cho mo - cho bo - ay leem A - do - - - - - noy,

502

mee ko - mo - cho ne - e - dor ba - ko - desh,

no - ro s'hil - los o - - - say . . . . fe - lay?

**Reader:**

Mal-chu-s'cho ro-u vo-ne-cho: ze Ayli o-nu v'-om'ru:
When Thy children beheld Thy sovereign power, they exclaimed: This
is my God; and they said:

**Together:**

The Lord shall reign forever and ever.

Ado - noy yim - loch l'o - lom vo - - ed.

# READING OF SCRIPTURE

**Reader:**

As Thou dost reveal Thyself in the power and beauty of the outer world, so dost Thou reveal Thyself in the world within. In the spirits of men Thou sowest Thy seeds of vision and of truth. Through generations and through centuries they sprout and grow, thrusting their way at last into the light, and bearing divine blossoms of wisdom and justice. So do we honor the Torah, the noblest flower upon the stem of Israel's past. We thank Thee for its words of inspiration and insight, for its laws of righteousness and goodness.

*(Congregation standing)*

**All Singing:**

G. Froelich

*Maestoso*

S'u sh'o - reem ro - shay - - - chem . . . u - s'-

u pis-chay o - lom, v' yo - vo me - lech hak - ko - vod, hak-

SOLI

ko - vod. Mee hu zeh me - lech, hak - ko - - vod;

*f* ALL

*rit.*

A - do - noy . . . ts'vo - os; . . . hu me - lech ha - ko - vod, se - lo.

**Reader:**

Happy are they who are upright in the way, who walk in the law of the Lord.

**Together:**

Hear, O Israel: The Lord our God, the Lord is One.
Sh'ma Yis-ro-ayl A-do-noy E-lo-hay-nu, A-do-noy e-chod.

**All Singing:**

Traditional

*f  Andante Maestoso*

Sh'ma Yis-ro-ayl A-do-noy E-lo-hay - nu A-do-noy e-chod.

Alois Kaiser

*f  Allegro maestoso*

L'-cho A-do-noy hag'-dul-lo v'hag-'vu-ro, . . . v'-hat-tif-

e - res v'han-ne-tsach v'ha-hod. Kee-chol bash-sho-ma-yim

u - vo - o - rets. L' - cho A - do - noy ham -

mam - lo - cho V'-ham - mis - nas - say... l'-chol l' - rosh.

*(Congregation seated)*

## Scriptural Reading (from Leviticus xxiii, 33–44)

RETURNING THE SCROLL

*(Congregation standing)*

**Reader:**

O magnify the Lord with me and let us exalt His name together.

(The Scroll is replaced in the Ark)

**Reader:**

It is a tree of life to them that lay hold of it, and the supporters thereof are happy. Its ways are ways of pleasantness and all its paths are peace.

**All Singing:**

S. Sulzer

Aytz cha-yeem hee la - ma-cha-zee-keem bo v' - som - che - ho v'-

506

som'-che-ho m'-u-shor, d'ro-che-ho dar-chay no-am

dar-chay no-am v'-chol n'-see-vo-se-ho sho-lom.

*(Congregation seated)*

Four children ascend the platform, each carrying one of the emblems of Succos.

### First Child, carrying Lulav:

This is the Lulav, a branch of the stately palm. It still sleeps enfolded, waiting for the sun of spring to wake it to life. It stands for pride in the history of Israel, in its staunch loyalty to faith in God.

### Second Child, carrying Hadassah:

This is the Hadassah, the myrtle, that bends in beauty toward the earth. It stands for the loveliness of a good heart, for the glory of a pure spirit.

### Third Child, carrying Arovoh:

This is the Arovoh, the willow, that droops beside the watercourses, bowing low as in sorrow. It stands for the myriads of the humble, who have lived and died upon earth, who have worshiped the God of Israel and obeyed His law, and whose memory is blessed.

### Fourth Child, carrying Esrog:

This is the Esrog, the fruit of a tree with lustrous leaves. It sheds sweet perfume on all who are near. Even so does the man in whose heart God dwells, bring goodness and light to the souls of those who know him.

The children bearing the four emblems march around the hall (Hakofoh) while the remainder of the children unite in singing one of the Succos Hymns, Nos. 180–188.

**Sermon**

**Hymn**

*(Congregation standing)*

**Reading Together:**

Let us adore the ever-living God, and render praise unto Him who spread out the heavens and established the earth, whose glory is revealed in the heavens above and whose greatness is manifest throughout the world. He is our God; there is none else.

We bow the head and bend the knee and magnify the King of kings, the Holy One, praised be He.

**All Singing:**

S. Sulzer

*mf Andante*

Va - a - nach-nu ko - r'-eem u-mish - ta - cha-veem u - mo-deem

lif - nay Me - lech mal-chay ham - lo-cheem ha - ko-dosh bo-ruch hu.

*(Congregation seated)*

**Reader:**

At the close of our service, we turn to Thee, O heavenly Father, imploring Thy continued blessing during the year. May the spirit of these holy days abide within our hearts. May we learn from them how to seek Thee and find Thee in the world within, and in the world without. Teach us how to draw ever nearer to Thee by the threefold pathway of truth, of beauty, and of goodness. Grant that the bountiful harvest Thou hast sent may be a harbinger of peace and plenty, that the earth may give her increase, so that there shall be no want nor scarcity among the sons of men. Even as we may behold the stars shining through the leaves and vines upon the Succah, so may we behold Thee in the beauty and the orderliness of Thy world.

Thine, O Lord, are the greatness and the power, the glory, and the victory, and the majesty; for all that is in the heaven and in the earth is Thine; Thine is the kingdom, O Lord, and Thou art exalted over all.

**Hymn**

**Benediction**

# FOR NEW YEAR

My heavenly Father, with solemn feelings I have come into Thy house to give praise unto Thee on this New Year Day. Though I have not traveled far nor long upon life's roadway, yet may this day remind me that in Thy wisdom Thou hast put a limit to the journey of our human life, and that, having passed another span of it, I am nearer to that limit. May it be Thy sovereign will that this New Year, which we are welcoming, be one of many that in Thy goodness may be granted unto me. But whether this be Thy decree or whether my years be fewer than I hope, may I be enabled by Thy grace to make noble use of the time that is given me, and to render my life worthy of all Thy loving-kindness.

Grant, O God, that this newborn year may be a joyous one for my beloved parents and dear ones, and that I may help to make it such. Do Thou give me strength to keep this growing life of mine free from sin and wrong at home or at school, in study or play, alone or in company with my school and playfellows. May I have no fear but the fear of offending Thee. May my heart be filled only with affection for my dear ones, with friendliness toward my fellow man, and with loving gratitude to Thee, so that there be in it no room for hatred or prejudice or envious complaining. Amen.

**Hymn No. 156, 157 or 161**

**Responsive Reading (Psalm cxlv):**

I will extol Thee, my God, O King; and I will bless Thy name forever and ever.

Every day will I bless Thee; and I will praise Thy name forever and ever.
Great is the Lord, and highly to be praised; His greatness is unsearchable.
One generation shall praise Thy works to another, and shall declare Thy mighty acts.

The glorious splendor of Thy majesty, and Thy wondrous works, will I rehearse.

And men shall speak of the might of Thy acts; and I will tell of Thy greatness.
They shall utter the fame of Thy great goodness, and shall sing of Thy righteousness.

The Lord is gracious, and full of compassion; slow to anger and of great mercy.

The Lord is good to all; and His tender mercies are over all His works.
All Thy works shall praise Thee, O Lord; and Thy saints shall bless Thee.

They shall speak of the glory of Thy kingdom, and talk of Thy might;
To make known to the sons of men His mighty acts, and the glory
of His majestic kingdom.
Thy kingdom is a kingdom for all ages, and Thy dominion endureth
throughout all generations.
The Lord upholdeth all that fall, and raiseth up all those that are
bowed down.
The eyes of all wait upon Thee, and Thou givest them their food in due
season.
Thou openest Thy hand, and satisfiest every living thing with favor.
The Lord is righteous in all His ways, and gracious in all His works.
The Lord is nigh unto all them that call upon Him, to all that call
upon Him in truth.
He will fulfill the desire of them that revere Him; He will hear their cry,
and save them.
The Lord preserveth all them that love Him; but all the wicked shall
be defeated.
My mouth shall speak the praise of the Lord.
And let all flesh bless His holy name forever and ever.  Amen.

**Reader:**

Praise ye the Lord, to whom all praise is due.
Bor-chu es A-do-noy ha-m'-voroch.

**Congregation:**

Praised be the Lord, to whom all praise is due forever and ever.

**All Singing:**

S. Sulzer

Bo - ruch A - do - noy  ha - m' vo - roch  l'o - lom  vo - ed.

**Reader:**

Praised be Thou, O Lord of the universe, by whose will the light of day
and the darkness of night are the ordered way of the world.  In mercy
Thou renewest day after day, the wonders of Thy creative power.  The
heavens declare the wisdom of Thy works, and the earth showeth Thy glory.

With great love hast Thou loved us, O our God, and exceeding compassion hast Thou showered upon us. As our fathers believed in Thee and accepted the Law which Thou gavest them, so may we revere Thy name and obey Thy Law. May our hearts cling to Thy Torah and our souls be filled with loving faith in Thee. With serene trust we rejoice in Thy salvation, and seek Thy help in the fulfillment of the sacred task Thou hast entrusted to us. May we do so in love, even as Thou hast chosen us in love.

*(Congregation standing)*

**Reader:**

Hear, O Israel: The Lord our God, the Lord is One.
Sh'ma Yis-ro-ayl A-do-noy E-lo-hay-nu, A-do-noy e-chod.

**All Singing:**

**Reader:**

Praised be His name whose glorious kingdom is forever and ever.
Bo-ruch shaym k'-vod mal-chu-so l'o-lom vo-ed.

**All Singing:**

*(Congregation seated)*

512

## Responsive Reading:

Thou shalt love the Lord thy God with all thy heart, with all thy soul
and with all thy might.
And these words which I command thee shall be upon thy heart.
Thou shalt teach them diligently to thy children.
Thou shalt speak of them when thou sittest in thy house, and when
thou walkest by the way;
When thou liest down and when thou risest up.
Thou shalt bind them for a sign upon thy hand and as frontlets between
thine eyes.
Thou shalt write them upon the doorposts of thy house and upon thy gates.
To the end that ye may remember and do all this commandment and
be holy unto your God.

## Reader:

Who is like Thee among the mighty, O God? Who is like unto Thee, glorified
in holiness, wondrous in praises?

## All Singing:

L. Lewandowski

Mee cho - mo - cho bo - ay - leem A - do - noy;

mee ko - mo - cho ne-e - dor — ba - ko - - - - desh

no - ro s'hil - los, o - say fe - - - lay?

**Reader:**

The Lord reigneth forever and ever.

**All Singing:**

A - do - noy yim - loch l'o - lom vo - - - ed.

**Reader:**

Our God and God of our fathers! Thou art supreme in all goodness and love. Thou dealest in kindness with all Thy creatures; Thou rememberest the virtues of the fathers, Thou redeemest their children in the fullness of Thy mercy. O remember us to life, Thou God of life, who art our helper and our shield, as Thou wast the shield of Abraham.

Thou art all-powerful to save, and in Thy loving-kindness Thou sustainest the living, Thou healest the sick; Thou settest the captive free, Thou fulfillest Thy promise of immortal life to those who sleep in the dust.

Praised be Thou, Father of mercy, who hast given unto us of Thine own eternal being. Amen.

Our God and God of our fathers! Let Thy presence be manifest to us in all Thy works, so that reverence for Thee may be in the hearts of all Thy creatures. May the children of men worship Thee with humble hearts, united in the desire to do Thy will and to proclaim that Thine alone are all power, dominion, and majesty.

Grant courage to Thy people that they may serve Thee with honor, hope and peace to all who seek to do Thy will, and joy and gladness to those who bear witness to the truth of Thy unity. May the righteous see and rejoice, and the just and the good sing aloud for joy, when falsehood shall be silenced in shame, and wickedness vanish like smoke and the reign of evil shall have passed away from all the earth, and Thou alone shalt rule in the hearts of men.

Then shall Thy kingdom be established and the nations be united in peace and brotherhood, and in joyous obedience to Thy word every living thing shall know that Thou art God, and Thy dominion is for all eternity. Amen.

### SANCTIFICATION

#### (K'DUSHAH)

*(Congregation standing)*

**Reader:**

Holy, holy, holy is the Lord of hosts; the whole earth is full of His glory.

**All Singing:**

S. Sulzer

Ko - dosh   ko - dosh   ko - dosh   A - do - noy   ts' - vo - os   m'lo   chol   ho - o - retz   k'-vo - - - do.

**Reader:**

In all places of Thy dominion, Thy name is praised and glorified.

**All Singing:**

S. Sulzer

Bo - ruch k' - vod A - do - noy mi - m' - ko - mo.

**Reader:**

The Lord will reign forever, thy God, O Zion, from generation to generation. Hallelujah.

**All Singing:**

S. Sulzer

*Moderato*

Yim - loch A - do - noy l' - o - lom E - lo - ha - yich Tsee - yon l' - dor vo - dor ha - l' - lu - yo.

*(Congregation seated)*

516

**Responsive Reading (Psalm xix):**

The heavens declare the glory of God, and the firmament showeth His
handiwork;
Day unto day uttereth speech, and night unto night showeth knowledge;
There is no speech nor language; their voice cannot be heard.
Yet their sound goeth forth to all the earth; and their words to the
end of the world.
The law of the Lord is perfect, restoring the soul:
The testimony of the Lord is sure, making wise the simple.
The precepts of the Lord are right, rejoicing the heart:
The commandment of the Lord is pure, enlightening the eyes.
The fear of the Lord is clean, enduring forever:
The judgments of the Lord are true, and righteous altogether.
More to be desired are they than gold, yea, than much fine gold;
Sweeter also than honey and the honeycomb.
Moreover by them is thy servant warned;
In keeping of them, there is great reward.
Who can discern his errors?
Clear thou me from hidden faults.
Keep thy servant also from presumptuous sins;
Let them not have dominion over me; then shall I be faultless,
And I shall be clear from great transgression.
May the words of my mouth and the meditation of my heart be accept-
able in Thy sight, O Lord, my Rock, and my Redeemer!

**Hymn**

**Meditation (to be read in unison):**

A year has gone. What it has taken with it can never be recovered. A
page in the book of life has been turned over, and it cannot be turned back
again, no matter how much we might wish and strive to do so. We look
back on the things that we did and the things that we said, and no doubt
for many of them we feel deep regret. But we cannot unsay them or undo
them. They remain for all time.

Yet the value of looking backward is to help one rightly to look forward.
The way to treat the mistakes of the past is not merely to sorrow for them,
but to correct them in the future. The leaf that has been turned for the
old year uncovers a clean page for the new year that is coming. The message of this hour is to begin this new year rightly, to inscribe upon that
clean page the record of only clean thoughts and clean acts. Let there be
in all our hearts a resolution for noble purpose and fine conduct. Mere
length of life does not mean nearly as much as the manner of living.

If I would live rightly, I must strive to make myself worthy of the privilege of living. I must strive to have each succeeding day find me seeking

to help my fellow man, and to make the world better for my having lived in it.  I must try to deal justly, to do the right, and to tell the truth.  I must try to fight against wrong and sin and lies and dishonesty, to be a true follower of the law of the God of Israel, and by my conduct declaring it to the world around me.

O my God and Father, help me in this effort, grant me strength and courage to do Thy will this coming year.  Amen.

## READING OF SCRIPTURE

**Reader (Psalm xxiv):**

Who shall ascend into the mountain of the Lord and who shall stand in His holy place?  He that hath clean hands, and a pure heart; who hath not taken My name in vain, and hath not sworn deceitfully.  He shall receive a blessing from the Lord, and righteousness from the God of his salvation.  Such is the generation of them that seek Thee; that seek Thy presence, O God of Jacob.

**All Singing:**

G. Froelich

*Maestoso*

S'u sh'o - reem ro - shay - - - chem . . . u - s' - u pis-chay o - lom, v' yo - vo me - lech hak - ko - vod, hak - ko - vod.  Mee hu zeh me - lech, hak - ko - - - vod;

A - do - noy ... ts'vo - os; ... hu me - lech ha - ko - vod, se - lo.

*(Congregation rises)*

**Reader (facing the Ark):**

The Lord, the Lord God is merciful and gracious, long-suffering and abundant in goodness and ever true; keeping mercy for thousands, forgiving iniquity, transgression and sin.

**All Singing:**

Response No. 313

**Reader, then Congregation:**

Our Father, our King, we have sinned before Thee.
Our Father, our King, we have no King but Thee.
Our Father, our King, grant unto us a year of happiness.
Our Father, our King, keep far from our country pestilence, war, and famine.
Our Father, our King, inscribe us for blessing in the book of life.
Our Father, our King, pardon and blot out our sins.
Our Father, our King, accept graciously our petitions.
Our Father, our King, be merciful and answer us; though we can plead no merit, deal with us according to Thy loving-kindness and help us. Amen.

Taking the scroll from the Ark

**Reader:**

Happy are they who are upright in the way; who walk in the Law of the Lord.
Hear, O Israel: The Lord our God, the Lord is One.

**Together:**

Sh'ma Yis-ro-ayl A-do-noy E-lo-hay-nu, A-do-noy e-chod.

(Alternative response, number 314)

Traditional

*f Andante Maestoso*

Sh'ma Yis - ro - ayl A - do - noy E - lo - hay - nu A - do - noy e - chod.

*f Allegro maestoso*

Alois Kaiser

L' - cho A - do - noy hag' - dul - lo v'hag - 'vu - ro, . . . v' - hat - tif -

e - res v'han - ne - tsach v'ha - hod. Kee - chol bash - sho - ma - yim

u - vo - o - rets. L' - cho A - do - noy ham -

mam - lo - cho ... V'-ham - mis - nas - say... l' - chol l' - rosh.

*(Congregation is seated)*

**Scriptural Reading from Genesis XXII:1–19**

## SHOFAR SERVICE

**Reader:**

O Lord, God of all the universe, Thou art beyond all measurements of time. A thousand years are in Thy sight but as yesterday which is gone, as a watch in the night when the morning has come. Before the mountains were born or Thou hadst formed the earth and the world, from everlasting to everlasting Thou art God. Compared to Thee our life is but as the fraction of the fraction of a moment. It is less than the lightning's fleeting flash across the heavens. Yet art Thou merciful to Thy human children for Thou knowest our weaknesses and our shortcomings. Therefore dost Thou invite us to Thy house on this New Year's Day, that we may be reminded that even that short span has been made the shorter by the passage of a year. With the solemn sounds of the Shofar, is this lesson brought home to us. It is as a trumpet of the heart, arousing us to the duties of life. It is as a voice calling Thy children to Thee in prayer and penitence. O may these sounds of the Shofar awaken in us the resolution for finer, truer life and nobler conduct. And do Thou grant us strength to carry out this resolution.

Praised be Thou, O King of the universe, who hast kept us alive, preserved us and permitted us to see this day.

The Shofar is sounded thrice. See Music Nos. 315, 316, 317

**Responsive Reading:**

Shout unto the Lord, all the earth, break forth and sing for joy, yea, sing praises.
With trumpets and the sound of the Shofar, cry aloud before the King, the Lord.

Exalted is God amidst the sound; the Lord amidst the sound of the Shofar.
Happy is the people that know the joyful sound; they walk, O Lord,
in the light of Thy countenance.
In Thy name do they rejoice all the day; and through Thy righteousness
are they exalted.
For Thou art the glory of their strength; and in Thy favor our horn
is exalted.
For the Lord is our shield, and the Holy One of Israel is our King.
All ye inhabitants of the world and ye dwellers on the earth, when the
Shofar is blown, hear ye.
Come ye and worship the Lord in His holy temple.

### Returning the Scroll to the Ark

*(Congregation rises)*

**Reader:**

O magnify the Lord with me and let us exalt His name together.

**All Singing:**

S. Sulzer

Ho - do al e - rets v' - sho - mo - yim Va - yo - rem

ke - ren l'am - - mo. T' - hil - loh l' - chol ... cha -

see - - - dov, Li - v' - nay Yis - ro - ayl am k' - ro -

vo. Ha - l' - lu - yo, ha - l' - lu - yo.

**Reader:**

The law of the Lord is perfect, restoring the soul; the testimony of the Lord is sure, making wise the simple. The precepts of the Lord are right, rejoicing the heart; the fear of the Lord is pure, enduring forever. Behold, a good doctrine has been given unto you; forsake it not. .

**All Singing:**

S. Sulzer

Aytz cha-yeem hee la-ma-cha-zee-keem bo v' - som - che - ho v'-

som'-che - ho m' - u - shor, d'ro - che - ho dar-chay no - am

dar - chay no - am    v'-chol n'-see - vo - se - ho  sho - lom.

*(Congregation is seated)*

**Hymn**

**Sermon**

**Hymn**

## ADORATION

*(Congregation rises)*

**Reader and Congregation:**

It is our duty to give praise to the great Creator of all things, whose will and whose wisdom are revealed in the heavens and the earth and the wonders of all the worlds. He is the supreme Soul of the universe, and to Him, praised be He, we bow the head and bend the knee and ascribe all glory and greatness.

**All Singing:**

S. Sulzer

Va - a - nach-nu   ko - r'-eem   u-mish - ta - cha-veem u - mo-deem

524

lif - nay Me - lech    mal-chay ham - lo-cheem    ha - ko-dosh    bo-ruch    hu.

*(Congregation seated)*

May the day soon come when Thy kingdom of righteousness will prevail over all the earth, when selfishness and bigotry will vanish from the minds of men, when tyranny and oppression will cease, and all the families of the earth will recognize the brotherhood of their common humanity.  Then shall justice flow as a mighty stream and righteousness as a river of many waters, to enrich the fields of human endeavor and give gladness to the lives of men.  Then shall Thy presence be in the hearts of men, and Thy law shall lead them forever and ever.  Amen.

**Hymn: Ayn Kay-lo-hay-nu** (No. 275 or 292)

**Responsive Reading (Psalm viii):**

Eternal God, our Lord! How excellent is Thy name in all the earth!
Thou who hast set Thy glory above the heavens.
When I consider the heavens, the work of Thy fingers, the moon and
the stars which Thou hast ordained:
What is man that Thou art mindful of him, and the son of man that
Thou carest for him?
Yet Thou hast made him a little less than divine, and hast crowned him
with glory and honor.
Thou hast given him dominion over the works of Thy hands; Thou
hast put all things under his feet:
All sheep and oxen; yea, and the beast of the fields;
The fowl of the air and the fish of the sea, whatsoever passeth through
the paths of the seas.

**Together:**

Eternal God, our Lord, how excellent is Thy name in all the earth!

**Prayer (Together):**

Almighty and most merciful God, in whose hands are the souls of all
the living, it is with humble and contrite hearts that we have come into
Thy house on this most sacred day. In loving-kindness Thou guidest and
governest all things. All worlds and all that is therein, from the tiniest
pebble on the ground to the mightiest stars that people the heavens, are
under the guidance of Thine infinite wisdom. In that wisdom, too, Thou
hast placed man as the chief among all Thy creatures, and given to him
the light of reason and understanding. Thou hast made known to him
the paths of good and evil, and hast also given to him freedom of will.
Thou hast shown him the way of righteousness, and the way that is pleasing
unto Thee, and accorded him the privilege of choice of action in the conduct
of his life.

Too often does man prove unworthy of Thy love and kindness. Led by his base desires and his selfishness, he strays from the paths of honesty and truthfulness. Yielding in the weakness of will to the strength of temptation, he disobeys Thy law and neglects Thy word.

Yet in great mercy, Thou dost give him the chance to correct his mistakes, to come back from his strayings unto Thy pathways again, for Thou hast compassion upon our weaknesses. Thou art our Maker and Thou knowest our frame. Thou sendest to us this Day of Atonement and Reconciliation to make us recognize our sins, to confess and repent them. As a father calleth his children from the outer darkness into the light of home, so dost Thou on this day call us into Thy house. We are indeed Thy children, and in penitence we come on this holy day humbly to seek shelter under the shadow of the wings of Thy mercy, and to find comfort in the embrace of Thy love. Grant, O God, that by our confession, our prayer and penitence, we may truly find ourselves at one with Thee and feel Thy presence within our hearts. May we learn to know this day as a wonderful friend, the messenger of Thy benign mercy and Thine all-unfolding love. Amen.

**Responsive Reading (Psalm I):**

Happy is the man who walketh not in the counsel of the wicked,
Nor standeth in the way of sinners, nor sitteth in the seat of scoffers;
But whose delight is in the law of the Lord; and in His law he meditateth day and night.
He shall be like a tree planted by the streams of water, that bringeth forth its fruit in its season,
Whose leaf also doth not wither: and all that he doeth shall prosper.
Not so the wicked; but they are like the chaff which the wind driveth away.
Therefore the wicked shall not stand in judgment, nor sinners in the congregation of the righteous.
For the Lord knoweth the way of the righteous; but the way of the wicked leadeth to ruin.

**Reader:**

Praise ye the Lord, to whom all praise is due.
Bor'-chu es A-do-noy ha-m'-voroch.

**Congregation:**

Praised be the Lord to whom all praise is due forever and ever.

S. Sulzer

*f Andante*

Bo - ruch A - do - noy ha - m' vo - roch l'o - lom vo - ed.

Praised be Thou, O Lord of the universe, by whose will the light of day and the darkness of night are the ordered way of the world. In mercy Thou renewest day after day the wonders of Thy creative power. The heavens declare the wisdom of Thy works, and the earth showeth Thy glory.

With great love hast Thou loved us, O our God, and exceeding compassion hast Thou showered upon us. As our fathers believed in Thee and accepted the Law which Thou gavest them, so may we revere Thy name and obey Thy Law. May our hearts cling to Thy Torah and our souls be filled with loving faith in Thee. With serene trust we rejoice in Thy salvation, and seek Thy help in the fulfillment of the sacred task Thou hast intrusted to us. May we do so in love, even as Thou hast chosen us in love.

*(Congregation standing)*

**Reader:**

Hear, O Israel: The Lord our God, the Lord is One.
Sh'ma Yis-ro-ayl A-do-noy E-lo-hay-nu, A-do-noy e-chod.

**All Singing:**

Traditional

*f Andante Maestoso*

Sh'ma Yis-ro - ayl A - do - noy E - lo - hay - nu A - do - noy e - chod.

528

**Reader:**

Praised be His name whose glorious kingdom is forever and ever.
Bo-ruch shaym k'-vod mal-chu-so l'-o-lom vo-ed.

**All Singing:**

*(Congregation seated)*

**Responsive Reading:**

Thou shalt love the Lord thy God, with all thy heart, with all thy soul
and with all thy might.
And these words which I command thee this day, shall be upon thy
heart.
Thou shalt teach them diligently to thy children.
Thou shalt speak of them when thou sittest in thy house, and when
thou walkest by the way;
When thou liest down and when thou risest up.
Thou shalt bind them for a sign upon thy hand and as frontlets between
thine eyes.
Thou shalt write them upon the doorposts of thy house and upon thy gates.
To the end that ye may remember and do all this commandment, and
be holy unto your God.

**Reader:**

Who is like unto Thee, O God, among the mighty?   Who is like unto
Thee, glorious in holiness, extolled in praises, working wonders?

**All Singing:**

L. Lewandowski

Mee cho - mo - cho bo - ay - leem A - do - noy;

mee ko - mo - cho ne-e - dor — ba - ko - - - - desh

no - ro s'hil - los, o - say fe - - - lay?

**Reader:**

The Lord reigneth forever and ever.

**All Singing:**

A - do - noy yim - loch l'o - lom vo - - - ed.

**Reader:**

O our God, and God of our fathers, Thou art supreme in all goodness and love. Thou dealest in kindness with all Thy creatures; Thou rememberest the virtues of the fathers; Thou redeemest their children in the full-

530

ness of Thy mercy. O remember us to life, Thou God of Life, who art our helper and our shield, as Thou wast the shield of Abraham.

Thou art all-powerful to save, and in Thy loving-kindness Thou sustainest the living; Thou healest the sick; Thou settest the captive free; Thou ful-fillest Thy promise of immortal life to those who sleep in the dust.

Praised be Thou, Father of mercy, who hast given unto us of Thine own eternal being. Amen.

## SANCTIFICATION
### (K'DUSHAH)

*(Congregation standing)*

**Reader:**

Holy, holy, holy is the Lord of hosts; the whole earth is full of His glory.

**All Singing:**

S. Sulzer

Ko - dosh ko - dosh ko - dosh A - do - noy ts' - vo - os m'lo chol ho - o - retz k'-vo - - - do.

**Reader:**

In all places of Thy dominion, Thy name is praised and glorified.

531

All Singing:

S. Sulzer

Bo - ruch k' - vod A - do - noy mi - m' - ko - mo.

**Reader:**

The Lord will reign forever, Thy God, O Zion, from generation to generation.   Hallelujah!

All Singing:

S. Sulzer

*Moderato*

Yim - loch A - do - noy l' - o - lom E - lo - ha - yich Tsee -

yon l' - dor vo - dor · ha - l' - lu - yo.

*(Congregation seated)*

532

**Reader:**

Our God and God of our fathers, let Thy presence be manifest to us in all Thy works, so that reverence for Thee may be in the hearts of all Thy creatures. May the children of men worship Thee with humble hearts, united in the desire to do Thy will and to proclaim that Thine alone are all power, dominion, and majesty.

Grant courage to Thy people that they may serve Thee with honor, hope and peace to all who seek to do Thy will, and joy and gladness to those who bear witness to the truth of Thy unity. May the righteous see and rejoice, and the just and the good sing aloud for joy, when falsehood shall be silenced in shame, and wickedness vanish like smoke and the reign of evil shall have passed away from all the earth, and Thou alone shalt rule in the hearts of men.

Then shall Thy kingdom be established and the nations be united in peace and brotherhood, and in joyous obedience to Thy word every living thing shall know that Thou art God, and Thy dominion is for all eternity. Amen.

**Hymn**

*Silent Devotion*

**Confession and Prayer:**

Heavenly Father, in Thy house, on this sacred day of Atonement, I am filled with shame as the sense of my sinfulness comes strongly to me. I am conscious of the wrong things that I have done, of disobedience to my dear parents, of the selfish and ugly acts of which I have been guilty in my conduct at home and at school and among my friends. I recall with sorrow the hurt that I gave to others, and the evil that I did in both words and acts. I realize now, in humiliation, that in all these things wherein I sinned against others, I sinned against Thee also, and was forgetful of Thy law. But Thou art most merciful, O my Father, for Thou dost provide this day for me, that I may come to Thee in penitence and seek forgiveness. Thou sendest the assurance of Thy compassion, and I turn to Thee in earnest prayer, that I may receive Thy forgiveness, that Thou wilt pardon my sins. May I be brave enough to seek out those whom I have wronged and make peace with them. May my heart be made clean from hate and envy and greed and all things evil. May I be strengthened to live a better life, and be more truly a devoted child of Israel, Thy servant and a witness of Thy word. Amen.

## CONFESSION
### (VIDUI)

**Reader:**

O Lord our God, let our prayers come before Thee. Pardon our sins and forgive our transgressions. We are not so bold and stubborn as to say before Thee that we have always done right and have not sinned. In truth we have sinned, we have done many evil things, we have turned aside from Thy path, we have neglected Thy law.

What shall we say before Thee who dwellest on high? Thou knowest all things, the hidden and the open. The secrets of all life are revealed to Thee and the most hidden thoughts of all the living are disclosed before Thee. Thine all-seeing eye searches the deepest recesses of our hearts.

May it be Thy will, O God our Father, to help us to turn ourselves from our wicked ways, to right the wrongs we have done, and to grant us pardon for our sins.

**Reader, then Congregation:**

For the sins which we have sinned against Thee willingly or unwillingly,

For the sins which we have sinned against Thee openly or secretly,

For the sins which we have sinned against Thee willfully or ignorantly,

For the sins which we have sinned against Thee by word of mouth or deed of hand,

For the sins which we have sinned against Thee in thought or in act,

For the sins which we have sinned against Thee by disrespect for parents and teachers, by false dealing with our fellowmen,

For all these sins, O God of pardon, pardon us; forgive us. Amen.

**Reader, then Congregation:**

We are Thy people, Thou art our King.

We are Thy children, Thou art our Father.

We are Thy possession, Thou art our Portion.

We are Thy flock, Thou art our Shepherd.

We are Thy vineyard, Thou art our Keeper.

We are Thy beloved, Thou art our Friend.

**Hymn No. 326**

## READING OF SCRIPTURE

**Reader (Psalm xxiv):**

Who shall ascend into the mountain of the Lord and who shall stand in His holy place? He that hath clean hands, and a pure heart; who hath not taken My name in vain, and hath not sworn deceitfully. He shall receive a blessing from the Lord, and righteousness from the God of his salvation. Such is the generation of them that seek Thee; that seek Thy presence, O God of Jacob.

*(Congregation standing)*

G. Froelich

Taking the Scroll from the Ark

**Reader:**

Happy are they who are upright in the way; who walk in the Law of the Lord.

**Together:**

Hear, O Israel: The Lord our God, the Lord is One.
Sh'ma Yis-ro-ayl A-do-noy E-lo-hay-nu, A-do-noy e-chod.

(Alternative response, number 314)

**All Singing:**

536

mam - lo - cho  V'-ham - mis - nas - say... l'-chol l' - rosh.

*(Congregation is seated)*

## Scriptural Reading (from Deuteronomy xxix, 9–14; xxx, 11–19; Haphtarah, Isaiah lviii, 1–8)

Returning the Scroll to the ark

*(Congregation standing)*

**Reader:**

O magnify the Lord with me and let us exalt His name together.

**All Singing:**

S. Sulzer

Ho - do al e - rets v'-sho - mo - yim Va - yo - rem

ke - ren l'am - mo. T'-hil - loh l' - chol... cha -

see - - - dov, Li - v'-nay Yis - ro - ayl am k' - ro -

537

vo. Ha - l' - lu - yo, ha - l' - lu - yo.

**Reader:**

The law of the Lord is perfect, restoring the soul; the testimony of the Lord is sure, making wise the simple. The precepts of the Lord are right, rejoicing the heart; the fear of the Lord is pure, enduring forever. Behold, a good doctrine has been given unto you; forsake it not.

**All Singing:**

S. Sulzer

Aytz cha-yeem hee la - ma-cha-zee-keem bo v' - som - che - ho v'-

som'-che - ho m' - u - shor, d'ro - che - ho dar-chay no - am

dar - chay no - am   v'-chol   n'-see - vo - se - ho   sho - lom.

*(Congregation seated)*

**Hymn**

**Sermon**

**Hymn**

### ADORATION

*(Congregation rises)*

**Reader and Congregation:**

It is our duty to give praise to the great Creator of all things, whose will and whose wisdom are revealed in the heavens and the earth and the wonders of all the worlds. He is the supreme Soul of the universe, and to Him, praised be He, we bow the head and bend the knee and ascribe all glory and greatness.

**All Singing:**

S. Sulzer

mf Andante

Va - a - nach-nu   ko - r'-eem   u-mish - ta - cha-veem u - mo-deem

lif - nay Me - lech mal-chay ham - lo-cheem ha - ko-dosh bo-ruch hu.

*(Congregation seated)*

May the day soon come when Thy kingdom of righteousness will prevail over all the earth, when selfishness and bigotry will vanish from the minds of men, when tyranny and oppression will cease, and all the families of the earth will recognize the brotherhood of their common humanity. Then shall justice flow as a mighty stream and righteousness as a river of many waters, to enrich the fields of human endeavor and give gladness to the lives of men. Then shall Thy presence be in the hearts of man, and Thy law shall lead them forever and ever. Amen.

**Hymn: Ayn Kay-lo-hay-nu (No. 275 or 292)**

# FOR PURIM OR CHANUKKOH

**Responsive Reading (Psalm cxiii):**

Hallelujah, praise, O ye servants of the Lord, praise the name of the Lord.
Blessed be the name of the Lord from this time forth and forever.
From the rising of the sun unto the going down thereof, the Lord's name
is praised.
The Lord is high above all nations, His glory is above the heavens.
Who is like the Lord our God, that is enthroned on high,
Who raiseth up the poor out of the dust, and lifteth up the needy from
his lowliness?
He maketh the forsaken to dwell in her house, a joyful mother of children.

**All Singing:**

Praise the Lord, all ye hosts, Hal - l' - lu - yah, A - men.

**Responsive Reading (Psalm cxviii):**

O give thanks unto the Lord for He is good, for His mercy endureth forever.
So let Israel now say, for His mercy endureth forever.
I called upon the Lord in distress; He heard and set me in a wide place.
The Lord is on my side, I will not fear; what can man do to me?
It is better to take refuge in the Lord than to trust in man.
It is better to take refuge in the Lord than to trust in princes.
I shall not die but live, and declare the works of the Lord.
This is the day which the Lord hath made; we will rejoice and be glad
in it.
O give thanks unto the Lord for He is good, for His mercy endureth
forever.

**All Singing:**

Adapted from Halevy's "Min Hamaytsar"

*Allegretto*

Let us with glad-some mind Praise the Lord for He is kind,
Ho - du la-do-noy kee-tov, kee l'o-lom chas - do

For His mer-cy shall en-dure Ev - er faith-ful ev - er sure.
Ho - du la-do-noy kee-tov, kee l'o - lom chas - do.

## FOR PURIM

**Reader and Congregation:**

Thou who guardest Israel in every peril, we remember now Thine aid in ancient days. When the wicked Haman made evil plans against us and sought to destroy the Israelites of Persia, how quickly came the help from Thee. Mordecai, wise and patient, Esther, beautiful and brave, arose to stand by the side of their people. With wisdom they planned and with courage they acted until Haman was punished and the danger removed from the people of Israel.

This day we pray to Thee, O Lord, who lovest peace, that all hatred among the children of men shall end forever. May no Hamans arise again. May no one ever try to arouse prejudice against any religion or race. Let all nations learn to recognize that they have the same Heavenly Father; and let the followers of all religions know that they are brothers.

Grant us a share of the courage of Esther and of the wisdom of Mordecai. May our hearts never harbor narrow prejudice. May we never mock any race, or scorn any nation. May we never hate anyone. With tolerant mind and friendly spirit, may we learn to be true children of the people of Israel, which has ever taught the hope that all men will be united in the worship of Thee. Amen.

(Or this prayer:)

On this day of joy, we adore Thee, Thou fount of joy. On this day which was for our fathers a day of merriment and laughter, we invoke Thy blessing on our own merriment and laughter. May it ever be a kindly laughter—laughing with others always, laughing at others never. Bless and sanctify all of our pleasures and enjoyments. Grant that they may be such as bring health and wholesomeness and never such as bring harm, shame, or ill. Bless the people who provide our pleasures—the musicians, actors, singers, performers, athletes, teachers, leaders and all who, with pure and thoughtful hearts, created and maintain worthy places of pleasure. May all of our enjoyments lead us nearer to Thee, O God, and none of them take us away from Thee. Comfort all who, because their hearts are heavy, cannot share our merriment. Deliver them from their sorrows. Speedily turn their mourning into joy, gladness and feasting.

Banish from our hearts all pride and arrogance lest we become, like Haman, proud and arrogant. Fill our souls with the beauty and the loyalty of an Esther, with the wisdom and devotion of a Mordecai. And may Thy name, O God, unwritten in that ancient story, be written on our hearts in letters of devotion, consecration, and love. Amen.

## Hymn No. 13 or No. 33 (Psalm 121)

## Reader and Congregation:

We gratefully acknowledge, O Lord our God, that Thou art our Creator and Preserver, the Rock of our life and the Shield of our help. We render thanks unto Thee for our lives which are in Thy hand, for our souls which are ever in Thy keeping, for Thy wondrous providence and for Thy continuous goodness, which Thou bestowest upon us day by day. Truly, Thy mercies never fail and Thy loving-kindness never ceases. Therefore in Thee, do we forever put our trust.

# FOR CHANUKKOH

**Reader and Congregation:**

Everlasting God, Protector and Guide of our fathers, we gather to thank Thee this day for all Thy wonderful deeds in days gone by. When a wicked king arose to destroy our people, to defile our holy Temple and to drive our fathers away from their worship of Thee, then didst Thou put courage into the hearts of Mattathias and his sons, and then didst Thou give them the strength to fight for their faith. Yet not merely by the strength of their arms did they conquer the foe, nor by the might of battle did they win their victories, but because they knew that Thy spirit was with them, and that Thy justice could not fail, did they overthrow the host of the oppressor and succeed in rededicating the Sanctuary on Zion.

In these days of Chanukkoh we think again of the gallant Maccabeans and of the undying light that burned in the Holy Temple. Now once more the lights are kindled here and in our homes, and the radiance of the ancient courage shines again in our hearts. May the faith for which our fathers lived and died, become all the more precious to us because of their self-sacrifice and unshaken devotion.

We pray to Thee, O Lord, to make us worthy of the heroic past. Teach us to purify the sanctuary of our hearts. May no evil desires mar our thoughts and may no falsehood abide within us. Let the light of truth shine eternally in our souls, so that our lives become a Temple made holy by Thy presence and dedicated to the service of Thee. Amen.

*(Or this prayer:)*

Our Heavenly Father, in whose light we shall see light, we beseech Thee on this feast of light to fill our souls with light. As day by day we add to the shining tapers, so may knowledge and goodness be added unto us day by day and may knowledge and goodness increase throughout the world. Now the nights cease to lengthen and the days begin to lengthen; O send into every sorrowing heart the assurance that, even after the longest night, hope's sunshine will return.

And on this day of dedication, we would again dedicate ourselves to Thee. Make our hearts clean as that new-built altar; forever let the sacred light of love glow within us. As Thou didst strengthen the Maccabees, strengthen also us. Help us fight the foes within our own bosoms—impatience, impurity, and all other temptations; and make us worthy of inscribing upon our spirit's banners: "Who among the mighty, O Lord, is like unto Thee?" Amen.

**Hymn Nos. 122, 123, or from the Chanukkoh group**

Blessed art Thou, O Lord our God, King of the universe, who hast sanctified us by Thy commandments and hast bidden us to kindle the lights of consecration.  (All sing No. 295.)

Blessed art Thou, O Lord our God, King of the universe, who didst do wonders for our fathers in days of old at this season.

Blessed art Thou, O Lord our God, King of the universe, who hast permitted us to live, hast enabled us to endure and hast brought us unto this time.

*The tapers are kindled*

**Hymn Nos. 205, 206, 207 or 208**

Turn to page 467 (continuing the Sabbath service with Silent Devotion).

# SERVICES FOR YOUTH AND HIGH SCHOOL

## I

### THE IDEA OF GOD

**The Call to Worship**

Canst thou by searching find out God? Canst thou find out the Almighty unto perfection?

**Response:**

Seek ye the Lord while He may be found; call ye upon Him while He is near.

**Reading from the Bible:**

To whom then will ye liken God?
Or what likeness will ye compare unto Him?
The image?
A workman hath cast it and the goldsmith overlaid it with gold!

Have ye not known? Have ye not heard?
Hath it not been told you from the beginning?

Who hath measured the waters in the hollow of His hand
And meted out the heaven with a span and comprehended the dust of the earth in a measure
And weighed the mountains in scales and the hills in a balance?

Who hath directed the spirit of God or, being His counselor, hath taught Him?

Behold nations are but as a drop of water and are accounted as a grain of dust in the balance!
It is He that sitteth above the circle of the earth and the inhabitants thereof are as grasshoppers;
That stretcheth out the heavens as a curtain
And spreadeth them out as a tent to dwell in;
That bringeth princes to naught; that maketh the juages oi tne earth as vanity.

Lift up your eyes on high and see
Who hath created these—
That bringeth out their hosts by number?
To whom then will ye liken Me, saith the Holy One. (Isaiah xl.)

**Reader:**

Meecho-mo-cho bo-ay-leem A-do-noy?

**Response:**

Who is like unto Thee among the mighty, O God?

**Reader:**

Ado-noy ts'vo-os, Hu Ayl
ba-sho-ma-yeem u-vo-o-rets
v'chol asher bom.   Hu
Ado-noy E-lo-hay-nu, ayn od.

**Response:**

The Lord God of Hosts is the Creator of the heavens and the earth and all that is in them.   He is the Lord our God and there is none else.

**Meditation (to be read silently):**

Great things have been achieved by the hand and the mind of men.

It is a great thing to have sought out and revealed the marvels of nature's power, to chain the winged lightning, to span the earth and air with flying messengers, to belt the world with the thoughts of man.   And yet—how pitiably small after all are the accomplishments of man!

We use the power of electricity but of its secret we know nothing.

No one can explain the miracle of the growth of a blade of grass or a flower—the hidden power that defies the heavy covering of earth, the magic hand that paints the beauty of a rose.

It is a greater thing to steal from night her glory and bathe the world in sudden and sublime light; to pierce the clouds with shafts of flaming glory and cleanse and purify the air; to anchor in the void each circling world and set it spinning through endless space held to its course by an immutable law.   What Will, through the revealing years, evolved from one nerveless cell this creature called man, with body, mind, and soul, man who struggles, who dreams, who aspires, who sacrifices, who loves?

We can best understand nature and man—the world without and the world within—if we accept the idea of God!

**Hymn**

**Together (Psalm viii):**

O God, our Lord!
How excellent is Thy name in all the earth
. Who hast set Thy glory in the heavens!
When I consider Thy heavens the work of Thy hands
The moon and the stars which Thou hast ordained—
What is man that Thou art mindful of him?
And the son of man that Thou thinkest of him?
Yet Thou hast made him but little lower than the angels
And hast crowned him with glory and honor.
Thou makest him to have dominion over the works of Thy hands
Thou hast put all things under his feet.
O God our Lord,
How excellent is Thy name, in all the earth!


### READING FROM JEWISH LITERATURE

What then can be the result of our efforts, when we try to obtain a knowledge of a Being that is free from substance, that is most simple, whose existence is absolute and not due to any cause, to whose perfect essence nothing can be superadded and whose perfection consists in the absence of all defects?

All we understand is the fact that He exists, that He is a Being to whom none of His creatures are similar, who does not include plurality, who is never too feeble to produce other beings and whose relation to the universe is that of a steersman to a boat; and even this is not a real simile, but serves only to convey to us the idea that God rules the universe, that He gives it duration and preserves its necessary arrangement.

In the contemplation of His essence, our comprehension and knowledge prove insufficient; in the examination of His works how they necessarily result from His will, our knowledge proves to be ignorance; and in the endeavor to extol Him in words, all our efforts in speech are mere weakness and failure!

If God did not exist—suppose this were possible—the universe would not exist. On that account God is called in the sacred language chay ha-olamim—the life of the universe.

(Maimonides—Guide to the Perplexed)

**Together:**

Hear, O Israel: The Lord our God, the Lord is One!
Sh'ma Yis-ro-ayl A-do-noy E-lo-hay-nu, A-do-noy e-chod.

**Prayer (Together):**

Almighty God who permittest Thyself
To be entreated and who payest heed
Unto the lowly, how long wilt Thou from me
Be far and hidden?  Night and day I turn
And with steadfast heart I call to Thee
And pour incessant gratitude for Thy
Excelling goodness.  O my King, with pain
For Thee my heart is torn, in Thee it trusts.
Dreaming this shut-in dream, it looks to Thee
For life's interpretation. This I ask
This is the plea to which I beg assent,
My sole petition neither more nor less.
(Gabirol—Tr. Zangwill)

**Reader:**

God is near to all who call upon Him
To all who call upon Him in truth.

**Meditation (to be read silently):**

O Thou great Spirit, help me to see Thee in all the wonder of nature, in
the pageantry of the passing seasons—summer with its abundant blessings
of fruit and harvest, autumn with its glory of color, winter with all its great
silences and spring with its lyric promise of life—life inextinguishable and
eternal.

Help me to sense Thee in the life of man as he suffers and struggles; as
he grows humble in achievement and tender in failure.

Help me to see Thee in my own heart as I feel there the urge to goodness
that will not let me rest!

**Reader and Congregation:**

May the words of our lips and the meditations of our hearts be acceptable
before Thee, our Strength and our Redeemer. . . . Amen.

# II

## JEWISH UNITY

**The Call to Worship**

Our God and God of our fathers, be with us as we gather in prayer to Thee and in praise of Thy great name.

**Response:**

May these moments of meditation strengthen the bonds that bind us to our people; may they deepen within us a sense of our responsibility as Jews.

**First Reader:**

A common past, a common history, common sacrifice and suffering, the same language and literature, a common hope and ideal and a common faith constitute the spiritual background of a people. But this is a spiritual allegiance and not a political loyalty. And our Christian brethren with their splendid background of Christian historic tradition will be able to understand it. Of course, with us there is this difference: in addition to the bond of believers in the same religion, Judaism, there is the consciousness that we belong to a people, the Jewish people. This consciousness is frequently lost willfully by renegade Jews or weakened in the process of adaptation; but the outside world, through prejudice or discrimination, or barriers in business and social life, forces upon us Jews—even upon those who would forget—the knowledge that we belong to a distinct people. The best type of Jew is eager to proclaim his fealty to Judaism; is willing to accept the discomforts of being a Jew.

If we are to be convicted because we are true to ourselves, true to the best in our past; if we are to be convicted because of our willingness to bend our necks to the slaughterer in refusal to relinquish Truth as we conceive it; then upon the nations of the earth who make the unholy claim be the blame—not upon us! It is our duty to be ourselves. The tragedy is greater in that many among us are not loyal to themselves, their people, and its ideals. On the other hand, we are not so narrow that we see only good in Jews, that we recognize no evil in the household of Israel. But we must be what we are, Jews, by the blood that flows in our veins, by the faith and sacrifice of our fathers.

The physical characteristics of the Jew may be lost as he reacts to the environment of freedom. The back may be straightened, the form heightened, the face lose its rugged, crude and elemental strength. But the Jewish heart throbs within him. The Jewish soul is unchanged!

**Second Reader:**

Would God my people would understand these things! Amos, Hosea, Isaiah, Jeremiah, ha-Levi,¹ Maimonides, Mendelssohn—all his people's seers and prophets and poets—live in the Jew of to-day. Their inspiration forms the fabric of his being. Their redeeming revelations are graven on his heart. He is born with them. They live again in him. The Jew's past is in his soul. He cannot forget it, no matter how much he would. He cannot blot it out. It is the heritage of his birth. It haunts him. It gives him no peace. God has chosen the Jew! God will not let him alone! The Jew abandons his God? Turns his back upon Him? Ah, he cannot! "Whither shall I go from Thy spirit? Or whither shall I flee from Thy presence? If I ascend into heaven, Thou art there; if I make my bed in the netherworld, behold Thou art there. If I take the wings of the morning and dwell in the uttermost parts of the sea, even there would Thy hand lead me and Thy right hand would uphold me." It is written. It is so. All the mighty imperatives of his tragic past, all the martyrdom of his people rise up to agonize his heart with a thousand discontents. He becomes restless, unhappy, a cynic—a lonely seeker who gropes blindly in the dark. But God comes into his soul and he is transfigured! The prophets live again. The poets sing. The Jew serves! He has answered the call of his God. He has fulfilled the divine purpose for which he was created. He is a blessing!

When all is said and done, prejudice cannot be fought with prejudice; but it can be met by courage; it can be conquered by love; it can be overcome by service. When the world hates us, let us love; when the world reviles us, let us serve! The only justification for our separateness is that which our history, our literature and our tradition teach us; to exemplify the reality of God in our daily lives and in our relations with our fellows.

**Hymn**

**Reading from the Bible (Isaiah xliv):**

Yet now hear, O Jacob, My servant;
And Israel, whom I have chosen:
Thus saith the Lord that made thee,
And formed thee from the womb, who will help thee:
Fear not, O Jacob, My servant;
And thou, Jeshurun, whom I have chosen,
For I will pour water upon him that is thirsty,
And floods upon the dry ground:
I will pour My spirit upon thy seed,
And they shall spring up among the grass,
As willows by the watercourses.
One shall say, I am the Lord's:
And another shall call himself by the name of Jacob;
And another shall subscribe with his hand unto the Lord,
And surname himself by the name of Israel.

**Meditation:**

"Judaism is something more than a badge, something more than birth-mark; it is a life. To be born a Jew does not declare any of us to be of the elect. God signs the covenant, but we have to seal it—to seal it by a life of service. 'What makes a man a Jew?' is a question that is often asked. The answer is two things: membership in the Jewish brotherhood and loyal fulfillment of the obligations which that membership imposes. To be Jewish, but to trample upon Jewish duty is to be faithless to Israel."

—Morris Joseph.

**Prayer**

**Together:**

Let us think of the blessed heritage that is ours. The past with the memories of common suffering, its endless sacrifice; the present with its stories of Jewish heroism, loyalty and sublime self-immolation; the future with its hopes for the realization of God's kingdom—past, present and future—bind us in common brotherhood the world over!

Let us heed the deepest imperatives of our soul, which, amid the misunderstandings of the world around us, in spite of years, lands, waters, and languages that divide us, whispers: He is thy brother Jew! Love him!

**Hymn**

**Response (in unison):**

May God bless us with strength,
May God charge us with loyalty.
May God fill us with faith in ourselves, in our people and in Him—God of our fathers. Amen.

# III

## HUMAN BROTHERHOOD

**The Call to Worship**

Let us seek that which is lost and bring again that which is driven away;

**Response:**

Let us bind up that which is broken and strengthen that which is weak.

**Responsive Reading:**

(From the Bible)

Ye shall do no unrighteousness in judgment.
Thou shalt not respect the person of the poor, nor honor the person of the great.

In righteousness shalt thou judge thy neighbor.

Thou shalt not go up and down as a talebearer among thy people.

Thou shalt not avenge nor bear any grudge against the children of thy people;

But thou shalt love thy neighbor as thyself.

And if a stranger sojourn with thee in thy land, ye shall not vex him.

As one born in the land among you, shall be unto you the stranger that sojourneth with you.

And thou shalt love him as thyself; for ye were strangers in the land of Egypt. (Leviticus xix)

And if thy brother become poor and fall in decay with thee; then shalt thou assist him;

Yea, a stranger or a sojourner, that he may live with thee.

And ye shall not overreach one another. (Leviticus xxv)

And Solomon prayed at the dedication of his Temple: But also to the stranger who is not of thy people Israel but cometh out of a far country for the sake of Thy name—

When he will come and pray at this house, mayest Thou listen in heaven And do according to all that the stranger will call on Thee for. (I Kings viii)

For My house shall be called a house of prayer for all nations. (Isaiah 56, 7)

(From Jewish Literature)

When God created Adam He gathered dust from all parts of the earth and with it He formed the parent of the human race. (Talmud Sanhedrin)

Thou shalt love thy fellow man—not thy fellow Jew only—but thy fellow man, as thyself. (Sifra)

For every human being—and not only the Jew—is beloved by God, since he is the creature of God, made in His image. (Aboth)

The Torah was intentionally and purposely revealed on Sinai in the wilderness that it might be the possession of all. (Mekilta)

The righteous among all nations shall have a share in the future world. (Sanhedrin)

If you accustom yourself to speak evil of or against your non-Jewish brother who is not of your nation or race, you will also slander the brother who is of your own people and faith. (Midrash)

Hymn

**Prayer:**

Almighty and merciful God, Thou hast called Israel to Thy service. O mayest Thou find us worthy to be Thy witness unto the peoples of the earth. Give us grace to fulfill this mission with zeal tempered by wisdom and guided by regard for other men's faith. May our lives prove the strength of our own belief in the truths we proclaim. May our bearing toward our neighbors, our faithfulness in every sphere of duty, our compassion for the suffering and our patience under trial show that He whose law we obey is indeed the God of all goodness, the Father of all men, that to serve Him is perfect freedom and to worship Him the soul's purest happiness.

O Lord, open our eyes that we may see and welcome all truth, whether shining from the annals of ancient revelations or reaching us through the seers of our own time; for Thou hidest not Thy light from any generation of Thy children that feel after Thee and seek Thy guidance.

We pray for the masters and teachers in Israel that they may dispense Thy truth with earnestness and zeal, yet not wanting in charity. May the law of love be found on their lips, and may they by precept and example lead many in the ways of righteousness.

Bless, O God, all endeavors, wherever made, to lift up the fallen, to redeem the sinful, to bring back those who wander from the right path and restore them to a worthy life. Truly, O God, we long to adore Thee in the temple of holiness, at the altar of truth and with the offerings of our love. O satisfy us early with Thy mercy, that we may rejoice and be glad all our days. Amen.

**Reader:**

May the time not be distant, O God, when Thy name shall be worshiped in all the earth, when unbelief shall disappear and error be no more. We fervently pray that the day may come when all men shall invoke Thy name, when corruption and evil shall give way to purity and goodness, when superstition shall no longer enslave the mind, nor idolatry blind the eye, when all inhabitants of the earth shall know that to Thee alone every knee must bend and every tongue give homage. O may all, created in Thine image, recognize that they are brethren, so that, one in spirit and one in fellowship, they may be forever united before Thee. Then shall Thy kingdom be established on earth and the word of Thine ancient seer be fulfilled: The Lord will reign forever and ever.

**Congregation:**

On that day the Lord shall be One and His name shall be One.

**Hymn**

**Prayer:**

O Thou who art from everlasting to everlasting,

Thou before whom the generations pass—

Fill our hearts with a sense of Thy certitude!

All the things to which we anchor our lives may pass.

Our wealth may be for a day; our influence may vanish with the coming year; our health and our strength are not our sure possessions. Tomorrow's sun may rise to find us here no more.

We are as shadows and shadows we pursue.

All men drink the same potion from the cup of life.

Uncertainty surrounds us every hour.

Help us to feel our common humanity;

In the pain of our own life, teach us to sense the pain of our brother;

In the struggle of our own life, reveal to us the struggle of our brother;

In the aspirations of our own life, discover for us the aspirations of our brother;

In the frustration of our own life, fill us with sympathy to understand the frustration of our brother.

O Thou who art the Father of us all—

Charge us with kindness and with courage, with friendliness and the spirit of helpfulness.

Tear from our souls the prejudices that close the hearts of men to one another—prejudices of race and religion and nation—

Let us see in our fellow man a reflection of ourselves

And help us to live a life of brotherhood and service!

**Congregation: Amen.**

# IV

## THE RATIONALITY OF JUDAISM
### (From the Book of Job)

**Reader:**

Canst thou, by searching, find out God? Canst thou find out the Almighty unto perfection? It is as high as heaven; what canst thou do? deeper than the netherworld; what canst thou know? The measure thereof is longer than the earth, and broader than the sea.

Man maketh an end of darkness, searching out to the uttermost bounds, stones of darkness and of deep shadow. He breaketh a shaft where none sojourn. They are forgotten of them that pass; afar from men, they hang;

they swing.  Out of the earth there cometh bread; and underneath, it is twisted by fire; a place of sapphires are its stones, and dust of gold is found there.  It is a path no vulture knoweth, and the falcon's eye hath not seen it; the boldest beast hath not trodden it; the lion hath not passed thereby. Man putteth his hand to the flinty rock; he overturneth the mountains by the roots.  He cutteth out channels among the rocks; and his eye seeth all that is precious.  He bindeth the streams that they weep not; and that which is hid, he bringeth to light.

But wisdom—where shall it be found?  And where is the place of knowledge?  Man knoweth not the price thereof; and it is not found in the land of the living.  The deep saith:  It is not in me; and the sea saith:  I have it not.  Treasure may not be given therefor, nor silver be weighed for its price.  It cannot be valued with the gold of Ophir, with costly onyx, or sapphire.  Coral or crystal cannot equal it; yea, the price of wisdom is greater than pearls.  The topaz of Ethiopia doth not equal it; it may not be matched with purest gold.  Wisdom—whence doth it come? and where is the home of knowledge which is hid from the eyes of all living, and concealed from the fowls of the air?  Destruction and death have said:  With our ears have we heard a rumor thereof.

God understandeth the way thereto, and He knoweth the home thereof. For He beholdeth the ends of the earth, and seeth all that is under the heavens; appointing to the winds their weight, and meting out the waters by measure; establishing for the rain a law, and a way for the bolt of the thunder.  He hath seen and numbered it; He established it, yea, and searched it out.  And to man He said:

> Behold, the fear of the Lord is wisdom;
> To refrain from evil is knowledge.

**Hymn: Adon Olom No. 276 or 311**

**Reader:**

### (From the Liturgy)

Lord of all the worlds!  Not in reliance upon righteousness or merit in ourselves do we make our supplications to Thee, but trusting in Thine infinite mercy alone.  For what are we, what is our life, what our goodness, what our power?  What can we say in Thy presence?  Are not all the mighty men as naught before Thee, and those of great renown as though they had never been; the wisest, as if without knowledge, and the men of understanding as if without discernment?  Behold, nations are but as a drop of water, and accounted as a grain of dust in the balance.  Many of our actions are vain; and our days pass away like shadows.  Our life would be altogether vanity, were it not for the soul which, fashioned in Thine own image, gives us assurance of our higher destiny, and imparts to our fleeting days an abiding value.

We, therefore, beseech thee, O our God, to help us banish from our hearts all pride and vain glory, all confidence in worldly possessions, all self-sufficient leaning on our own reason. O give us the spirit of meekness and the grace of modesty, that we may become wise in Thy fear. May we never forget that all we have and prize is but lent to us, that we may use worthily every gift that cometh from Thee, to Thine honor, and the good of our fellowmen.

**Reader:**

### (From Jewish Literature)

The object of this treatise is to enlighten a religious man who has been trained to believe in the truth of our holy Law, who consciously fulfills his moral and religious duties and at the same time has been successful in his philosophic studies. Human reason has attracted him to abide within its sphere; and he finds it difficult to accept as correct the teaching based on the literal interpretation of the Law. . . . Hence he is lost in perplexity and anxiety. If he is guided solely by reason . . . he would consider that he had rejected the fundamental principles of the Law; and if, instead of following his reason, he abandons its guidance altogether, it would still appear that his religious convictions have suffered loss and error. . . .

(From Maimonides—Guide to the Perplexed)

The great Jewish thinker then goes on to discuss the difficulties which occur when one attempts to take the Bible language literally. He pleads for a figurative, metaphorical interpretation and declares that the Bible authors used similes and allusions and figures of speech which must be appreciated to be understood. He quotes the phrase of the Rabbis—the Torah speaks the language of men—and declares that we can only understand God by applying to Him the highest that we know in our own experience—that expressions like God's arm or hand, or His sitting or dwelling are but metaphorical descriptions.

He declares, however, that there are things which man cannot know; a boundary is undoubtedly set to the human mind which it cannot pass. But a proposition which can be proved by evidence is not subject to dispute, denial or rejection; none but the ignorant would contradict it. . . .

Thus our great teacher lifts high the torch of reason in the midst of an age which was darkened by dogmatism.

It has ever been so in Judaism. The intellect of man is regarded as a God-given endowment; it is obligatory upon man to use it. If he does not use his mind, he may dam up the flow of God's revelation which proceeds through the mind of man. Another Jewish teacher said that nothing which is unreasonable has a place in authoritative Jewish thought and that reason is the great corrective which continually purifies our faith, eliminating evermore of error and superstition and expanding more and more toward the perfect truth.

To be a liberal Jew, then, does not require one to forego his reason. In

confessing our Judaism we are not asked to relinquish the use of our reason. Judaism has nothing to fear from science or the scientific method. Judaism and science march along together in perfect harmony. The discoveries of science according to liberal Jewish thought but enrich and enlarge the idea of God by revealing how "wonderful are His works!"

**Hymn (Psalm xix, No. 57)**

**Meditation:**

Judaism does not demand blind faith. As Moses Mendelssohn pointed out in his *Jerusalem*, there is no command in the Bible "Thou shalt believe," but only, "Thou shalt do" or "Thou shalt not do." Mendelssohn, therefore, points out that the foundation of Judaism is rooted in reason and understanding. He was but following along the lines laid down by Maimonides who declares that the fundamental teaching of Judaism is to know there is one God. . . .
Unanimity of thought was never demanded. . . . A member of the Beth Din who was in the minority was not prevented from propagating his views so long as he did not stir up the people to act against the decision of the majority. . . .
But for liberty of thought and liberty of speech, Jewish literature might never have had the writings of Abraham ibn Ezra, who in one place boldly declares that the command, "And thou shalt write them for a sign upon thy hand," like that other, "And thou shalt write them on the tablets of thy heart" is not to be taken literally, but only symbolically! Such liberty of speech has not undermined Judaism, but its existence shows that the history of liberty of thought among Jews is a continuous record from the earliest times to the golden age in Spain. . . .
The constitution of the human mind is such that men differ in their views of ethics, politics, and religion. Judaism is strong enough and broad enough to tolerate all results of free inquiry, if only the spirit in which they are carried out is honest and the aim in view the furtherance of the Jewish conception of holiness, justice, and goodness. "Some may forbid and some allow; yet both are the words of the living God."

(From Benammi, *Essays, Second Series*)

**Reader:**

We bow the head and bend the knee and adore Him who is beyond the power of the mind to comprehend, the Eternal Spirit of life, the mind and will and love in the universe whom we call God.

**Congregation:**

Va-anachnu kor'eem umishtachaveem umodeem lifnay Melech malchay ham'locheem, hakodosh boruch hu.

**Prayer (Together):**

O God, I stand before Thee, knowing all my deficiencies and overwhelmed by Thy greatness and majesty. But Thou hast commanded me to pray to Thee and hast suffered me to offer homage to Thine exalted name according to the measure of my knowledge. . . . Thou knowest what is for my good. If I recite my wants, it is not to remind Thee of them but only so that I may understand better how great is my dependence upon Thee. If then I ask Thee for the things that make not for my well-being, it is because I am ignorant; Thy choice is better than mine and I submit myself to Thine unalterable decrees and Thy supreme direction. O Lord, my heart is not haughty nor mine eyes lofty; neither do I exercise myself in great matters or in things too wonderful for me. Surely I have stilled and quieted my soul; like a child with his mother. Amen.

(Bachya ibn Pakudah, 11th century)

# V

**Hymn**

**Responsive Reading (Micah vi):**

Hear ye, now what the Lord saith:
   Arise, contend thou before the mountains;
Hear O ye mountains the Lord's controversy;
   And ye enduring rocks, the foundations of the earth,
For the Lord hath a controversy with His people,
   And He will plead with Israel.
I brought thee out of the land of Egypt, ˋ
   And redeemed thee out of the house of bondage.
And I sent before thee Moses, Aaron, and Miriam,
   That ye may know the righteous acts of the Lord.
Wherewith shall I come before the Lord,
   And bow myself before God on high?
Shall I come before Him with burnt offerings,
   With calves of a year old?
Will the Lord be pleased with thousands of rams;
   With ten thousands of rivers of oil?
It hath been told, O man, what is good;
   And what the Lord doth require of thee:
Only to do justly and to love mercy,
   And to walk humbly with thy God.

(From Psalm cxix, 9–16):

> Wherewithal shall a young man keep his way pure?
> By taking heed thereto according to Thy word.
> With my whole heart have I sought Thee;
> O let me not err from Thy commandments.
> Thy word have I laid up in my heart,
> That I might not sin against Thee.
> Blessed art Thou, O Lord; teach me Thy statutes.
> With my lips have I told all the ordinances of Thy mouth.
> I have rejoiced in the way of Thy testimonies,
> As much as in all riches.
> I will meditate in Thy precepts,
> And have respect unto Thy ways.
> I will delight myself in Thy statutes;
> I will not forget Thy word.

**Reader:**

Praise ye the Lord, to whom all praise is due.
Bor'-chu es A-do-noy ha-m'-voroch.

**Together:**

Praised be the Lord, to whom all praise is due forever and ever.
Bo-ruch A-do-noy ha-m'-voroch l'-o-lom vo-ed.

**All Singing:**

S. Sulzer

Bo - ruch A - do - noy ha - m' vo - roch l'o - lom vo - ed.

**First Reader:**

Praised be Thou, O Lord our God, Ruler of the world, who in Thy mercy makest light to shine over the earth and all its inhabitants, and renewest daily the work of creation. How manifold are Thy works, O Lord! In wisdom hast Thou made them all. Thou formest light and darkness, ordainest good out of evil, bringest harmony into nature, and peace to the heart of man.

**Second Reader:**

With great love hast Thou loved us, O our God. Our fathers believed and trusted in Thee; therefore Thou didst teach them the laws of life and show them the way of wisdom. O merciful Father, grant us discernment that we may understand and fulfill all the teachings of Thy word.

Hear, O Israel: The Lord our God, the Lord is One.

Sh'ma Yis-ro-ayl, A-do-noy E-lo-hay-nu, A-do-noy e-chod.

**All Singing:**

Traditional

*f* *Andante Maestoso*

Sh'ma Yis-ro-ayl A-do-noy E-lo-hay-nu A-do-noy e-chod.

**Responsive Reading:**

Truth eternal is Thy word which Thou hast spoken through Thy prophets.
    Thou art the living God, Thy words bring life and light to the soul.
Thou art the strength of our life, the rock of our salvation;
    Thy kingdom and Thy truth abide forever.
May Thy law rule in the hearts of all Thy children;
    And Thy truth unite them in bonds of fellowship.

**Together:**

Who is like unto Thee, O God, among the mighty? Who is like unto Thee, glorious in holiness, extolled in praises, working wonders.

L. Lewandowski

Mee cho - mo - cho bo - ay - leem A - do - noy;
mee ko - mo - cho ne-e - dor — ba - ko - - - - desh
no - ro s'hil - los, o - say fe - - - lay?

**First Reader:**

Praised be Thou, O Lord our God, God of our fathers Abraham, Isaac, and Jacob, great, mighty, and revered God.

**Second Reader:**

Thou art mighty forever, O Lord. In loving-kindness Thou sustainest the living, Thou upholdest the falling, healest the sick, and loosest the chains of the captives. Thou wilt fulfill Thy promise of immortal life unto those who sleep in the dust.

**Reader:**

Holy, holy, holy is the Lord of hosts; the whole earth is full of His glory.

**All Singing:**

S. Sulzer

Ko - dosh ko - dosh ko - dosh A - do - noy ts' - vo - os m'lo chol ho - o - retz k'-vo - - - do.

**Reader:**

In all places of Thy dominion, Thy name is praised and glorified.

**All Singing:**

S. Sulzer

Bo - ruch k' - vod A - do - noy mi - m' - ko (mo.'

**Reader:**

The Lord will reign forever, thy God, O Zion. from generation to generation.   Hallelujah.

**All Singing:**

S. Sulzer

Yim - loch  A - do - noy  l' - o - lom  E - lo - ha - yich  Tsee -
von  l' - dor  vo - dor  ha - l' - lu - yo.

**Reader:**

O eternal Spirit, we seek Thy presence, for Thou art the soul of the world.
At the heart of nature's mystery in the growth of living things, through the
beauty dwelling in sea and land and day by day, within the searching mind
of man, art Thou revealed.   Humbly we stand before Thee, that we may
learn to do justice and love mercy.

Lord our God, lead us in Thy ways, that Thy name may be honored, and
Israel be blessed by our works.   May we remain firm in our devotion to Thee
and never fall into temptation and shame.   May our better nature always
prompt us to do good deeds with a willing heart and faithfully to fulfill our
duties.   Gird us with strength to govern our inclinations and to rule them
according to Thy will.   Grant, O Father, that all our life and work may be
a blessing to our fellowmen and win favor in Thine eyes.

**Silent Devotion:**

O God, keep my tongue from evil and my lips from speaking guile. Be my support when grief silences my voice, and my comfort when woe bends my spirit. Plant humility in my soul, and strengthen my heart with perfect faith in Thee. Help me to be strong in trial and temptation and to be meek when others wrong me, that I may readily forgive them. Guide me by the light of Thy counsel, my Rock and my Redeemer. Amen.

Lord of all, reign Thou supreme within my heart. Be Thou with me in all my ways. As I meditate on Thy holiness may all my thoughts be purified and ennobled. Realizing Thy great goodness may I be grateful for Thy manifold blessings. Knowing Thy love for all Thy children, may selfishness never keep me from useful service to my fellow man. Lead me, I pray Thee, from strength to strength that I may dedicate myself to truth, knowledge, and goodness, whereby I may be a blessing to all Thy children, and thus be truly serving Thee. Amen.

**Hymn**

**Sermon**

**Hymn**

**Benediction (Psalm cxix):**

Give us understanding, O Lord, that we may keep Thy Law, and observe it with our whole heart. Amen.


## BIRTHDAY SERVICE

**Reader:**

Blessed be he that cometh in the name of the Lord.

**Congregation:**

We bless you out of the house of the Lord.

**Prayer (Together):**

To Thee, O heavenly Father, we give our thanks this day. Many are the gifts which we have received from Thee. Thou hast blessed us with parents whose unfailing love protects us, with teachers from whom we have learnt what is true and good, and with playmates and friends who have been our good companions. Our hearts are filled with happiness as we voice our gratitude to Thee.

Bless us, O Father, in the years that are to come. Grant us health. Keep us from sorrow and pain. May each year bring us greater knowledge and deeper friendship. Teach us to bring joy to those who love us and to do Thy will with all our hearts. Amen.

## All Singing:

Isabella Hess  J. H. Rogers

*mf Andante con moto*

(this) (child —)
Fath - er bless these birth-day child-ren Let the day bring joy - ous cheer,

(his) (her) (his) (her) (he) (she) (holds)
Bless their go - ing and their com - ing Bless with peace all they hold dear.

## Reader:

Boruch At-toh Adonoy, Elo-hay-nu Me-lech ho-olom, she-he-che-yo-nu, v'kee-y'mo-nu v'hi-gee-o-nu la-z'man ha-zeh.

Praised be Thou, O Lord our God, who has kept us in life. sustained us, and brought us to this day.

**All Singing:**

Bo - ruch At - to A - do - noy E - lo - hay - nu Me - lech ho -

o - lom, she - he - che - yo - nu v' - keey' - mo - nu, v' -

hi - gee - o - nu la - z' - man ha - zeh.

# UNION HYMNAL

## PART IV

## INDEXES

# GENERAL INDEX AND FIRST LINES

The last two columns in this table are for the purpose of helping those who have favorite hymns in the preceding two editions of the Union Hymnal and who wish to find such hymns in the present edition. All references are to the second edition (1914) unless where the first edition (1897) is specifically noted.

| FIRST LINE | NO. | COMPOSER | AUTHOR | CROSS REFERENCE FOR SECOND EDITION* | |
|---|---|---|---|---|---|
| | | | | WORDS | MUSIC |
| A little kingdom I possess.... | 251 | J. H. Rogers | L. M. Alcott | | |
| A message sweet the breezes.. | 133 | S. Hecht | F. Switton | 195 | 195 |
| A new shrine stands in....... | 213 | J. G. Heller | L. Marshall | 211 | |
| A noble life, a simple........ | 225 | C. H. Grimm | A. S. Isaacs | 115 | |
| A week within the succah.... | 189 | H. Schalit | I. R. Hess | | |
| ditto | 190 | J. Weinberg | ditto | | |
| Again as evening's shadow.... | 11 | A. W. Binder | S. Longfellow | 44 | |
| Ah well it is that God........ | 89 | G. Neumark—har. by J. S. Bach | G. Aguilar | 97 | 97 |
| All as God wills............. | 88 | J. Barnby | J. G. Whittier | | |
| All living souls shall......... | 55 | S. Alman | P. Moise | | |
| All praise to Thee we........ | 203 | P. Jassinowsky | M. D. Klein | | |
| All the world shall come..... | 63 | A. W. Binder | I. Zangwill | 150 | |
| All things bright and........ | 252 | H. R. Shelley | C. F. Alexander | | |
| All through the long bright... | 186 | J. Singer | B. J. Singer | | |
| All wise, all great whose..... | 218 | J. Singer | A. Dobson | 208 | |
| Almighty Father, God of..... | 6 | H. Schalit | | | |
| Almighty God in humble..... | 28 | C. H. Grimm | J. Montgomery | | |
| Almighty God, who hearest... | 53 | L. Lewandowski | A. Lucas | 99 | 99 |
| Arise to praise the Lord...... | 74 | A. W. Binder | J. K. Gutheim | 26 | |
| Around the weary world...... | 17 | N. L. Norden | D. Levy | | |
| As birds unto the genial...... | 113 | M. Grauman | D. Levy | | |
| As pants the hart for........ | 30 | R. R. Rinder | "New" Version | 66 | |
| | 40 | A. Kaiser | | | |
| At midnight so the sages..... | 175 | Fr. G. F. Handel | A. S. Isaacs | 96 | 96 |
| Behold, it is the............. | 129 | Traditional | A. Lucas | 162 | 162 |
| Believe not those who say.... | 231 | S. Alman | A. Brontë | 117 | |
| Blessed art Thou, O Lord.... | 15 | D. Nowakowsky—ad. A. W. Binder | Author unknown tr. A. Lucas | | |
| Blessed, O blessed moment... | 153 | A. W. Binder | M. Jastrow, st. 2 composite | 200 | |
| ditto | 154 | A. Kaiser | | | |
| Blest is the bond of.......... | 219 | J. G. Heller | P. Moise | 207 | |
| Bow down Thine ear, Lord... | 35 | J. Beimel | H. H. Mayer | 83 | |
| Come forth, my friend....... | 108 | D. Nowakowsky | tr. A. Lucas | | |
| Come, let us praise our...... | 201 | C. H. Grimm | F. Montefiore | | |
| Come let us sing in sweet.... | 217 | M. Grauman | L. Stern | 214 | |
| Come, O holy Sabbath....... | 105 | P. Jassinowsky | H. H. Mayer | | |
| Come, O Sabbath day and ... | 118 | A. W. Binder | G. Gottheil | 156 | |
| Come ye faithful servants.... | 101 | B. Levenson | J. L. Levy | 143 | |
| Courage brother do not...... | 87 | F. Mendelssohn | N. Macleod | 126 | 66—1st ed** |
| Create in this weak form..... | 170 | Arr. by A. Lieber | L. Weitzman | 113 | 113 |
| Dear Father, here Thy....... | 257 | J. G. Heller | A. R. Rosewater | | |

| FIRST LINE | NO. | COMPOSER | AUTHOR | CROSS REFERENCE FOR SECOND EDITION* | |
|---|---|---|---|---|---|
| | | | | WORDS | MUSIC |
| Descend, descend, O........ | 107 | D. Nowakowsky—arr. by A. W. B. | A. Cohen | 154 | |
| Despise not, Lord, my....... | 162 | R. K. Miller | A. Lucas—tr. fr. Judah Ha-Levi | 184 | 184 |
| Dim mine eyes with many.... | 173 | Traditional | Mrs. I. L. Rypins | | 100 |
| Early will I seek Thee....... | 18 | S. Sabel | G. Gottheil—tr. fr. Solomon ibn Gabirol | 7 | |
| Earth with all thy.......... | 64 | Ad. fr. Lewandow- ski by A. W. B. | E. Churton—abr. | 63 | |
| Ere space exists, or earth..... | 159 | A. W. Binder | tr. by S. Solis-Cohen | | |
| Father, again to Thee our...· | 177 | M. Grauman...... | J. Ellerton | | |
| Father as the day I greet..... | 241 | P. Jassinowsky | I. R. Hess | | |
| Father, hear the pray'r....... | 42 | J. Singer | L. M. Willis | 72 | |
| Father, let Thy blessing...... | 102 | R. K. Miller | A. A. Ogden | 46 | 46 |
| Father of mercies, God of Love | 185 | S. Alman | A. Flowerdew | | |
| Father, see Thy suppliant children.................. | 150 | Mrs. S. E. Munn | Hamburg Temple Hymnal | 201 | 201— 2nd tune |
| ditto | 151 | A. Rubin | Tr. by F. Adler | 201 | 201— 1st tune |
| ditto | 152 | A. W. Binder | Tr. by F. Adler | 201 | |
| Father, to Thee we look in all | 96 | F. Mendelssohn | F. L. Hosmer | 78 | 78 |
| Father, to Thy dear name I lift | 85 | A. W. Binder | J. L. Levy | 27 | |
| Firm this cornerstone be laid.. | 212 | E. J. Stark | P. Moise | 209 | 209 |
| Fling wide the gates of....... | 132 | Ad. by A. W. B. | Composite | 22 | |
| For garnered fields and meadows.................. | 182 | P. Jassinowsky | J. Leiser | | |
| Forgive us, Lord, we turn to Thee.................. | 163 | S. Alman | F. Montefiore | | |
| For mother-love and father-care.................. | 242 | J. H. Rogers | Author unknown | | |
| For the golden sun and the darting................. | 184 | P. Jassinowsky | I. R. Hess | | |
| Fortress, Rock, my God, my Aid.................. | 208 | Old Synagogal melody | F. de Sola Mendes | 190 | 190 |
| Friend after friend departs.... | 223 | C. H. Grimm | J. Montgomery | 217 | |
| From heaven's height........ | 124 | B. Jacobsohn | H. H. Mayer | 163 | 163 |
| From heaven's height the thunder.................. | 142 | L. Lewandowski | I. M. Wise | 169 | |
| From Sinai's height a fountain | 143 | J. Beimel | J. K. Gutheim | 106 | |
| Gird us, O God, with humble might................. | 24 | J. Singer | W. H. Foulkes | | |
| God is in His holy Temple.... | 4 | H. W. Hawkes | Anonymous | 35 | |
| God is my strong salvation... | 95 | A. W. Binder | J. Montgomery | 69 | |
| God moves in a mysterious way | 83 | A. W. Binder | W. Cowper | | |
| God of grace, O let Thy light.. | 75 | E. Haile | E. Churton | 17 | |
| God of Israel, keep us faithful. | 52 | A. W. Binder | H. H. Mayer | 206 | |
| God of might, God of right... | 125 | Trad. "Addir Hu" | Composite | 164 | 164 |
| God of our fathers whose almighty................. | 263 | G. W. Warren | D. C. Roberts | | |
| God of the nations near and far | 226 | P. C. Lutkin | J. H. Holmes | 151 | 151 |

| FIRST LINE | NO. | COMPOSER | AUTHOR | CROSS REFERENCE FOR SECOND EDITION* | |
|---|---|---|---|---|---|
| | | | | WORDS | MUSIC |
| God send us men whose aim shall................... | 233 | B. Levenson | F. J. Gillman | | |
| God supreme! To Thee we pray.................... | 93 | J. Achron | P. Moise—st. 1 & 2 E. Calisch—st. 3 & 4 | 98 | |
| God that doest wondrously... | 176 | Arr. by A. W. Binder | S. Solis-Cohen | | |
| God the All-Merciful....... | 265B | A. T. Lwoff | H. F. Chorley, J. Ellerton | | |
| Grant me strength when skies are..................... | 48 | J. Weinberg | L. Weitzman | 90 | |
| Great Arbiter of human fate.. | 209 | E. Samuel | P. Moise | 191 | 191 |
| Great Lord of life who lives in | 243 | A. W. Binder | J. E. Sampter | | |
| Hail the glorious Golden City. | 227 | Composer unknown | F. Adler | 147 | 147 |
| Happy he that never wanders. | 100 | A. W. Binder | tr. by F. Adler | 125 | |
| Happy he who walketh ever.. | 25 | H. Fabisch | J. Voorsanger | 116 | 116— 2nd tune |
| | 27 | A. W. Binder | J. Voorsanger | 116 | |
| Happy who in early youth.... | 253 | Arr. fr. L. M. Gottschalk | tr. by J. K. Gutheim | 199 | 199 |
| Hark the voice of children.... | 146 | Har. by G. H. Loud | S. H. Sonnenschein St. 1 & 2—L. Wolsey—St. 3 | 205 | 205 |
| Haste not! Haste not! do not rest.................... | 43 | Arr. fr. J. Blumenthal | tr. by C. C. Cox | 130 | 79—1st ed** |
| Hatikvah................... | 266 | | | | |
| Hear my pray'r, O hear my pray'r.................. | 168 | J. Weinberg | I. R. Hess | | |
| Hear us, Eternal King,....... | 136 | F. Giardini | E. Davieson | 131 | |
| Here let Thy people come, dear | 5 | A. W. Binder | R. Loveman | 95 | |
| His flock our Shepherd feeds.. | 111 | Ad. by M. Grauman | tr. by A. Lucas | | |
| How blest the man who fears to | 26 | J. Kinross | B. H. Kennedy | 122 | 122 |
| How good it is to thank the Lord.................... | 109 | H. Gideon | F. Weisberg | 13 | |
| ditto | 110 | Lewandowski's "L'cho Dodi" | F. Weisberg | 13 | |
| How goodly is Thy house, O Lord ................. | 1 | W. A. Mozart | H. S. Jacobs | 38 | 38 |
| How lovely are Thy dwellings | 3 | F. Mendelssohn | J. Milton | 42 | 81 |
| How lovely are Thy dwellings | 2 | Arr. fr. Schumann | J. Milton | 34 | 140 |
| How wondrous is Thy world, O Lord.................. | 56 | J. Singer | A. Lucas | | |
| I bless Thee Father, for the grace.................... | 115 | A. Epstein | G. Aguilar | 160 | 160 |
| I hope for the salvation of the | 92 | J. G. Heller | tr. by A. Lucas | | |
| I leave the burdens of my life. | 221 | B. Levenson | S. Navra | | |
| I lift mine eyes unto the hills.. | 33 | J. Achron | C. M. C. | 81 | |
| If our God had not befriended. | 123 | J. Weinberg | E. Churton | 194 | |
| In God the holy, wise and just | 73 | H. R. Shelley | P. Moise | 15 | |
| In many a stone bound city... | 180 | J. Beimel | J. E. Sampter | | |
| In mercy, Lord, incline Thine ear.................... | 211 | A. W. Binder | I. M. Wise | 210 | |

| FIRST LINE | NO. | COMPOSER | AUTHOR | CROSS REFERENCE FOR SECOND EDITION* | |
|---|---|---|---|---|---|
| | | | | WORDS | MUSIC |
| In sunshine and in storm, O God | 90 | B. Levenson | H. H. Mayer | | |
| In the candles' rays I see..... | 206 | A. W. Binder | E. E. Levinger | | |
| Into the tomb of ages past.... | 156 | J. G. Heller. | P. Moise | 175 | |
| ditto | 157 | A. W. Binder, Trad. melody | P. Moise | 175 | |
| Into Thy hands my spirit I commend................. | 14 | C. Hartog | L. Weitzman | 89 | 89 |
| It singeth low in every heart.. | 220 | C. H. Grimm | J. W. Chadwick | 220 | |
| Kindle the taper like the ..... | 204 | J. Singer | E. Lazarus | 192 | |
| ditto | 205 | A. W. Binder | E. Lazarus | 192 | |
| Let Israel trust in God alone.. | 139 | W. Lowenberg | Tr. J. K. Gutheim | 142 | 142 |
| Let there be light, at dawn of. | 141 | J. S. Mombach | I. M. Wise | 170 | 33 |
| Let there be light, Lord God.. | 232 | J. Singer | W. M. Vories | | |
| Let us with a gladsome mind.. | 58 | Fr. Braham & Nathan's "Hebrew Melodies" | J. Milton | 2 | 2 |
| Little children, Lord, are we.. | 249 | J. H. Rogers | | | |
| Lo, as the potter molds his clay | 172 | "Kee hinnay kachomer" | Tr. by E. Davis | 68 | 68 |
| Lo, our Father's tender care.. | 82 | J. H. Rogers | J. K. Gutheim | 88 | |
| Lo! the earth rejoices........ | 248 | A. W. Binder | | | |
| Lord, do Thou guide me on my | 22 | J. G. Heller | A. Lucas | 92 | |
| Lord God whose breath the... | 37 | Theme fr. D'Andrieux | A. Lucas | | |
| Lord in this sacred hour ..... | 112 | H. R. Shelley | S. G. Bulfinch | | |
| Lord, into Thy sacred dwelling | 144 | M. Grauman | H. Berkowitz | | |
| Lord of hosts, whom all adore | 178 | Arr. by A. W. Binder | tr. by A. Lucas | | |
| Lord of the harvest ......... | 188 | C. H. Grimm | J. H. Gurney | | |
| Lord what offering shall we bring.................. | 148 | J. Weinberg | J. Taylor | 202 | |
| Lord, written in rocks and in.. | 39 | J. G. Heller | I. R. Hess | | |
| Lord, Thine humble servants hear.................... | 169 | J. Weinberg | tr. by S. Solis-Cohen | | |
| Loud let the swelling anthems rise.................... | 78 | N. L. Norden | tr. by F. Adler | 24 | |
| Magnify th' Eternal's name... | 59 | Arr. fr. G. F. Handel | J. Montgomery | 166 | 166 |
| May He who kept us through the.................... | 10 | J. H. Rogers | A. Lucas | 28 | |
| Men, whose boast it is that ye | 121 | "Az Yasheer" | J. R. Lowell | 128 | |
| My country 'tis of thee...... | 264 | Henry Carey | S. F. Smith | 226 | 226 |
| My faith shall be my rock of might.................. | 200 | J. Beimel | A. Lucas | | |
| Not alone for mighty empire.. | 229 | W. A. Mozart | W. P. Merrill | 224 | 224 |
| Now bless the God of all..... | 81 | F. H. Cowen | I. Abrahams | 64 | 71 |
| Now upon the earth descending | 236 | J. Beimel | D. Levy | | |
| O beautiful for spacious skies. | 262 | S. A. Ward | K. L. Bates | 222 | |
| O bless the Lord, my soul.... | 62 | Arr. by A. W. Binder | I. Watts | 4 | |

| FIRST LINE | NO. | COMPOSER | AUTHOR | CROSS REFERENCE FOR SECOND EDITION* | |
|---|---|---|---|---|---|
| | | | | WORDS | MUSIC |
| O deem not that earth's crowning | 51 | L. Spohr | W. H. Burleigh | 78—1st ed.** | 78—1st ed.** |
| | 98 | J. H. Rogers | W. H. Burleigh | | |
| O Father, Thou who givest all | 250 | N. L. Norden | J. H. Holmes | | |
| O God, all gracious! | 45 | F. Dunkley | P. Moise | 112 | 176 |
| ditto | 50 | Composer unknown | P. Moise | | 112 |
| O God, my ever constant Friend | 192 | J. Singer | H. H. Mayer | | |
| O God our help in ages past... | 47 | W. Croft | I. Watts | 52 | |
| O God the Rock of Ages..... | 32 | J. Achron | E. H. Bickersteth | 61 | |
| O God whose law from age to age | 97 | J. Singer | J. H. Holmes | | |
| O holy joy that raises........ | 104 | A. Kaiser | | 10—1st ed. | 39, 10—1st ed. |
| O holy Sabbath day draw near | 117 | J. Beimel | I. S. Moses | | |
| O Lord be near me when I pray | 19 | H. R. Shelley | T. Tallis—ad. by F. E. Falch | | |
| O Lord my God to Thee I pray | 29 | Arr. fr. S. Sulzer | tr. by J. K. Gutheim | 123 | 123 |
| O Lord of heaven and earth and..................... | 66 | M. Grauman | C. Wordsworth | | |
| O Lord our King how bright Thy.................... | 72 | S. Alman | B. H. Kennedy | 58 | |
| O Lord Thy all discerning eyes | 38 | H. R. Shelley | J. Q. Adams | 53 | |
| O Lord to Thee who dwell'st | 196 | A. Kaiser | G. Jacobs | 40 | 40 |
| O Lord where shall I find Thee | 21 | J. Weinberg | tr. by S. Solis-Cohen | | |
| O rain depart with blessings.. | 128 | P. Jassinowsky | S. Solis-Cohen | | |
| O render thanks to God above | 194 | A. W. Binder | | 19 | |
| O say can you see by the dawn's | 265 | | F. S. Key | 226a | 226a |
| O sometimes gleams upon my sight.................... | 94 | A. W. Binder | J. G. Whittier | 108 | |
| O Soul supreme above us..... | 46 | A. W. Binder | L. I. Newman | | |
| O sound the loud timbrel o'er. | 131 | J. Weinberg | T. Moore | | |
| O worship the king, all-...... | 60 | F. J. Haydn | R. Grant | 16 | 16 |
| Of all the thoughts of God.... | 224 | M. Deutsch | E. B. Browning | 219 | 219 |
| Oh Thou whose presence moved | 216 | J. G. Heller | J. H. Holmes | | |
| On mighty wings rush swiftly. | 161 | M. Grauman | tr. by J. K. Gutheim | 171 | |
| Once more, O Lord, do I awaken | 7 | J. Weinberg | L. Weitzman | 29 | |
| Once more the lib'ral year.... | 181 | J. G. Heller | J. G. Whittier | 197 | |
| One God! One Lord! One mighty.................... | 140 | G. A. Rossini | P. Moise | 56 | 56 |
| Onward brothers, march still.. | 230 | L. van Beethoven | H. Ellis | 146 | 146 |
| Our Father we beseech Thy grace.................... | 145 | H. Schalit | I. Goldstein | 203 | |
| Our Fortress strong art Thou. | 165 | F. Dunkley | Mrs. Goulston | 176 | 176 |
| Our pious fathers built their.. | 215 | M. Grauman | F. de Sola Mendes | | |
| Our Shepherd is the Lord..... | 84 | P. C. Lutkin | Tr. by F. Adler | 93 | 64 |
| Out of the depths, O Lord.... | 164 | A. W. Binder | A. Lucas | 36 | |
| Pledging our lives and our.... | 149 | A. Epstein | H. H. Mayer | 135 | 135—1st tune |
| Praise the Lord! one accord... | 130 | Trad. "Addir Hu" | Tr. by I. S. Moses | | |
| Praise to the living God...... | 54 | Trad. Leoni "Yigdal" | N. Mann ad. fr. Heb. | 77 | 77 |
| Praise ye the Lord! for it is... | 65 | L. M. Isaacs | P. Moise | 3 | 3 |
| Pray when the morn unveileth | 8 | F. Brandeis | P. Moise | 39 | 72 |

| FIRST LINE | NO. | COMPOSER | AUTHOR | CROSS REFERENCE FOR SECOND EDITION* WORDS | MUSIC |
|---|---|---|---|---|---|
| Rejoice and offer thanks to God | 259 | J. Singer | H. H. Mayer | | |
| ditto | 260 | A. W. Binder | H. H. Mayer | | |
| Remember Him, the only One. | 44 | M. Henle | E. Lazarus | 49 | 49 |
| Rest in the Lord, my soul.... | 91 | A. W. Binder | M. D. Babcock | 84 | |
| Rock of Ages, let our song.... | 207 | "Mooz Zur" | M. Jastrow, G. Gottheil—ad. fr. Ger. | 189 | 189 |
| | | | | | |
| See, O God, we children come. | 147 | Traditional | D. Philipson | 204 | 204 |
| Sing to the sov'reign of the... | 67 | B. Levenson | tr. by F. Adler | 14 | |
| Sound the loud timbrel...... | 131 | J. Weinberg | T. Moore | | |
| Splendor of the morning...... | 9 | M. Tintner | F. Adler | 30 | 30 |
| Summer suns are glowing..... | 155 | A. W. Binder | W. W. How | 196 | |
| Sweet hymns and songs will I. | 23 | Trad. "Omnon Kayn" | Tr. by A. Lucas | 1 | 1 |
| Sweet Sabbath! day of sacred. | 116 | R. K. Miller | B. H. Maurice | 152 | 152 |
| | | | | | |
| Take unto you the boughs.... | 187 | S. Alman | A. Lucas | 187 | |
| Ten thousand martyrs died... | 135 | J. Weinberg | M. Meyerhardt | 133 | |
| Tent-like this day the King... | 160 | E. Samuel | Tr. by I. Zangwill | 174 | 174 |
| The day is done, the night.... | 12 | B. Levenson | L. Weitzman | 32 | |
| The God that to the fathers.. | 234 | L. M. Isaacs | M. J. Savage | 145 | |
| The heav'ns, O God, Thy glory | 57 | L. M. Isaacs | B. H. Kennedy | 59 | |
| | 77 | L. van Beethoven | B. H. Kennedy | 59 | |
| The lifting of my (for choir).. | 174 | S. Alman | tr.by N.D.Salaman | 182 | |
| The Lord my Shepherd still has | 86 | A. W. Binder | A. Lucas | 94 | |
| The Lord of all who reigns.... | 76 | S. Sulzer | tr. by F. de Sola Mendes | 74 | 74—1st tune |
| | 80 | A. W. Binder | | | |
| The Lord, the Lord of glory.. | 71 | S. Rappaport | Mrs. Follen | 216 | 216 |
| The Sabbath light is burning.. | 106 | A. W. Binder | J. E. Sampter | | |
| The sun goes down, the...... | 179 | J. Stark | Composite | 185 | |
| The voice of God is calling... | 238 | B. Levenson | J. H. Holmes | | |
| The wise may bring their..... | 246 | J. H. Rogers | | | |
| There is a joy the heart can... | 79 | B. Levenson | R. Loveman | | |
| There is a mystic tie that..... | 137 | J. Achron | M. Meyerhardt | 138 | |
| ditto | 138 | Sephardic "Hallel" | M. Meyerhardt | | 138 |
| There is an Eye that never... | 68 | E. Haile | J. C. Wallace | | |
| There lives a God!.......... | 61 | O. Lob | tr by J.K.Gutheim | 51 | 51 |
| These things shall be!........ | 237 | B. Levenson | J. A. Symonds | | |
| Think gently of the erring.... | 239 | Gesangbuch | J. F. Carney | 121 | |
| This child we dedicate to..... | 240 | J. Singer | Tr. by S. Gillman | | |
| This feast of the law all...... | 199 | J. Beimel | I. Zangwill | | |
| Thou ever-present Perfect.... | 41 | R. R. Rinder | L. I. Newman | | |
| Thou knowest my tongue, O.. | 31 | J. G. Heller | Tr. by S. Solis-Cohen | | |
| | 34 | H. Schalit | | | |
| Thou, O Almighty, knowest... | 158 | J. Beimel | Tr. by A. Lucas | | |
| Though our hearts dwell..... | 228 | Arr. fr. J. Blumenthal | S. Sternberg | 139 | 139 |
| Throughout the night, O God. | 244 | G. Ephros | I. Wise | | |
| Thy faithful servant, Lord.... | 167 | H. R. Shelley | Tr. by A. Funk | 183 | |
| Thy praise, O Lord, will I.... | 183 | N. L. Norden | A. Lucas | 188 | |
| Thy word is to my feet a..... | 36 | P. Jassinowsky | "New" Version | 119 | |
| | 191 | J. Weinberg | ditto | 119 | |
| 'Tis not the large, the huge... | 235 | J. G. Heller | A. Cronbach | | |
| 'Tis winter now; the fallen.... | 198 | J. G. Heller | S. Longfellow | 198 | |

| FIRST LINE | NO. | COMPOSER | AUTHOR | CROSS REFERENCE FOR SECOND EDITION* | |
| --- | --- | --- | --- | --- | --- |
| | | | | WORDS | MUSIC |
| To Bethel came the patriarch. | 49 | M. Grauman | F. de Sola Mendes and N. Stern | | |
| To-day while the sun shines... | 258 | A. W. Binder | N. Douty | | |
| To the God of all creation.... | 20 | Arr. fr. L. van Beethoven | W. W. Hull | 11 | 11 |
| To Thee above all creatures... | 126 | E. Haile | Tr.by J.K.Gutheim | 167 | |
| To Thee we give ourselves.... | 166 | Kee hinay kachomer | G. Gottheil | 178 | 178 |
| To worship God in truth..... | 214 | fr. Lyra Anglo-Judaica | H. H. Mayer | 213 | 213 |
| 'Twas like a dream, when by.. | 120 | R. Schumann | "Scottish" Version | 140 | 140 |
| ditto | 122 | Ad. by A. W. Binder | | | |
| Unto the hills I lift mine..... | 13 | J. Beimel | A. Lucas | | |
| Unveil mine eyes that of..... | 202 | F. Belmont | Scottish Version | 102 | 102 |
| Uplift the song of praise...... | 261 | J. H. Rogers | F. L. Hosmer | 225 | |
| We build our school on Thee.. | 254 | J. H. Rogers | S. W. Mayer | | |
| We hear the call of Israel's.... | 256 | J. Achron | A. R. Rosewater | | |
| We meet again in gladness.... | 255 | S. Hecht | Anonymous | 23 | 23 |
| We plough the fields and..... | 195 | C. H. Grimm | Tr. by J. M. Campbell | | |
| We thank Thee, Lord, for.... | 193 | J. Singer | G. E. L. Cotton | | |
| When Israel of the Lord...... | 119 | J. Beimel | Sir W. Scott | 132 | |
| When Israel to the wilderness. | 127 | J. Beimel | M. Meyerhardt | 136 | |
| When the Sabbath peace..... | 114 | J. Beimel | M. Jastrow, alt. | 158 | |
| When the stars at set of sun.. | 245 | M. Grauman | | | |
| When there is peace, where... | 16 | A. W. Binder | T. A. Davis | | |
| When this song of praise..... | 103 | E. J. Stark | W. C. Bryant | 47 | 47—1st tune |
| When thy heart with joy..... | 197 | J. G. Heller | T. C. Williams | | |
| When warmer suns and bluer. | 134 | N. L. Norden | | | |
| Where Judah's faithful sons... | 210 | S. Alman | H. H. Mayer | 193 | |
| While yet the earth mid'st | 99 | J. Singer | Mrs. I. L. Rypins | | |
| Who is like Thee, O Universal. | 69 | A. W. Binder | J. K. Gutheim | 55 | |
| Who taught the bird to build. | 247 | A. W. Binder | | | |
| Whose works, O Lord, like... | 222 | I. Warren | A. Lucas | 218 | 218 |
| Why art thou cast down, my. | 171 | A. W. Binder | Tr.by J.K.Gutheim | 186 | |
| With the voice of sweet song.. | 70 | F. H. Cowen | H. H. Mayer | 10 | 10 |

* The Second Edition of the Union Hymnal was published in 1914.
** The First Edition of the Union Hymnal was published in 1897.

# INDEX OF PSALMS

| PSALM | NUMBER | PSALM | NUMBER |
|-------|--------|-------|--------|
| 1 | 25, 26, 27 | 93 | 71 |
| 8 | 72 | 95 | 20 |
| 19 | 57, 77 | 103 | 62 |
| 23 | 84, 86 | 104 | 60 |
| 27 | 95 | 106 | 194 |
| 37 | 87 | 107 | 59 |
| 42 | 30, 40 | 118 | 132 |
| 51 | 170 | 119 | 36, 191, 202 |
| 66 | 64 | 121 | 13, 33 |
| 67 | 75 | 124 | 123 |
| 82 | 2 | 126 | 120, 122 |
| 84 | 3 | 130 | 164 |
| 86 | 35 | 136 | 58 |
| 90 | 32, 47 | 139 | 38 |
| 92 | 109, 110 | | |

# INDEX OF MUSICAL SERVICES

| RESPONSE | NUMBER | IN RELIGIOUS SCHOOL SERVICES—PAGE |
|----------|--------|-----------------------------------|
| Adon Olom | 276 | |
| | 311 (for Rosh Hashonoh and Yom Kippur) | |
| Adonoy, Adonoy | 313 | |
| Adonoy Mo Odom | 334 | |
| Adonoy Yimloch | 271 | 435, 445, 480 |
| | 282 | |
| | 284 | |
| | 294 (for Chanukoh) | |
| | 296 (for Sh'vuos) | |
| | 299 (for Succos) | |
| All Ye Dwellers (Shofar) | 317 | |
| Amens | 341 | |
| Ayn Kaylohaynu | 275 | |
| | 292 | |
| Ayn Komocho | 304 | |
| Ayts Chayeem | | 472, 484 |
| Blessings over Chanukoh Lights | 297 | 545 |
| Blessings over the Lulov | 303 | 507 |
| Bor'chu | 268 | 433 |
| | 279 | 437 |
| | 305 (for Rosh Hashonoh and Yom Kippur) | |
| | | 443 |
| Boruch K'vod | 286 | 440 |
| Boruch Shaym | 306, 314, 331 | 434, 438 |
| Finale Day of Atonement | 338 | |
| | 339 | |
| | 340 | |
| For the Mountains (Shofar) | 316 | |
| Harneenu | 308 | |
| Hayom T'am'tsaynu | 333 | |
| Hodo and Ono | 302 | 471 |
| Hodo al Eretz | | 471 |
| Kee Onu Amecho | 326 | |
| Kee Vayom | 322 | |
| Kee L'olom chasdo | | 477 |

577

| RESPONSE | NUMBER | IN RELIGIOUS SCHOOL SERVICES—PAGE |
|---|---|---|
| Kodosh | 285 | 439, 481 |
| Kol Nidre | 318 | |
| L'cho Adonoy | 291 | 469, 482, 494 |
| L'cho Dodee | 267 | |
| Lift Up Your Heads | 289 | |
| May the Words | 273 | 435, 441 |
| Mee Chomocho | 270 | 434 |
| | 281 | 444 |
| | 283 | 479 |
| | 293 (for Chanukoh) | |
| | 295 (for Sh'vuos) | |
| | 298 (for Succos) | |
| | 307 | |
| Olaynu | 329 | |
| O Lord, What Is Man! | 335 | |
| Ono Adonoy Kapper No | 330 | |
| Our Father, Our King | 309 | |
| Praise the Lord | | 541 |
| Priestly Benediction | 301 | |
| P'sach Lonu | 337 | |
| Shehecheyonu | 352 | 567 |
| Shiveesee | 336 | |
| Sh'ma Yisroayl | 269 | 433 |
| | 280 | 438 |
| | 290 | 443 |
| | | 494 |
| Sholom Alaychem | 278 | |
| S'lach No | 320 | |
| S'u Sh'oreem | 288 | 468, 481, 493 |
| The Lord Reigneth (Shofar) | 315 | |
| Tovo l'fonecho | 324 | |
| Un'saneh tokef | 328 | |
| Va-anachnu | 274 | |
| | 310 | |
| V'al kulom | 325 | |
| Vay'dabayr Moshe | 300 | |
| Vayomer Adonoy | 321 | |
| V'nislach | 319 | |
| V'shom'ru | 272 | |
| We Are Thy People | 326 | |
| Yaa'leh | 323 | |
| Y'vorechecho | 301 | |
| Yigdal | 277 | |
| | 327 | |
| Yimloch | 287 | 440 |
| Yimloch Adonoy | 332 | |
| Zochraynu | 312 | |

# CROSS REFERENCE FOR SECOND EDITION

This index is for the purpose of enabling one to find in this Hymnal the hymns and verses in the first two editions of the Union Hymnal. Unless otherwise indicated, the numbers in the first two columns refer to the second edition.

| WORDS | MUSIC | NUMBERS IN THIS HYMNAL | WORDS | MUSIC | NUMBERS IN THIS HYMNAL |
|---|---|---|---|---|---|
| 1 | 1 | 23 | 74 | — | 76, 80 |
| 2 | 2 | 58 | — | 74-1st tune | 76 |
| 3 | 3 | 65 | 77 | 77 | 54 |
| 4 | — | 62 | 78-1st ed. | 78-1st ed. | 51 |
| 7 | — | 18 | 78-1st ed. | — | 98 |
| 10 | 10 | 70 | 78 | 78 | 96 |
| 11 | 11 | 20 | — | 79-1st ed. | 43 |
| 13 | — | 109, 110 | 81 | — | 33 |
| 14 | — | 67 | — | 81 | 3 |
| 15 | — | 73 | 83 | — | 35 |
| 16 | 16 | 60 | 84 | — | 91 |
| 17 | — | 75 | 88 | — | 82 |
| 19 | — | 194 | 89 | 89 | 14 |
| 22 | — | 132 | 90 | — | 48 |
| 23 | 23 | 255 | 92 | — | 22 |
| 24 | — | 78 | 93 | — | 84 |
| 26 | — | 74 | 94 | — | 86 |
| 27 | — | 85 | 95 | — | 5 |
| 28 | — | 10 | 96 | 96 | 175 |
| 29 | — | 7 | 97 | 97 | 89 |
| 30 | — | 95 | 98 | — | 93 |
| 32 | — | 12 | 99 | 99 | 53 |
| — | 33 | 141 | 100 | 100 | 173 |
| 34 | — | 2 | 102 | 102 | 202 |
| 35 | — | 4 | 106 | — | 143 |
| 36 | — | 164 | 108 | — | 94 |
| 38 | 38 | 1 | 112 | — | 45, 50 |
| 39 | — | 8 | — | 112 | 50 |
| — | 39 | 104 | 113 | 113 | 170 |
| 40 | 40 | 196 | 115 | — | 225 |
| 42 | — | 3 | 116 | — | 25, 27 |
| 44 | — | 11 | — | 116-2nd tune | 25 |
| 46 | 46 | 102 | 117 | — | 231 |
| 47 | 47-1st tune | 103 | 119 | — | 36, 191 |
| 49 | 49 | 44 | 121 | — | 232, 239 |
| 51 | 51 | 61 | 122 | 122 | 26 |
| 52 | — | 47 | 123 | 123 | 29 |
| 53 | — | 38 | 125 | — | 100 |
| 55 | — | 69 | 126 | — | 87 |
| 56 | 56 | 140 | 128 | — | 121 |
| 58 | — | 72 | 130 | — | 43 |
| 59 | — | 57, 77 | 131 | — | 136 |
| 61 | — | 32 | 132 | — | 119 |
| 63 | — | 64 | 133 | — | 135 |
| 64 | — | 81 | 135 | 135-1st tune | 149 |
| — | 64 | 84 | 136 | — | 127 |
| 66 | — | 30, 40 | 138 | — | 137, 138 |
| — | 66-1st ed. | 87 | — | 138 | 138 |
| 68 | 68 | 172 | 139 | 139 | 228 |
| 69 | — | 95 | — | 140 | 2, 120 |
| — | 71 | 81 | 140 | — | 120, 122 |
| 72 | — | 42 | 142 | 142 | 139 |
| — | 72 | 8 | 143 | — | 101 |

| WORDS | MUSIC | NUMBERS IN THIS HYMNAL |
|---|---|---|
| 145 | — | 234 |
| 146 | 146 | 230 |
| 147 | 147 | 227 |
| 150 | — | 63 |
| 151 | 151 | 226 |
| 152 | 152 | 116 |
| 154 | — | 107 |
| 156 | — | 118 |
| 158 | — | 114 |
| 160 | 160 | 115 |
| 162 | 162 | 129 |
| 163 | 163 | 124 |
| 164 | 164 | 125 |
| 166 | 166 | 59 |
| 167 | — | 126 |
| 169 | — | 142 |
| 170 | — | 141 |
| 171 | — | 161 |
| 174 | — | 160 |
| 175 | — | 156, 157 |
| — | 176 | 45 |
| 176 | 176 | 165 |
| 178 | 178 | 166 |
| 182 | — | 174 |
| 183 | — | 167 |
| 184 | 184 | 162 |
| 185 | — | 179 |
| 186 | — | 171 |
| 187 | — | 187 |
| 188 | — | 183 |
| 189 | 189 | 207 |
| 190 | 190 | 208 |
| 191 | 191 | 209 |
| 192 | — | 204, 205 |

| WORDS | MUSIC | NUMBERS IN THIS HYMNAL |
|---|---|---|
| 193 | — | 210 |
| 194 | — | 123 |
| 195 | 195 | 133 |
| 196 | — | 155 |
| 197 | — | 181 |
| 198 | — | 198 |
| 199 | 199 | 253 |
| 200 | — | 153, 154 |
| 201 | — | 150, 151, 152 |
| — | 201-2nd tune | 150 |
| — | 201-1st tune | 151 |
| 202 | — | 148 |
| 203 | — | 145 |
| 204 | — | 147 |
| 205 | 205 | 146 |
| 206 | — | 52 |
| 207 | — | 219 |
| 208 | — | 218 |
| 209 | 209 | 212 |
| 210 | — | 211 |
| 211 | — | 213 |
| 213 | 213 | 214 |
| 214 | — | 217 |
| 216 | 216 | 71 |
| 217 | — | 223 |
| 218 | — | 222 |
| 219 | 219 | 224 |
| 220 | — | 220 |
| 222 | — | 262 |
| 224 | 224 | 229 |
| 225 | — | 261 |
| 226 | 226 | 264 |
| 226a | 226a | 265 |

# INDEX OF HEBREW TUNES AND MODES IN THE HYMNS

| | NUMBER |
|---|---|
| Addeer Hu | 125, 130 |
| Adon Olam | 157 (Rosh Hashonoh) |
| Akdamos | 56, 143 |
| Ashkenazi | 58, 214 |
| Az Yasheer | 62, 121 (Sephardic) |
| Bemotzoay (Sephardic) | 173 |
| Eliyahu Hanavi | 42 |
| Grace | 111 |
| Hakofos | 199 |
| Hallel (Sephardic) | 138 |
| Hatikvo | 266 |
| Kee Hinay Kachomer | 166, 172 |
| L'cho Dodee (Lewandowski) | 110 |
| Mee Chomocho (Shevuos) | 142 |
| Min Hamaytsar (Halevy) | 132 |
| Mooz Tsur | 207, 208 |
| N'eelah | 177, 179 |

| | NUMBER |
|---|---|
| Omnon Ken | 23 |
| Oveenu Malkaynu | 161 |
| Rosh Hashonoh Chant | 157, 158, 159 |
| Sabbath Mode | 114, 117 |
| Sephardic | 80, 121, 138, 176, 178, 258 |
| Sheer Hamaalos | 122 |
| Sheer Hasheereem | 105, 192 |
| Simchas Torah | 200 |
| Song of Songs | 105, 192 |
| Succos | 180, 187 |
| S'u Sh'oreem (Lewandowski) | 64 |
| Synagog Chant | 101 |
| Tal | 128 |
| V'al Kulom | 171 |
| Yigdal (Leoni) | 54 |
| Yom Kippur Mode | 163 |

# INDEX OF COMPOSERS

NUMBER

Achron, Joseph.........32, 33, 93, 137, 256
Alman, Samuel, 55, 72, 163, 174, 185, 187, 210, 231
Barnby, Joseph...................... 88
Beimel, Jacob, 13, 35, 114, 117, 119, 127, 143, 158, 180, 199, 200, 236, 312, 323, 326
Belmont, F........................ 202
Binder, A. W., 5, 11, 15, 16, 27, 46, 52, 62, 63, 64, 69, 74, 77, 80, 83, 85, 86, 91, 94, 95, 100, 106, 107, 108, 118, 122, 132, 142, 152, 153, 155, 157, 159, 164, 171, 176, 178, 194, 205, 206, 211, 243, 247, 248, 258, 260, 267, 273, 277, 279, 280, 283, 288, 290, 293, 297, 300, 301, 303, 304, 305, 307, 308, 309, 311, 314, 315, 322, 325, 327, 330
Blumenthal, Jacques...............43, 228
Braham & Nathan's "Hebrew Melodies"  58
Brandeis, F........................ 8

Carey, Henry...................... 264
Cohen, Francis L.........319, 329, 338, 341
Cowen, Frederic H................70, 81
Croft, William.................... 47

D'Andrieux........................ 37
Deutsch, M........................ 224
Dunkley, Ferdinand..............45, 165

Ephros, Gershon.................244, 291
Epstein, A......................115, 149

Fabisch, H........................ 25
Freudenthal, Julius............... 292

Gerovitch, Eliezer............. 276, 313
Giardini, Felice.................. 136
Gideon, Henry.................... 109
Goldfarb, I....................... 278
Goldstein, M...................... 274
Gottschalk, Louis M............... 253
Grauman, Max, 49, 66, 111, 113, 144, 161, 177, 215, 217, 245
Grimm, C. Hugo, 28, 188, 195, 201, 220, 223, 225
Haendel, George F...............59, 175
Haile, Eugen..................68, 75, 126
Halevy, J. F...................... 302
Halpern, M....................... 334
Hartog, Cecile.................... 14
Hawkes, H. W...................... 4
Haydn, Franz J.................... 60
Hecht, Simon...................133, 255
Heller, James G., 22, 31, 39, 92, 156, 181, 197, 198, 213, 216, 219, 235, 257, 335
Henle, M.......................... 44

NUMBER

Isaacs, Lewis M.............57, 65, 234
Jacobsohn, B...................... 124
Jassinowsky, Pinchos, 36, 105, 128, 182, 184, 203, 241, 324
Kaiser, Alois...........40, 104, 154, 196
Kinross, J........................ 26
Leoni............................. 277
Levenson, Boris, 12, 67, 79, 90, 101, 221, 233, 237, 238
Lewandowski, Louis, 53, 64, 110, 142, 267, 270, 272, 275, 295, 298, 307, 320, 322, 333
Lieber, Arthur.................... 170
Lob, Otto......................... 61
Loud, George...................... 146
Lowenberg, William................ 139
Lutkin, Peter C..................84, 226
Lwoff, Alexis T................... 265B

Mendelssohn, Felix..........3, 87, 96
Miller, Russell King.........102, 116, 162
Mombach, J. S..................... 141
Mozart, W. A....................1, 229
Munn, Mrs. S. E................... 150

Naumburg, S................. 288, 309, 328
Neumark, Georg.................... 89
Norden, N. Lindsay.....17, 78, 134, 183, 250
Nowakowsky, David...........15, 107, 108

Rappaport, S...................... 71
Rinder, Reuben R................30, 41
Rogers, James H., 10, 82, 98, 242, 246, 249, 251, 254, 261
Rossini, G. A..................... 140
Rubin, A.......................... 151

Sabel, S.......................... 18
Samuel, Edward................160, 209
Schalit, Heinrich........6, 34, 145, 189
Schumann, Robert................2, 120
Shelley, Harry Rowe, 19, 38, 73, 112, 167, 252
Singer, Jacob, 24, 42, 56, 97, 99, 186, 192, 193, 204, 218, 232, 240, 259, 289
Spohr, L.......................... 51
Stark, E. J....................103, 212
Stark, Josef...................179, 337
Sulzer, Solomon, 29, 76, 268, 269, 285, 286, 287, 306, 310, 336

Tintner, M........................ 9

Unknown.......................50, 227
Van Beethoven, Ludwig.........20, 77, 230
Ward, Samuel Augustus............. 262
Warren, George W.................. 263
Warren, Ivor...................... 222
Weinberg, Jacob, 7, 21, 48, 123, 131, 135, 148, 168, 169, 190, 191

# INDEX OF AUTHORS

NUMBER

Abrahams, Israel................ 81
Adams, John Quincy............. 38
Adler, Felix, 9, 67, 78, 84, 100, 151, 152, 227
Aguilar, Grace.................89, 115
Alcott, Louisa M............... 251
Alexander, Cecil Frances........ 252

Babcock, Maltbie D............. 91
Bates, Katherine Lee........... 262
Berkowitz, Henry............... 144
Bickersteth, Edward H.......... 32
Brontë, Anne................... 231
Browning, Elizabeth Barrett..... 224
Bryant, William Cullen......... 103
Bulfinch, Stephen Greenleaf..... 112
Burleigh, William Henry........51, 98

C. M. C........................ 33
Calisch, Edward N.............. 93
Campbell, Jane M............... 195
Carney, Julia Fletcher......... 239
Chadwick, John W............... 220
Chorley, Henry F...............265B
Churton Edward................64, 75, 123
Cohen, Aaron................... 107
Cotton, George E. L............ 193
Cowper, William................ 83
Cox, C. C...................... 43
Cronbach, Abraham.............. 235

Davieson, Eve.................. 136
Davis, Elsie................... 172
Davis, T. A.................... 16
Dobson, Austin................. 218
Douty, Nicholas................ 258

Ellerton, John................ 177, 265B
Ellis, Havelock................ 230

Flowerdew, Alice............... 185
Follen, Mrs.................... 71
Foulkes, William Hiram......... 24
Funk, Addie.................... 167

Gillman, F. J.................. 233
Gilman, Sam.................... 240
Goldstein, Ida................. 145
Gottheil, Gustav...........18, 118, 166, 207
Goulston, Mrs.................. 165
Grant, Robert.................. 60
Gurney, John Hampden........... 188
Gutheim, James K., 29, 61, 69, 74, 82, 126,
    139, 143, 161, 171, 253

Hess, Isabella R., 39, 168, 184, 189, 190, 241
Holmes, John Haynes..97, 216, 226, 238, 250
Hosmer, F. L...................96, 261
How, William Walsham.......... 155

NUMBER

Hull, W. W..................... 20

Imber, N. H.................... 266
Isaacs, A. S...................175, 225

Jacobs, George................. 196
Jacobs, Henry S................ 1
Jastrow, M.............114, 153, 154, 207

Kennedy, B. H...........26, 57, 72, 77
Key, Francis Scott............. 265
Klein, Max D................... 203

Lazarus, Emma..........44, 204, 205
Leiser, Joseph................. 182
Levinger, Elma Ehrlich......... 206
Levy, David.............17, 113, 236
Levy, J. Leonard...........85, 101
Longfellow, Samuel.........11, 198
Loveman, Robert................5, 79
Lowell, James Russell.......... 121
Lucas, Alice, 10, 13, 15, 22, 23, 37, 53, 56, 86,
    92, 108, 111, 129, 158, 162,
    164, 178, 183, 187, 200, 222
Macleod, Norman................ 87
Mann, Newton................... 54
Marshall, Louis................ 213
Maurice, Bertha Helena......... 116
Mayer, Harry H., 35, 52, 70, 90, 105, 124,
    149, 192, 210, 214, 259, 260
Mayer, Sebastian W............. 254
Mendes, F. de Sola......49, 76, 80, 208, 215
Merrill, William P............. 229
Meyerhardt, Max........127, 135, 137, 138
Milton, John...................2, 3, 58
Moise, Penina, 8, 45, 50, 55, 65, 73, 93, 140,
    156, 157, 209, 212, 219
Montefiore, Florence...........163, 201
Montgomery, James..........28, 59, 95, 223
Moore, Thomas.................. 131
Moses, Isaac S.................117, 130

Navra, Sophia.................. 221
Newman, Louis I................41, 46

Ogden, Althea A................ 102
Philipson, David............... 147

Roberts, Daniel C.............. 263
Rosewater, Adeline R...........256, 257
Rypins, Mrs. Isaac L...........99, 173

Salaman, Nina Davis............ 174
Sampter, Jessie E........106, 180, 243
Savage, Minot J................ 234
Scott, Sir Walter.............. 119
Singer, Barbara Joan........... 186
Smith, Samuel F................ 264

Solis-Cohen, Solomon, 21, 31, 34, 128, 159, 169, 176

Sonnenschein, S. H. ..................... 146
Stern, Louis ........................... 217
Stern, Nathan ......................... 49
Sternberg, Sadye ...................... 228
Switton, Florence ..................... 133
Symonds, J. Addington .............. 237

Taylor, John .......................... 148

Voorsanger, Jacob .................. 25, 27
Vories, William Merrell .............. 232

Wallace, James Cowden ............... 68
Watts, Isaac ......................... 47, 62
Weisberg, Florence ................. 109, 110
Weitzman, Lily ............ 7, 12, 14, 48, 170
Whittier, John G. ............. 88, 94, 181
Williams, Theodore Chickering ......... 197
Willis, L. M. ......................... 42
Wise, Isaac M. ................ 141, 142, 211
Wise, Isidor ......................... 244
Wordsworth, Christopher ............. 66

Zangwill, Israel ............... 63, 160, 199

# INDEX OF SUBJECTS

**Adversity** (See Faith, Trust, and Courage)

**Anniversary of Congregation or Rabbi**

Come let us sing in sweet accord ........ 217
Oh Thou, whose presence moved before .. 216
Our pious fathers built their shrine ...... 215
To worship God in truth .............. 214

**Aspiration**

Ah well it is that God ................ 89
Almighty Father, God of love .......... 6
Almighty God, in humble prayer ....... 28
As pants the hart .................... 30, 40
At midnight so the sages tell ........ 88, 175
Bow down Thine ear, Lord, ........... 35
Dim mine eyes with many tear-drops .... 173
Early will I seek Thee ............... 18
Father, hear the pray'r we offer! ....... 42
Gird us, O God, with humble might ..... 24
God of Israel, keep us faithful ........ 52
Grant me strength when skies are azure .. 48
Happy he who walketh ever .......... 25, 27
Haste not! Haste not! ............... 43
How blest the man who fears to stray ... 26
I lift mine eyes unto the hills .......... 33
Lord, do Thou guide me .............. 22
Lord God whose breath .............. 37
Lord, written in rocks and in woodland .. 39
O deem not that earth's crowning bliss .. 51, 98
O God, all gracious! ................ 45, 50
O God, our help in ages past, ......... 47
O God, the Rock of Ages ............. 32
O Lord, be near me when I pray, ....... 19
O Lord, my God, to Thee I pray ....... 29
O Lord, Thy all discerning eyes ........ 38
O Lord, where shall I find Thee ........ 21
O Soul supreme above us ............. 46
Remember Him, the only One ......... 44
Splendor of the morning sunlight ....... 9
Sweet hymns and songs .............. 23
Thou ever-present Perfect Friend ....... 41
Thou knowest my tongue, O God, ..... 31, 34

Thou O Almighty knowest all ......... 158
Thy word is to my feet a lamp ...... 36, 191
To Bethel came the patriarch .......... 49
To the God of all creation ............ 20
Unto the hills ....................... 13

**Atonement, Day of** (See also Penitence)

Create in this weak form of mine ....... 170
Despise not, Lord, my lowly penitence ... 162
Dim mine eyes with many tear-drops .... 173
Forgive us, Lord, we turn to Thee ...... 163
Hear my pray'r, O hear my pray'r ...... 168
Lo as the potter molds his clay ......... 172
Lord, Thine humble servants hear ...... 169
On mighty wings rush swiftly by ....... 161
Our fortress strong art Thou ........... 165
Out of the depths, O Lord, ........... 164
The lifting of my hands (for choir) ...... 174
Thy faithful servant, Lord, ............ 167
To Thee we give ourselves today; ...... 166

**Atonement, Day of** (N'eelah)

Father, again to Thee ................. 177
God, that doest wondrously ........... 176
Lord of Hosts, whom all adore ......... 178
The sun goes down, ................. 179
Why art thou cast down, my soul ....... 171

**Autumn (and Harvest)**

All through the long bright days ........ 186
Father of mercies, God of love ......... 185
For garnered fields .................. 182
For the golden sun ................... 184
Lo the earth rejoices ................. 248
Lord of the harvest .................. 188
Once more the lib'ral year ............ 181
We plough the fields ................. 195
When thy heart with joy ............. 197

**Bar Mitzwah**

God of Israel, keep us faithful ......... 52
This child we dedicate to Thee ........ 240

**Blessing the Child**

This child we dedicate to Thee.........240

**Booths, Feast of**

A week within the Succah green.....189, 190
All through the long bright days........186
Father of mercies, God of love..........185
Fling wide the gates...................132
For garnered fields....................182
For the golden sun....................184
God of grace O let Thy light..........75
In many a stone bound city............180
Lo the earth rejoices..................248
Lord of the harvest...................188
Once more the lib'ral year.............181
O rain depart with blessings...........128
Take unto you the boughs..............187
Thy praise, O Lord, ..................183

**Brotherhood** (See also Social Progress)

Hear us, Eternal King.................136
These things shall be!.................237
Think gently of the erring one.........239

**Call to Worship**

Again, as evening's shadow falls........11
God is in His holy temple..............4
Here let Thy people come,.............5
How goodly is Thy house,..............1
How lovely are Thy dwellings fair.......3
How lovely are Thy dwellings Lord.....2
Sweet hymns and songs...............23

**Chanukkoh**

Fortress, Rock, my God, my Aid........208
Great Arbiter of human fate............209
If our God had not befriended..........123
In the candles' rays I see,.............206
Kindle the taper...................204, 205
Rock of Ages, let our song............207
'Twas like a dream.................120, 122
Where Judah's faithful sons............210

**Charity** (See also Social Progress)

Almighty God, in humble prayer........28
The voice of God is calling.............238
When thy heart with joy..............197

**Children's Hymns** (See also Religious School)

A little kingdom I possess..............251
All things bright and beautiful..........252
Almighty Father, God of love..........6
Courage brother do not stumble........87
Dear Father, here Thy children.........257
Early will I seek Thee.................18
Father as the day I greet,.............241
Father, let Thy blessing...............102
Father, to Thy dear name..............85
For mother-love and father-care........242

God is in His holy Temple.............4
God is my strong salvation............95
Great Lord of life who lives...........243
Happy who in early youth............253
Haste not! Haste not!................43
Here let Thy people come,............5
In God the holy, wise and just.........73
Let Israel trust in God................139
Little children, Lord, are we...........249
Lo our Father's tender care...........82
Lo the earth rejoices.................248
Lord God whose breath...............37
May He who kept us.................10
O Father, Thou who givest all.........250
O holy joy that raises................104
O Lord, be near me when I pray.......19
O Lord, my God, to Thee I pray.......29
O render thanks to God above.........194
Our Shepherd is the Lord.............84
Pray when the morn unveileth,........8
Splendor of the morning..............9
The wise may bring their learning......246
Throughout the night, O God above....244
Thy praise, O Lord, ................183
Today while the sun shines ...........258
To the God of all creation............20
We hear the call of Israel's children.....256
We plough the fields and scatter.......195
When the stars at set of sun..........245
When this song of praise shall cease.....103
Who taught the bird to build her nest...247
With the voice of sweet song..........70

**Close of Service**

Father, let Thy blessing...............102
O holy joy that raises................104
When this song of praise..............103

**Conclusion, Feast of**

A week within the Succah green.....189, 190
Thy word is to my feet a lamp.......36, 191

**Confirmation**

Blessed, blessed moment most holy...153, 154
Father, see Thy suppliant children,150, 151, 152
God of Israel keep us faithful..........52
Happy who in early youth............253
Hark the voice of children............146
Lord, into Thy sacred dwelling........144
Lord, what off'ring shall we bring.....148
Our Father we beseech Thy grace......145
Pledging our lives...................149
See, O God, we children come,........147

**Cornerstone, Laying of**

Firm this cornerstone be laid..........212
In mercy, Lord, incline Thine ear.......211

**Courage** (See Faith, Trust and Courage)

584

### Dedication of Temple

A new shrine stands in beauty reared.... 213
Our pious fathers built their shrine...... 215
Though our hearts dwell lovingly....... 228
To worship God in truth.............. 214

### Evening

Again, as evening's shadow falls........ 11
Almighty Father, God of love.......... 6
Around the weary world.............. 17
Blessed art Thou, O Lord of all,........ 15
Early will I seek Thee................ 18
How good it is to thank the Lord....109, 110
Into Thy hands my spirit I commend... 14
The day is done,..................... 12
Throughout the night, O God above..... 244
Unto the hills I lift mine eyes.......... 13
When there is peace.................. 16

### Faith, Trust, and Courage

Ah, well it is that God............... 89
Arise to praise the Lord.............. 74
Around the weary world.............. 17
As pants the hart...................30, 40
At midnight, so the sages tell........88, 175
Bow down Thine ear, Lord,........... 35
Courage, brother, do not stumble....... 87
Dim mine eyes with many tear-drops.... 173
Father, hear the pray'r............... 42
Father, to Thee we look.............. 96
Father, to Thy dear name............. 85
Gird us, O God,..................... 24
God is my strong salvation............ 95
God supreme! To Thee we pray....... 93
I hope for the salvation.............. 92
I leave the burdens of my life.......... 221
I lift mine eyes unto the hills.......... 33
In God the holy..................... 73
In sunshine and in storm, O God....... 90
Into Thy hands...................... 14
Lord, written in rocks and in woodland.. 39
O deem not that earth's crowning bliss.51, 98
O God, all gracious...................45, 50
O God whose law from age to age....... 97
O Lord, Thy all discerning eyes........ 38
O sometimes gleams upon my sight...... 94
Rest in the Lord, my soul;............ 91
The Lord, my Shepherd still has been... 86
There lives a God.................... 61
Thou O Almighty knowest all.......... 158
Unto the hills....................... 13
When there is peace.................. 16
Why art thou cast down, my soul,...... 171

### Feast of Conclusion (See Conclusion, Feast of)

### Feast of Lights (See Chanukkoh)

### Feast of Lots (See Purim)

### Feast of Tabernacles (See Booths)

### Feast of Weeks (See Weeks, Feast of)

### Freedom

From heaven's height.................. 124
God of might, God of right............ 125
Hear us, Eternal King................ 136
If our God had not befriended.......... 123
Loud let the swelling anthems.......... 78
Men, whose boast it is that ye.......... 121
'Twas like a dream,................120, 122
When Israel of the Lord beloved........ 119

### Funeral, The

Friend after friend departs............ 223
I leave the burdens of my life.......... 221
It singeth low in every heart.......... 220
Of all the thoughts of God............ 224
Whose works O Lord like Thine can be.. 222

### God—His Fatherhood and Love

How wondrous is Thy world........... 56
Lo our father's tender care............ 82
O God, my ever constant Friend,....... 192
O render thanks to God above,........ 194
The Lord my Shepherd still has been.... 86
The Lord, the Lord of glory reigns..... 71
There is an Eye that never sleeps....... 68
Thou ever-present Perfect Friend....... 41
Why art thou cast down, my soul,...... 171

### God—His Majesty

O Lord, Thy all discerning eyes........ 38
O Lord where shall I find Thee........ 21
O worship the King.................. 60
The Lord of all.....................76, 80
The Lord, the Lord of glory........... 71

### God—His Providence

All living souls shall bless............. 55
From heaven's height................. 124
God moves in a mysterious way........ 83
Lo our Father's tender care............ 82
O God, my ever constant Friend....... 192
O God, whose law from age to age...... 97
O Lord of heaven, and earth, and sea.... 66
Our Shepherd is the Lord............. 84
Praise to the living God.............. 54
Rest in the Lord.................... 91
There is an Eye that never sleeps....... 68
To Thee above all creatures' gaze....... 126
'Twas like a dream.................120, 122
With the voice of sweet song.......... 70

### God—His Unity

Come, let us praise our God........... 201
Let there be light, Lord God........... 232
One God! One Lord! One mighty King! 140
Remember Him, the only One.......... 44

NUMBER

The Lord of all.....................76, 80
Who is like Thee, O Universal Lord..... 69

## God—His Works in Nature

All living souls shall bless............. 55
Lord, written in rocks and in woodland.. 39
O worship the King, all glorious above... 60
The heav'ns, O God, Thy glory tell....57, 77
The Lord, my Shepherd still has been... 86
The Lord, the Lord of glory reigns...... 71
There lives a God.................... 61
To the God of all creation............. 20
We plough the fields.................. 195
While yet the earth mid'st chaos........ 99

## Grace after Meals

His flock our Shepherd feeds.......... 111

## Harvest (See Autumn)

## Immortality

Friend after friend departs............ 223
Into Thy hands my spirit I command.... 14
It singeth low in every heart.......... 220
Whose works, O Lord, like Thine can be 222

## Israel

All praise to Thee we bring............ 203
Come let us praise our God........... 201
Come ye faithful servants............. 101
From heaven's heights the thunder...... 142
God of Israel, keep us faithful......... 52
Great Arbiter of human fate........... 209
Hear us, Eternal King............... 136
If our God had not befriended......... 123
Let Israel trust in God alone.......... 139
Let there be light.................. 141
Magnify th' Eternal's name........... 59
One God!  One Lord!............... 140
Sing to the sov'reign of the skies....... 67
Ten thousand martyrs died........... 135
There is a joy the heart can feel....... 79
There is a mystic tie..............137, 138
Though our hearts dwell lovingly ....... 228
To Bethel came the patriarch.......... 49
To Thee above all creatures' gaze...... 126
We hear the call of Israel's children..... 256
When Israel of the Lord beloved....... 119
When Israel to the wilderness........ 127
Where Judah's faithful sons........... 210

## Law, The

All praise to Thee we bring............ 203
Come, let us praise our God........... 201
From Sinai's height a fountain......... 143
Happy he who walketh ever.........25, 27
How blest the man who fears to stray... 26
My faith shall be my rock of might..... 200
The heav'ns, O God, Thy glory tell....57, 77
This feast of the Law................ 199

NUMBER

Thy word is to my feet a lamp.......36, 191
Unveil mine eyes that of Thy law....... 202

## Light (See Truth and Light)

## Lights, Feast of (See Chanukkah)

## Lots, Feast of (See Purim)

## Marriage, The

All wise and great.................... 218
Blest is the bond of wedded love........ 219

## Morning

Almighty Father, God of love.......... 6
Father as the day I greet,............. 241
May He who kept us.................. 10
Once more, O Lord, do I awaken....... 7
Pray when the morn unveileth.......... 8
Splendor of the morning.............. 9

## Motherhood

Rejoice and offer thanks to God......259, 260

## Nation, The

God of our fathers,................... 263
God, the All-Merciful................ 265B
Hatikvah........................... 266
My country, 'tis of thee.............. 264
Not alone for mighty empire.......... 229
O beautiful for spacious skies.......... 262
O say, can you see................... 265
Uplift the song of praise to Him........ 261

## N'eelah (See Atonement, Day of—N'eelah)

## New Year

Ere space exists, or earth or sky........ 159
Into the tomb of ages past.........156, 157
On mighty wings rush swiftly by........ 161
Tent-like this day.................... 160
Thou O Almighty knowest all.......... 158

## Opening of Service (See Call to Worship, Aspiration)

## Passover

Behold, it is the springtide............ 129
Fling wide the gates.................. 132
From heaven's height................. 124
God of might, God of right............ 125
Hear us, Eternal King................. 136
If our God had not befriended......... 123
Men, whose boast it is that ye......... 121
O rain depart with blessings,.......... 128
O sound the loud timbrel............. 131
Praise the Lord!  One accord.......... 130
To Thee, above all creatures' gaze...... 126
'Twas like a dream................120, 122
When Israel, of the Lord beloved...... 119
When Israel to the wilderness......... 127

**Passover** (Seventh Day)

O sound the loud timbrel.............. 131

**Patriotic Days** (See Nation, The)

**Paysach** (See Passover)

**Peace**

God of the nations near and far......... 226
Hail the glorious Golden City.......... 227
Let there be light,.................... 232
Not alone for mighty empire........... 229
Now upon the earth descending......... 236
These things shall be................. 237

**Penitence** (See also Atonement, Day of)

Create in this weak form of mine....... 170
Despise not, Lord,.................... 162
Dim mine eyes with many tear-drops.... 173
Forgive us Lord, we turn to Thee....... 163
Hear my pray'r,...................... 168
Lord God whose breath................ 37
Lord Thine humble servants hear....... 169
Out of the depths,................... 164
The lifting of my hands............... 174
Thy faithful servant Lord............. 167
Who is like Thee..................... 69

**Pentecost** (See Weeks, Feast of)

**Praise**

All living souls shall bless............. 55
All the world shall come.............. 63
Almighty God, who hearest pray'r...... 53
Arise to praise the Lord.............. 74
Blessed art Thou, O Lord of all........ 15
Earth, with all thy thousand voices..... 64
Fling wide the gates.................. 132
From heaven's height................. 142
God of grace, O let Thy light.......... 75
How good it is to thank the Lord....109, 110
How wond'rous is Thy world,......... 56
In God the holy, wise, and just........ 73
Let us with a gladsome mind.......... 58
Loud let the swelling anthems rise..... 78
Magnify th' Eternal's name........... 59
Now bless the God of all.............. 81
Now upon the earth descending........ 236
O bless the Lord, my soul............. 62
O Lord of heaven, earth and sea,....... 66
O Lord our King how bright........... 72
O Lord! to Thee who dwell'st above..... 196
O Lord, where shall I find Thee........ 21
O render thanks to God above,......... 194
O worship the King,.................. 60
Praise to the living God.............. 54
Praise ye the Lord!.................. 65
Sing to the sov'reign of the skies....... 67
Sweet hymns and songs will I recite..... 23
The heav'ns, O God, Thy glory tell....57, 77

The Lord of all, who reigns supreme....76, 80
The Lord, the Lord of glory reigns...... 71
There is a joy the heart can feel........ 79
There is an Eye that never sleeps....... 68
There lives a God!................... 61
To Bethel came the patriarch.......... 49
'Twas like a dream.................120, 122
Uplift the song of praise.............. 261
Who is like Thee, O Universal Lord..... 69
With the voice of sweet song.......... 70

**Purim**

God is my strong salvation............ 95
If our God had not befriended......... 123

**Rejoicing of the Law** (See Law, The)

**Religious School, The**

A little kingdom I possess.............. 251
All things bright and beautiful......... 252
Come ye faithful servants............. 101
Dear Father here Thy children come.... 257
Father as the day I greet.............. 241
Father let Thy blessing............... 102
Father to Thy dear name.............. 85
For mother-love and father-care....... 242
Fortress, Rock, my God............... 208
God is my strong salvation............ 95
Great Lord of life.................... 243
Hail the glorious Golden City.......... 227
Happy who in early youth............. 253
Hear us Eternal King................. 136
In the candles' rays.................. 206
Kindle the taper..................204, 205
Let Israel trust in God................ 139
Lo the earth rejoices................. 248
O Father Thou who givest............. 250
O holy joy that raises................ 104
O Lord to Thee...................... 196
O render thanks to God above......... 194
One God! One Lord!................. 140
Onward brothers..................... 230
Rock of Ages........................ 207
The wise may bring their learning...... 246
Think gently of the erring one......... 239
Though our hearts dwell lovingly...... 228
Throughout the night O God above..... 244
Thy praise, O Lord................... 183
Today while the sun shines............ 258
We build our school on Thee........... 254
We hear the call..................... 256
We meet again in gladness............. 255
We plough the fields.................. 195
We thank Thee, Lord................. 193
When Israel to the wilderness.......... 127
When the stars....................... 245
When this song of praise.............. 103
Who taught the bird.................. 247

**Resignation** (See Faith, Trust, and Courage)

NUMBER

**Righteousness**
A noble life, a simple faith............ 225
Come, ye faithful servants............ 101
Courage, brother do not stumble......... 87
God! send us men whose aim shall be.... 233
Hail the glorious Golden City.......... 227
Happy he who walketh ever...........25, 27
Onward brothers....................... 230
We thank Thee, Lord,.................. 193

**Rosh Hashonoh** (See New Year)

**Sabbath Eve**
Come forth, my friend.................. 108
Come, O holy Sabbath evening.......... 105
Descend, descend, O Sabbath Princess... 107
How good it is to thank the Lord....109, 110
O Holy Sabbath day draw near......... 117
The Sabbath light is burning bright..... 106

**Sabbath, The**
As birds unto the genial homeland...... 113
Come, O Sabbath day and bring......... 118
I bless Thee, Father, for the grace...... 115
Lord, in this sacred hour............... 112
O holy Sabbath day draw near.......... 117
Sweet Sabbath! Day of sacred joy...... 116
When the Sabbath peace inviting........ 114

**Scriptures, the Holy** (See Law, The)

**Seasons** (See also Winter, Spring, Summer, Autumn)
Father of mercies, God of love.......... 185
With the voice of sweet song........... 70

**Service** (See Charity, Social Progress)

**Sh'vuos** (See Weeks, Feast of)

**Sh'meenee Atseres** (See Conclusion, Feast of)

**Simchas Torah** (See Law, The)

**Social Progress**
Believe not those who say.............. 231
Come, ye faithful servants............. 101
God! send us men whose aim shall be.... 233
Hail the glorious Golden City.......... 227
Let there be light,..................... 232
Men, whose boast it is that ye.......... 121
Not alone for mighty empire............ 229
Now upon the earth descending......... 236
O sometimes gleams upon my sight...... 94
Onward, brothers,...................... 230
The God that to the fathers............ 234
The voice of God is calling............. 238
These things shall be.................. 237
Think gently of the erring one. ........ 239
Though our hearts dwell lovingly....... 228
'Tis not the large, the huge............ 235

**Spring**
A message sweet the breezes bring...... 133
Behold it is the springtide.............. 129
From heaven's height.................... 124
Praise the Lord! One accord........... 130
When warmer suns and bluer skies...... 134

**Succos** (See Booths, Feast of)

**Suffering** (See Faith, Trust, and Courage)
O deem not that earth's crowning bliss..51, 98

**Summer**
Summer suns are glowing.............. 155

**Thankfulness**
All living souls shall bless.............. 55
Father of mercies, God of love.......... 185
For garnered fields and meadows cropped 182
For mother-love and father-care........ 242
For the golden sun and the darting rain.. 184
How good it is.....................109, 110
Lord of the harvest, Thee we hail....... 188
Loud let the swelling anthems rise...... 78
Not alone for mighty empire........... 229
O Father, Thou who givest............. 250
O God, my ever constant Friend........ 192
O Lord of heaven, and earth,........... 66
O Lord! to Thee who dwell'st........... 196
O render thanks to God above.......... 194
Once more the lib'ral year.............. 181
We plough the fields and scatter........ 195
We thank Thee, Lord,................. 193

**Trust** (See Faith, Trust, and Courage)

**Truth and Light**
Come, ye faithful servants.............. 101
Happy he that never wanders........... 100
O Lord, my God, to Thee I pray........ 29
Thy word is to my feet a lamp........36, 191
While yet the earth mid'st chaos........ 99

**Weeks, Feast of**
All praise to Thee..................... 203
Come, let us praise our God............ 201
Fling wide the gates.................. 132
From heaven's heights the thunder...... 142
From Sinai's height a fountain.......... 143
"Let there be light"................... 141
Lord, into Thy sacred dwelling......... 144
My faith shall be my rock.............. 200
Unveil mine eyes...................... 202

**Winter**
'Tis winter now; the fallen snow........ 198

**Wisdom**
Almighty God, in humble prayer........ 28

**Word of God, the** (See Law, The)

**Worship** (See Call to Worship)

**Yom Kippur** (See Atonement, Day of)